READING NATIVE
AMERICAN WOMEN

CONTEMPORARY NATIVE AMERICAN COMMUNITIES
Stepping Stones to the Seventh Generation

Acknowledging the strength and vibrancy of Native American people and nations today, this series examines life in contemporary Native American communities from the point of view of Native concerns and values. Books in the series cover topics that are of cultural and political importance to tribal peoples and that affect their possibilities for survival, in both urban and rural communities.

SERIES EDITORS:
Troy Johnson, American Indian Studies, California State University, Long Beach, Long Beach, CA 90840, trj@csulb.edu

Duane Champagne, Native Nations Law and Policy Center, 292 Haines Hall, Box 951551, University of California, Los Angeles, Los Angeles, CA 90095-1551, champagn@ucla.edu

BOOKS IN THE SERIES

READING NATIVE AMERICAN WOMEN

Critical/Creative Representations

EDITED BY INÉS HERNÁNDEZ-AVILA

ALTAMIRA PRESS
A Division of Rowman & Littlefield Publishers, Inc.
Lanham • New York • Toronto • Oxford

AltaMira Press
A division of Rowman & Littlefield Publishers, Inc.
A wholly owned subsidary of The Rowman & Littlefield Publishing Group, Inc.
4501 Forbes Boulevard, Suite 200
Lanham, MD 20706
www.altamirapress.com

PO Box 317, Oxford OX2 9RU, UK

British Library Cataloguing in Publication Information Available

Library of Congress Cataloging-in-Publication Data
Reading Native American women : critical/creative representations / edited by Inés Hernández-Avila.
    p. cm. — (Contemporary Native American communities)
Includes bibliographical references.
ISBN 0-7591-0371-2 (cloth : alk. paper) — ISBN 0-7591-0372-0 (pbk. : alk. paper)
1. American literature—Indian authors—History and criticism. 2. American literature—Women authors—History and criticism. 3. Indian women—United States—Intellectual life. 4. Women and literature—United States. 5. Indian women—Intellectual life. 6. Indian women in literature. 7. Indians in literature. I. Hernández-Avila, Inés. II. Title. III. Series.
PS153.I52R425 2005
810.9'9287'08997—dc22

2004028337

Printed in the United States of America

∞™ The paper used in this publication meets the minimum requirements of American National Standard for Information Sciences—Permanence of Paper for Printed Library Materials, ANSI/NISO Z39.48-1992.

CONTENTS

For the courageous, fierce love of our Wise women,
Strong women, Powerful women,
grandmothers, mothers, sisters, daughters,
grand-daughters, lovers, friends
For our peoples, our nations, for the good ancestor spirits,
for the future generations

Acknowledgments

I deeply appreciate the support I received to put this manuscript together. Before I took over as director of the Chicana/Latina Research Center (C/LRC) at the University of California, Davis, I received funding from the C/LRC to hire student assistants to help me with manuscript preparation. On two separate occasions, I also participated in a summer mentoring/research partnership program with California State University, Chico, whereby I received the help of graduate students in completing work on the manuscript. I'm especially grateful to all of the students who helped me with correspondence, transcriptions, filing, mailing, scanning, reformatting, duplicating, and various other work. These students are, from CSU-Chico, Dorette English and Barbara Rigby, and from UC Davis, Gricelda Espinosa, Carolina Montufar, Silvia Soto, Sarah Ramirez, Joel Tena, Marcos Guerrero, Liliana Aguilar, and Laura Barajas. I want to say a special thank-you to Bettina Schneider, graduate student in Native American Studies, and Sandra Gómez, graduate student in Cultural Studies, at UC Davis. Bettina became the book's godmother in the final stages of gathering permissions from all of the contributors and working with the staff of AltaMira to make sure things were done smoothly. Sandy became the second godmother getting us successfully through the copyediting stage. I thank the series editors, Duane Champagne and Troy Johnson, for their immediate enthusiasm for the manuscript and Rosalie Robertson for committing to the book. A special thanks to the AltaMira staff, particularly Kristina Razmara and Jehanne Schweitzer, for their patience and good energy.

Remember

Remember the sky that you were born under,
know each of the star's stories.
Remember the moon, know who she is.
Remember the sun's birth at dawn, that is the
strongest point of time. Remember sundown
and the giving away to night.
Remember your birth, how your mother struggled
to give you form and breath. You are evidence of
her life, and her mother's, and hers.
Remember your father. He is your life, also.
Remember the earth whose skin you are:
red earth, black earth, yellow earth, white earth
brown earth, we are earth.
Remember the plants, trees, animal life who all have their
tribes, their families, their histories, too. Talk to them,
listen to them. They are alive poems.
Remember the wind. Remember her voice. She knows the
origin of this universe.
Remember that you are all people and that all people
are you.
Remember that you are this universe and that this
universe is you.
Remember that all is in motion, is growing, is you.
Remember language comes from this.
Remember the dance language is, that life is.
Remember.

Joy Harjo

Introduction

The essays in this collection give centrality and visibility to some of the major driving forces behind the intellectual and creative work of Native women today. Perhaps what is most telling (for specialists in now mainstream feminist studies) is that the work of these women is not ancillary to Women's Studies but instead core to Native American Studies. Native American Studies, as an inter/multidisciplinary field, provides the historical, political, economic, social, and cultural frameworks by which to understand Native peoples in relation to their communities and nations. Native American women scholars who focus on or foreground gender and sexuality in their work contribute to a space that brings us full force to questions of Native women's consciousness, power, and vision in relation to both academia and our communities at large. In her challenging work *Why I Can't Read Wallace Stegner and Other Essays*, Elizabeth Cook-Lynn considers "the American Indian Woman in the Ivory Tower" and posits a series of questions that pertain to "the appropriate female role[s] in modern Indian society," one of which is "What is the role of scholarship and academic participation in native life?"[1] *Reading Native American Women* offers some directions for approaching this question. Furthermore, these essays contribute to conceptualizing the idea of Native American Women's Studies: What are Native women studying and why? What are the critical perspectives by which to "study" (the work of) Native women?

Cook-Lynn says, "The model [of Indian studies] itself revitalizes, not only by permitting [the Native woman] to pursue the intellectual, philosophical, political, and social matters essential to the survival of her Indian nation, but by requiring that she undertake the responsibilities she rightfully acknowledges as hers" (100). This undertaking, at once arduous, deeply painful, and healing, demands a constant process of critical and creative reflection, a continuing re-encounter with the self, so that each Native woman discovers what is essential to her own survival as an indigenous intellectual at the beginning of the twenty-first century. It might sound contradictory, but it is not. For the survival of Indian nations, we Native women scholars must also discern for ourselves what will keep us strong, sane, inspired, and nourished as we pursue these paths we have chosen, these paths we are creating. Each time we confront, reconcile, and draw strength and courage from our own personal histories (contextualized by our family and tribal histories and nuanced by factors of race/ethnicity, class, gender, sexuality, nation, and culture), we gain acute insight into our resounding need to tell, to write, to be engaged, with commitment, rigor, and compassion. More important, we gain insight into and are guided by our people's (and other indigenous peoples') cultural responses over time to the experience(s) of colonization and decolonization. The reverse is true as well. Each time a Native woman seeks, unearths, brings forth, and defends her people's history, political identity, and cultural teachings, she finds increasingly discrete parts of herself.

How does this process take place? Gloria Bird says in her essay in this volume, "In order to move out of colonizing instances of interiorized oppression, we first have to identify those moments in which we reinforce those useless paradigms and search for new approaches to the way we speak of ourselves in relation to our histories and stories. To imagine a future." In imagining a future, we also imagine our past as we contemplate and enact our present. The imagination realized is praxis, and it is an imagination profoundly informed, as so many Native writers have said, by memory, by spirit, and by the land. The word and Native woman made one in self- (and community) realization and action/reflection.[2] The word. The responsible word. The accountable word. The continuing, transforming, flowering word. Joy Harjo says it beautifully in her poem "Remember," which provides the graceful entrance to this collection: "Remember that all is in motion, is growing, is you. / Remember language comes from this."

We look to the women, and the men, of our own communities, our own nations, to remember and imagine ourselves, to give our ancestors and elders their place in the shaping of the critical and creative social, political, cultural, spiritual consciousness that has brought us this far. Cook-Lynn says, "What a modern Indian woman in the [present] is doing is very likely dependent upon what her female ancestors and relatives have done. She walks the road smoothed for her by the women who preceded her. She does not, contrary to public opinion, operate in a vacuum, and she is not without precursors" (100). We are recovering the stories of our precursors, and in doing so, we walk beside them. For some, for many, their stories have been hidden, overlooked. It is time for them to come out.

A great part of the work of Native American women scholars is the formal recollection and recording of the lives and work of these ancestor precursors, the recovery of the languages of sign, silence, gesture, example, song, food, arts, performance, and testimony—the many languages that have pertained to Native women historically within their own specific cultural, *national* (Native nation) contexts. The power of language is known by Native people in the deepest sense from an old-time community perspective (old-time because in these "new times" the threat of cultural devastation, erasure of memory, and the worst, loss of sovereignty, have exacted a heavy toll on us, still violently dislocating us from our foundations by displacing us from our lands and languages and destroying our autonomy). Language, the oral tradition, the treaties, the early writings, and the formal scholarship all point to Native women and men naming, considering, discussing, interpreting, strategizing on behalf of the people, on behalf of ourselves, and, most important, on our own terms. Reid Gómez explores the language of sovereignty in her essay, emphasizing that "our method of engaging with the world informs the manner in which we theorize that world and understand its scope and our place within that scope." The people speak with each other and name the problems, facing the complexities of the (countless) struggles through language.

History is an imperative element in the interpretation and analysis of issues pertaining to Native women. There can be no understanding without recourse to appropriately specific historical contextualizations. Joanne Marie Barker and Teresia Teaiwa's essay, "Native InFormation," can be read as a performance piece, wherein the two establish their "aim . . . to interrupt the ways in which the narratives of the Vanishing Indian have intersected with our respective identities, communities, and histories as two mixed-bloods of American Indian and Pacific Islander ancestry." Victoria Bomberry's contribution to this volume subverts the "profoundly disturbing" official history of Oklahoma with her grandmother's secret stories of the turn-of-the-century (Muscogee) Crazy Snake Rebellion. In "Rape and the War against Native Women," Andrea Smith documents and testifies to past and present atrocities committed against Native women; her essay places in relief the cherished understandings of womanhood that are at stake when Native women are targeted for violence. In contrast, Deborah Miranda's essay speaks to the erotic in Native women's literature as a heightened form of subversion and creative resistance, while Carolyn Dunn's pursuit of the Coyotesse also manifests the creative, playful energy of Native women.

In what ways have Native American women historically represented ourselves? How have Native American women contributed to the overall struggles of our communities, and around what issues? What avenues have Native American women chosen for creative, cultural, and political expressions? When and how have women's issues been foregrounded and articulated? How do the interrelated and differentiated factors of nation, history, culture, race/ethnicity, gender, class, and sexual orientation give contour to our multiple and multiply shifting experiences as

Native women? On whose behalf are we speaking and writing? Are there points of convergence between Native American feminisms and "other" feminisms? As Native women scholars and artists, how do we position ourselves with respect to similarly "new" disciplines such as Women's Studies, other Ethnic Studies (especially the women of color who are working in these areas), and Cultural Studies, as well as the more traditional academic disciplines? There are so many powerful Native women scholars, writers, and artists, in this collection and beyond. As we articulate our own positions around issues such as identity (race, ethnicity, gender, sexuality), community, sovereignty, culture, and representation, we unlayer the complexities of Indian women's identity, including spirit, not only in the United States but also in this hemisphere. We recognize and acknowledge the political charge of our work.

When Luana Ross addresses the issue of prisonization and its relationship to other forms of institutionalization, including academization, she makes us aware of the notion of social control that permeates in specific ways our lives as Native people in U.S. society. Her essay is a companion piece to her award-winning work *Inventing the Savage: The Construction of Native American Criminality*. Similar analysis is being done by other women of color in relation to their own communities (a fruitful area of comparative investigation). Chicana historian Antonia Castañeda's work[3] speaks with Ross's essay to the construction of people of color, women of color, as the enemy—in effect, as those in need of punishment and behavior modification. This prescription is not without its parallels within the academy, given the seeming compulsion to punish, ignore, and erase Ethnic Studies for altering (challenging, threatening) the traditional disciplines by not conforming to the pre-established privileging of largely Euro-American critical perspectives and for daring to be disciplined in "other" ways.

Castañeda focuses on the systematic indoctrination of subjugated children as cultural translators in a way that disrupts their childhood and inverts the parent-child relationship, making them the "tongues, the lifeline, the public voice of parents, family, and sometimes communities" (203). She continues, "How do [these children] negotiate the culture they must translate for their parents—the culture that assaults and violates them, their families, and their communities with its assumptions and attitudes about them as well as with its language and other lethal weapons?" (203). Her question has relevance to us as Native scholars as well, in relation to our own work and to the essays in this volume; it is directly related to the question posed by Cook-Lynn, which is how and why we do what we do. The practice of deliberately subverting the authority of parents in homes where English is not the only or even first language has, as we know, continued into the present. As we bring our knowledge and information into present time (i.e., as we attune ourselves to the historical and contemporary nuances of our own multiple backgrounds as Native people, as Native women scholars), we shape those creative pedagogies, "personalized methodologies" (to borrow from Ross), and critical perspectives that ground us in our particular communities yet allow us our own ways of collaboration and exchange, with each other, with those who seek alliance with us, and even with those who would presume us invisible.

For Native scholars, women and men, two-spirit and straight, there is a clear understanding of the need for our work to be informed by our political realities and by our distinct cultural disciplines and protocols, which are quite complex and deserving of our lifetime's commitment to articulation. At the same time, we are aware of how historically, and in the present, this ideology of containment has been continually (re)enforced by rigorous "denaturalization" and "deculturiza-tion" processes at all levels of our educational institutionalization, as Janice Gould's and Victoria Bomberry's essays demonstrate. Inés Hernández-Avila's essay explores the connections between the interrelated ideas of home(land), language, and the re-inscription of our historical and cultural identities, as well as broadens the idea of Nativeness to be inclusive of indigenous peoples in other parts of the hemisphere. Hulleah Tsinhnahjinnie's photographic memoirs provide powerful vi-sual readings of the themes that are interwoven through these essays; she takes a stance as an aboriginal savant, pushing the boundaries to create a transformative formula based on her certainty and vision of, as she says, Native intelligence.

The increasing transnationalization or mobilization of indigenous people throughout the hemisphere since 1992 has implications for those of us who are members of Native communities, as well as those of us who are engaged in in-digenous (women's) research. Many of the Native communities from the south (e.g., the Maya, the Mixtec, the Purepecha) transport their modes of social or-ganization with them when they come to the U.S., ironically crossing a border that immediately erases their indigenousness as they become classified as Hispanic or Latina/o. And once again, the school system will attempt to erase language and identity and otherwise "denaturalize" them. Their presence, though, points to ex-citing potential collaborations between them and Native communities in the north as, in effect, the borders collapse, including the borders of Native American or Indigenous Women's Studies. As the borders collapse, the women of each nation will determine for themselves what they want to say about themselves and how they want to say it, just as they look to each other in solidarity and collaboration. Native American or Indigenous Women's Studies can be the space of creation for Muscogee Women's Studies, Maidu Women's Studies, Dakota Women's Studies, Cherokee Women's Studies, Apache Women's Studies, and so on, throughout the hemisphere and the globe. It is fitting that Jean LaMarr's image on the cover of this book shows us standing, dancing together to an eagle song.

What is our source of inspiration? How do we signal the role of intuition in precipitating a broader investigation that marks as it reaffirms that initial intuitive spark? The place of creativity, the link to our origins, to our life-giving originality as individuals and as peoples, is clear among so many Native writers. We go back to our own, not in essentialist or romantic terms, but with the wisdom that brings to bear what we have learned from our various forms of training, filtered through Native eyes. This is what Cherokee scholar Mary Churchill has done in her essay, wherein she establishes a "dialogical model generated from Cherokee mythic, ritual, and cosmological conceptions" as a way to interpret Cherokee women's literature. The creative spirit takes us always back to our loved ones, to their spirits—which sustain ours as we lovingly sustain theirs—and as Janice Gould suggests, to "the considered attention the heart pays to the earth." Cook-Lynn honors her grandmother in a prose poem, saying in beautiful, inspired language,

> Grandmother, today your landscape is light pursuing light, forever a human mirror in memory unblemished and close to the heart; when I walk to your place from the flat prairie above I can depend on your horses fraught with the destiny of us all following me through the dark discovering my presence. (101)

Native people have not vanished; on the contrary, we are a living presence, nourished by memory, nourishing memory, acting on behalf of the generations. Our nations are not on any periphery. Each nation has its own center, its own history, and its own vision of what it gives the earth and all of humanity.

Inés Talamantez, known for her work in the development of Native American religious traditions, writes, "This work is not just a research project: it is part of my life. I am connected to these women and their truths. . . . This narrative of inquiry requires deep reflection. It is an exploration in both humility and authority. Insight is gained through analysis, interpretation, and critique." She is right. This work is part of our lives, and our writings as Native women represent the intellectual, artistic, and political claiming of space on behalf of the women of our nations. It is an honor for me to introduce the words of the scholars and artists included in this volume.

Notes

1. Elizabeth Cook-Lynn, *Why I Can't Read Wallace Stegner and Other Essays: A Tribal Voice* (Madison: University of Wisconsin, 1996), p. 100.

2. My reference to praxis is indebted to Paulo Freire's development of the idea in *Pedagogy of the Oppressed* (New York: Continuum, 1970).

3. Antonia Castañeda, "Language and Other Lethal Weapons: Cultural Politics and the Rites of Children as Translators of Culture," in *Mapping Multiculturalism*, ed. Avery F. Gor-

don and Christopher Newfield (Minneapolis: University of Minnesota Press, 1996), p. 207. This essay describes her project (a social history of Tejana farmworkers) and points to "the decade of the 1950's [when] cold-war politics and gender, racial, class, and sexual politics of containment further converted people of color—and in this case specifically women of color—into 'the enemy within'" (p. 207). Her focus is Mexican farmworker children, but she draws the connections with boarding schools and mission schools.

Telling Stories to the Seventh Generation: Resisting the Assimilationist Narrative of *Stiya*

I

JANICE GOULD

> *We scrub the sidewalks down because it's shameful work. Our brushes cut the stone in watered arcs and in the soak frail outlines shiver clear a moment, things us kids pressed on the dark face before it hardened, pale, remembering delicate old injuries, the spines of names and leaves.*

—LOUISE ERDRICH, "INDIAN BOARDING SCHOOL: THE RUNAWAYS"

As I watched Chicana artist Celia Herrera Rodriguez conduct a workshop in storytelling at the University of Northern Colorado, where I was teaching in March of 1997, I understood something. She had brought with her to the classroom a large Mexican blanket in deep rainbow colors of green, yellow, white, and blue on a wine-colored background. Along with the blanket, Celia brought a basket of objects—small things she had collected, with our permission, from around the house my partner and I shared—among them a spoon, a cup, a doll, a tiny book, a shell, feathers, a votive candle, and the hand stone of the metate that had passed into my possession some years ago, which I had brought with me from California. Celia took this colorful blanket, unfolded it, and carefully spread it on the floor of the performance space whose use we had arranged for the afternoon. In the middle of the blanket she laid a small cloth, and taking the objects one by one from the basket, she placed each artifact on what became a kind of altar.

As Celia prepared the stage, the students looked on quietly. No one said a word. Though Celia transformed the classroom into a theater and occupied the space of performance, a sole actor on this floor-level stage, her actions could not be considered acting—there was nothing contrived in her demeanor, no particular elicitation of response from the audience that watched her. But she was performing. She had, in the moment of walking out onto the stage before an audience, created with her imagination a site for the possibility of storytelling, the possibility of truth telling.

After the blanket was spread and the objects laid down, Celia, barefoot and standing on the blanket, looked up at the audience and invited people to come down from their seats and take a place on the floor at the blanket's edge. A dozen or so students did this. Celia looked around at them. "This," she said, gesturing at the blanket and the "altar" with its objects, "is all that I own. This is my home. You are welcome here, and you are welcome to these things. But whatever object you pick up, I ask you to treat it with respect. I ask you to treat my home with respect."

I have thought about this moment many times. For one thing, it was of critical importance to witness how Celia exemplified the storytelling tradition through the claiming of place. In retrospect, I realize the sharp contrast between the Native storytelling tradition, with its naturalness and grace, and the national narratives of violence, conquest, and exclusion that have been institutionally imposed upon Native peoples since colonization. Celia's setting the stage as a home place powerfully reminded me that self-sovereignty does not preclude openness to and acceptance of others.

Celia asked the students to each take one object, hold it in his or her hands, look at it, and listen for the story it would tell. They were not to describe the objects; they were merely to listen and then share what they heard, what the objects told them. This is an exercise used in some form by many good writing teachers, but what I liked about what Celia did is that she created what I would call an indigenous space for storytelling. Out of her imagination she placed in front of us what is always already there: the sacred space where the heart's truth can be found.

The students selected their objects reverently and shyly, and the first to speak was a young Chicano. I noticed right away that he had reached for the hand stone of the metate. When it came his turn to talk in the story circle, he told us that he really liked this stone and that he heard it tell him something that came from his grandfather, who had died the summer before. Through the stone his grandfather had told him, "Be strong."

Perhaps the stone whispered other things to the Chicano student as well, but that was one of the important truths he learned and shared as he made himself available to the grief he held for his grandfather—true grief can sever the heart. Stories from stones must be among the oldest. The hand stone of the metate would have probably been held by many, many people, used far off in time. I want to believe that if we feel the grief of (and for) our ancestors, we may feel, too, the healing though sometimes lacerating love they still hold for us.

Dine poet Luci Tapahonso was invited to visit a Hohokamki archeological site being excavated in Phoenix for a new expressway. Surveying the gash in the earth that revealed the place the Hohokamki had lived, Tapahonso listened for the heart's truth to emerge. She writes:

> The presence of pottery pieces, clothing fibers, bone shards—signs of former village life—were imperceptible.
>
> Yet the Hohokamki had been there. As part of the arts team, I saw the small paper sacks of excavated remains standing upright in the bright sun. All these centuries later, we stood in the center of their homes. I sat now under the trees in the heavy silence, still wanting to talk, to laugh, to share stories.
>
> "We are all still here," I said to the Hohokamki whose homes were disturbed. "And we are still the same," I said. At that moment, it was obvious that there are memories and stories too powerful for things as new as cement and asphalt to destroy.
>
> The worlds I had entered that morning were the prayers and hopes the Hohokamki had thrown ahead for all of us. It is the same now. We pray several times a day for ourselves, our ancestors, our children, and our grandchildren. The Kiowas call this "throwing our prayers"—we cast our prayers seven generations ahead. (26)

"We cast our prayers seven generations ahead." Many Native people say this. Also we say that we listen to the ancestors, so we cast our prayers seven generations behind, too, as we try to hear the memories that come before the individual memories we believe are our own. We are, of course, someone's seventh generation. Back in the spiral of time, somebody prayed for us and hoped we would listen and hear. Our stories create our world. The heart's responsibility in all this is to hear, hold, and translate the stories it receives from memory and from the small beautiful objects of our world that probably never come to the attention of the rational, cognitive mind.

The legacy of colonization of indigenous people seeks to replace or change the people's stories, to excise the heart's knowledge, rendering it deaf and dumb. Without the considered attention the heart pays to the earth, without the homage of respect for our Mother, we lose the understanding of true sovereignty, the sovereignty of earth—its soil, water, and air, its plants and animals—and the sovereignty of the distinct Native Nations who, it is said, were entrusted with their particular landbases by the Supreme Being.

Stories, then, and prayers and songs are basic to an understanding of sovereignty, to the indigenous imagination that is rooted in place. And conversely, place is the formative element for story. Native homelands are literally still quite vulnerable to the colonizing impulse of military-industrial, transnational capitalism. When place is denigrated, when our homes—both inner and outer sanctuary—are derided, dismissed, and destroyed due to the colonizer's hatred and fear of our tie to the earth, our connection to story may be damaged.

At the end of the nineteenth century, the effort to sever Native people's ties to the land was enormous. "Break up the reservation, decapitate tribal authority," was the cry of reformers who called themselves "friends of the Indian." Many are aware that federally run Indian boarding schools, promoted by reform activists, were instrumental in trying to cut Indian children's tribal affiliation to family, home, and land. At Carlisle Indian School in Pennsylvania, a small propaganda book titled *Stiya: A Carlisle Indian Girl at Home* was issued to the Carlisle graduates who were returning to their home reservations as a way to "inoculate" them against their family's influence.

Laguna writer Leslie Silko has written about *Stiya* and Carlisle Indian School in a recent book of essays titled *Yellow Woman and a Beauty of the Spirit*. Silko tells about her great-grandmother, whom she calls Grandma A'mooh, and her Aunt Susie, both of whom attended Carlisle. In this boarding school, opened in 1879 under the direction of Captain Richard Henry Pratt, the oral tradition of story-telling was presumably displaced by an institutional method of educating children. However, the power of books had long been impressed upon Silko's relatives. Books had conferred protection of tribal land—through land grant laws. "So," writes Silko, "very early, the Pueblo people realized the power of written words and books to secure legitimate title to tribal land" (160). Property held in common by the tribe and secured to the Laguna people under law helped ensure continuance in the traditional Pueblo practice of farming, as well as in ceremonial usage. The land remains available as a source from which to draw physical and spiritual sustenance. Silko comments, "No wonder the older folks used to tell us kids to study: learn to read and to write for your own protection" (160).

The theme of protection comes up again in Silko's essay when she describes an argument that takes place between Grandma A'mooh and Aunt Susie, Grandma A'mooh's daughter-in-law. The quarrel was over the book *Stiya*. Because of the emphasis placed on harmony and cooperation in the Pueblo tradition, the argument must have been distressing for both women. Grandma A'mooh was upset by the book's untruths and its racist stereotyping: she wanted to burn the thing, "just as witchcraft paraphernalia is destroyed" (164). Aunt Susie, on the other hand, felt that *Stiya* should be preserved as "important evidence of the lies and the racism and bad faith of the U.S. government with the Pueblo people" (164). The argument was resolved when Aunt Susie asked her mother-in-law to give her the copy of this text. "According to Pueblo etiquette," writes Silko, "it would have been unthinkable for my great-grandmother to refuse her daughter-in-law's request for the book" (164). Thus, the volume was handed over to Aunt Susie and so lost to Silko's side of the family. Years later Silko came across a copy of *Stiya* "in the rare book room of the University of New Mexico Library in Albuquerque" (165).

I want to take this opportunity to correct some minor errors in Silko's essay about this book, *Stiya*. Possibly because Silko was writing from memory and hearsay, and not from a firsthand text, she incorrectly states that the author was "Marion Bergess, a white woman who worked as a teacher and dormitory matron at Carlisle" (162). The author was indeed a white woman, and her name was Mariana Burgess. She was a foot soldier in Captain Pratt's arsenal of educators at Carlisle and a champion of Pratt's theory of assimilation. It seems she authored not only *Stiya* but probably also most, if not all, of the weekly newspaper produced at Carlisle that was called, under her editorship, *The Red Man and Helper*.[1] Burgess may have referred to herself, in her capacity as editor of the school newspaper, as "the-Man-in-the-Bandstand," a play on the initials of her name, M. B. Her initials also provided her with the pseudonym "Embe," under which she wrote *Stiya*.[2]

Burgess's writing, in both the newspaper and the novel, always purports to be the authentic experiences of an Indian child (or children).[3] The pen name she chose, "Embe," obscures her social identity and offers her a way of passing herself off as an Indian. Despite this dissembling, Burgess states in a preface to the novel that "the story of Stiya and her trials is woven out of the experiences of girls at various times members of the Indian Industrial School at Carlisle, Pa." Though based on the collective experience of some of Carlisle's "returned" students,[4] *Stiya* is a work of fiction by a non-Indian author.

The narrative of *Stiya* concerns the homecoming of a Pueblo girl to her reservation and her trials and tribulations as she encounters first the "backwardness" of her parents and then the "cruelty and injustice" of the tribal authority in her pueblo. As Silko suggested previously, the purpose of the book was to provide the returning student with a way of dealing with her shock, surprise, and disappointment upon her arrival back to the reservation from Carlisle; it modeled "appropriate" feelings of discomfort for a now "civilized young lady." The text was meant to bolster a young woman's determination to hold onto the teachings and values with which she was inculcated in the boarding school so as to overcome any temptation upon coming home to "go back to the blanket."

The theme of the book was based on Pratt's guiding philosophy of "killing the Indian but saving the man" (Adams, 52). Carlisle School was relentless in its determination to eradicate all vestiges of Indian life, culture, and appearance in its students. To be Indian was to be savage: inwardly deviant and dishonest, outwardly filthy, stupid, and ungodly. The only good Indian was one willing to commit internal suicide, annihilating everything associated with one's former tribal life. The rich reward of such inward self-destruction was transformation of the Indian into a "true" individual woman or man with Anglo-Saxon Protestant bourgeois values, the epitome of civilization.

With its emphasis on female domesticity, the text of *Stiya* was clearly intended for a female audience. As Tsianina Lomawaima points out in her recent volume on Chilocco Indian School, "The roots of domestic education for all American women makes clear the underlying federal agenda, which was to train Indian girls in subservience and submission to authority" (81). Though Stiya initially feels despair upon coming home, in the tradition of the spunky heroine, she meets the challenges of dealing with backward-thinking parents and the tyrannical pueblo governor with bravery, pride, and self-assertion, just as any good red-blooded American would dare to do. She does not submit to the "despotism" of Native tribalism. Of course, Stiya is responsive to the values and beliefs of the white Western culture, but this is made to seem like freedom rather than subservience. Stiya does not submit to false authority; she throws off the yoke of an oppression steeped, as Pratt would say, in ignorance and superstition.

In the first chapter of the novel, titled "Disappointment," we find Stiya traveling merrily along with other Carlisle students as they return west on the train. Stiya's parents are waiting at the station to greet her when her train arrives. As she steps off the train and her parents rush to embrace her, Stiya narrates with brutal candor:

> Was I as glad to see them as I thought I would be?
>
> I must confess that instead I was shocked and surprised at the sight that met my eyes.
>
> "My father? My mother?" cried I desperately within. "No, never!" I thought, and I actually turned my back upon them.
>
> I had forgotten that home Indians had such grimy faces.
>
> I had forgotten that my mother's hair always looked as though it had never seen a comb.
>
> I had forgotten that she wore such a short, queer-looking black bag for a dress, fastened over one shoulder only, and such buckskin wrappings for shoes and leggings.
>
> "My mother?" I cried, this time aloud.
>
> I could not help it, and at the same time I rushed frantically into the arms of my school-mother, who had taken me home, and I remembered then as I never did before how kind she had always been to us. I threw my arms around her neck and cried bitterly, and begged of her to let me get on the train again.
>
> "I cannot go with that woman," I pleaded. (2–3)

Stiya's "school-mother," however, tells her to "stop crying" and "shake hands" with her parents, and Stiya, obedient and "dutiful," does so. But, she says, her father "never shall know how I suffered with mortification and regret that he was such an Indian" (4).

Historian David Wallace Adams has shown that some students did indeed experience culture clash upon returning home. He cites Polingaysi Qoyawayma's memoir. After Qoyawayma returned from the Sherman Institute, she asked her parents, "Why haven't you bought a white man's bed to sleep on? And a table? You should not be eating on a floor as the old ones did" (277).

Qoyawayma could have just finished reading her copy of *Stiya*, for interestingly Stiya's first meal at home is marked, like Qoyawayma's, with resistance to her mother's food preparation and the family's way of eating. Her mother makes a mutton stew from meat that had been hanging to dry inside their one-room dwelling. This meat, narrates Stiya, was covered with "thousands upon thousands" of flies. When the stew is ready, her mother places it on the floor at Stiya's feet. The fact that she would have to eat out of a bowl placed on the floor nauseates the girl. "'I was hungry,' she remarks, 'but could not eat; and excusing myself with a headache went outside and stood . . . in the bright moonlight and pure clear air, and thought'" (15). Outside in the "pure clear air" she notices "'human beings stretched on blankets on the tops of adjoining houses. They thus come out in the cool air to sleep and escape the vermin inside of their filthy abodes,'" says Stiya (15).[5]

In Silko's critique of Burgess's text, she also cites Polingaysi Qoyawayma's autobiography. Silko acknowledges that readjustment to village life was not easy but says that both Qoyawayma and Helen Sekaquaptewa, another returned Hopi student, clearly felt "overwhelming love and respect . . . for their families and communities despite the numerous conflicts that did arise between the boarding school graduates and village traditionalists" (Silko, 164).

By contrast, writes Silko, "the Stiya character Bergess [sic] created is detached from land and from village life. The Stiya character has no affection for any family member; every aspect of Pueblo life is repugnant. . . . she has only loathing for the traditional Pueblo ways . . . and wonders how she can possibly endure the squalor" (163). Pratt would have encouraged students in such questioning, for as Silko observes, "It was never too late for a Carlisle graduate to move to the city" (163).

Pratt preferred that his students not go home. His "Outing Program," which provided employment for students on white people's farms or in their communities, presumably allowed some Carlisle students the opportunity to stay away from their home reservations for as many as five years. The boarding school's slogan, after all, was another "Prattism": "To civilize the Indian, get him into civilization. To keep him civilized, let him stay" (quoted in Adams, 55).[6] Stiya, in spite of her return home, remains "civilized."

This is proved in the climax of the book, when Stiya and her parents are beaten by the governor of the pueblo because of her adamant refusal to don the traditional Pueblo women's clothing and attend the first ceremonial dance of the season. Stiya's disgust and disdain for traditional dress is apparent in the antipathy she feels for her mother's clothing, remarked on before but now elaborated in the following way:

> I watched my mother put on her shoes, for I had almost forgotten how she did it; but when I saw her winding yards and yards of buckskin around her ankles and saw how very neatly she did it, not a wrinkle showing in all that great winding, I remembered well, but I thought she had the funniest, clumsiest looking ankles I ever saw. Her ankles when wrapped were as thick and as straight as hitching posts. (39)

Leslie Silko writes, "The traditional clothing of Pueblo women emphasized a woman's sturdiness. Buckskin leggings wrapped around the legs protected her from scratches and injuries while she worked. The more layers of buckskin, the better. All those layers gave her legs the appearance of strength, like sturdy tree trunks" (68). Though at first Stiya seems somewhat intrigued and admiring of the "neatness" of her mother's leggings, we find instead that her feelings are closer to ridicule and shame. Burgess's little book is shot through with a hatred for the mother and traditional modes of Pueblo female work.

The dance that Stiya was "required" to attend in the novel would have been part of a ceremonial cycle that ensured the return of rain and the restoration of the earth. True to form, Stiya disdainfully tells her friend Annie that Indian dances are "disgraceful" and "shameful." Although we are never apprised of exactly what is so "disgraceful" about Indian dances, it may be that Burgess had heard about, or even witnessed, the antics of sacred clowns at dances whose defiling or sexually explicit behaviors no doubt sent shudders of horror down her spine. Obviously, the religious significance of Pueblo dances had to be denounced for the cause of Christian civilization. Before the showdown with the governor occurs, Stiya lectures her father about dances in the following manner, hoping to convince him of the error of his ways and gain his support:

> These dances are not good for our people. Our white friends, who know what we need better than we know ourselves, advise us to give up all our superstitious dances, and especially this low-down kind that is going on this afternoon. Somebody must begin to stay away from them." (79)

Stiya and her parents are beaten and jailed for refusing to obey the "cruel" governor, but this only increases their determination to change. In a switch in roles, clearly sanctioned and intended in the project of indoctrinating Indian children, the wiser daughter leads her parents out of their benighted traditions. When they return home, in a symbolic act of defiance to Pueblo ways, Stiya makes her parents sit with her at the table she bought with her "Outing" income, and "instead of the Mexican tortilla that my mother and all the Pueblo women know so well how to make, I made Carlisle biscuit, and baked them in a pan covered with hot ashes" (96). After this communion, Stiya and her father discuss leaving the "thousand-year-old . . . Pueblo[,] where there are so many who want to go in the old Indian way," for the "progressive" community of Seama, where there is a day school (98). Inspired by his daughter's "courage," her father speeds away to find work, and while her mother naps, Stiya, ever industrious, busies herself washing dishes. The moment provides Burgess with an opportunity to demonstrate Stiya's resourcefulness while making another outrageous claim about the "filth" of Pueblo life. Because Stiya has washed the dishes with water instead of letting the dog clean the dishes the way her mother would have done, Stiya must now find a way to dry them. She remembers that her school-mother packed some of the calico dresses she had brought with her from the pueblo. In another symbolic act that distances Stiya from her "savage" past, the girl takes an old dress from her Carlisle trunk and tears it into rags for cleaning and drying the dishes:

> As I sat by the fireplace on the floor . . . I could not help thinking how shocked my farm-mother would be if she saw me that minute washing dishes on the floor with a piece of calico dress, and drying them with another piece, when she had taught me to keep the dish-cloth in a certain place, and it must be so clean, and the dish towels were kept as white as snow all the time.
>
> "Well," I said to myself, "this is the very best I can do just now. If I do the very best I can all the time, I don't care what any one says. I will keep these calico rags clean at least, if they are not white." (103)

Though Stiya, too, can never be white, she can at least be clean, purified of "backward" and "heathenish" traditions by "enlightened" and "progressive" ideas. In the denouement of the story, Stiya and her father both secure jobs—her father shovels coal at the railway station, and Stiya works for the trader's family. They save their money and eventually buy a new home at Seama. Stiya delights her parents by baking pies for them and cooking "meat and eggs and potatoes and cabbage and other good things," which she sets on her table spread with a cloth and napkins (115). The book concludes with Stiya remarking that she "never regretted having braved the first hard steps that led me out of the accursed home slavery and made me a free woman" (115).

I am inclined, with Leslie Silko's Grandma A'mooh, to believe that Mariana Burgess's priceless book of propaganda should be burned as an artifact of incredible witchery. Like Aunt Susie, I am also inclined to preserve my Xeroxed copy and, as I have just done, write about and cite from it so that we may all be reminded of the lethal aspects of the federal program of indoctrination and assimilation of Indian children. It was no easy matter to "erase" the Indian child's past and replace it with writing more to the colonizer's liking. It was no easy matter to make into "Stiyas" all the little Indian girls who left their homes for boarding school excited and happy at a new adventure or terrified, homesick, and depressed at leaving their families and communities. Ultimately, what Indian girls were to learn they could not have foreseen. They would never have suspected that they would be required to internalize the hatred and antipathy the white world felt toward them and to return home with the goal of leading their parents out of the "degradation" of their "heathen ways." They would never have suspected that to view themselves as whole and beautiful women, they would, from a white perspective, have to see their mothers and grandmothers as ugly, filthy, and ridiculous.

Fortunately, even for Carlisle graduates such as Silko's relatives, the indoctrination was resisted so that in Silko's generation—and hopefully seven generations hence—the beauty and harmony of traditional thought is preserved. Silko honors female power and persistence in her homage to Kochininako, Yellow Woman. The value and importance of American Indian literature is that it continues to provide a way of exploring the heart's truth through storytelling. It reminds us that wherever we walk in this world we enter what was once—and often still is—someone's home, someone's heart and sacred space. We ask only that it be treated with respect.

Notes

I would like to thank Barbara Landis, Virginia Carney, and Mimi Wheatwind for their help with this essay.

This chapter was previously published as "Telling Stories in the Seventh Generation: Resisting the Assimilationist Narrative of *Stiya*," in *Engendering Communication*, edited by Suzanne Wertheim, Ashlee C. Baily, and Monica Corston-Oliver, University of California Berkeley Women and Language Conference Publication, 1998. Reprinted by permission.

1. The newspaper went through a number of name changes, and there may have been more than one newspaper being published, at least at first. The earliest paper, titled *School News*, was edited by a Native student named Samuel Townsend, and text seems to have been largely supplied by students themselves. A second paper seems to have begun publication, possibly under Pratt's editorship, during the first year of Carlisle's operation. It was named *Eadleh Keatah Toh* (Big Morning Star) and later renamed *The Red Man*, then *The Red Man and Helper*. See Littlefield and Parrins.

2. Silko writes that the author of *Stiya* "wrote the novel under the fake Indian name Tonke" (162). Burgess did inscribe the book as follows: "To Tonke, who shared the pleasures and sorrows of a trip among the Pueblos, this little book is lovingly dedicated by The Author." It is not clear whether "Tonke" is an Indian or not; I suspect not. My guess is that "Tonke" is the nickname or "Indian" pseudonym of a close friend and possibly fellow teacher of Burgess's at Carlisle. Silko also writes that the book was published by "the U.S. War Department in 1881." This seems to be incorrect, too. The copyright on my copy of *Stiya* is 1891. Although earlier versions of the text may have been published, corroborating evidence from a recent paper by Isleta scholar Ted Jojola states that the novel was published in 1891 (Landis, e-mail commu-

nication). Also, the administration of the Indian Office or Indian Bureau was overseen by the Department of the Interior after 1849, so the book was probably not published under the War Department's auspices. Indeed, my copy states that the publisher is Cambridge and that the printing was done "at the Riverside Press."

3. To add to the aura of authenticity about the novel, and perhaps give the impression that the book is an autobiographical fiction, Burgess provides the reader with a photograph of "Stiya" as a frontispiece. Though there was a Stiya Kowkura/Koykuri who attended Carlisle—and who was Pueblo—the young Indian woman in the photo is an Apache student named Lucy Tsisnah (personal correspondence with Barbara Landis, librarian at the Cumberland State Historical Society). In the photo she is perhaps sixteen or seventeen years old. She stands erect, her arms folded on the arm of a high-backed Victorian settee. Her hair is pulled back in a neat bun, and over a heavy floor-length skirt "Stiya" wears a military-style jacket with a cadet collar. This was probably the "dress uniform" distributed to girls at Carlisle, in contrast to the less elegant work clothes dispensed to them for daily wear. Burgess/"Embe" writes on the title page of the text that the story we are about to read is "Founded on the Author's Actual observations," but since we don't know who exactly the author is (is Embe a real person?; is Stiya?), we are encouraged to read the text as the work of a single American Indian student. The word *observations* suggests that the events contained in the narrative were merely witnessed and recorded rather than physically or emotionally lived.

Pratt commissioned before-and-after photographs of these students, showing their "savage" condition when they first entered the school and contrasting it with their appearance some time later. One of Pratt's supporters, Merrill E. Gates, was enthusiastic about the apparent "transformation" of Indian children, as evidenced by the photographs. In his report to the Board of Indian Commissioners in 1885, he states, "The years of contact with ideas and with civilized men and Christian women so transform them that their faces shine with a wholly new light, for they have indeed 'communed with God.' They came children; they return young men and young women; yet they look younger in the face than when they came to us. The prematurely aged look of helpless heathenish has given way to that dew of eternal youth which marks the difference between the savage and the man who lives in the thoughts of an eternal future" (quoted in Prucha, 54).

4. I use David Wallace Adams's term "returned student." See chapter 9, "Home," in his book *Education for Extinction: American Indians and the Boarding School Experience, 1875–1928* (Lawrence: University Press of Kansas, 1995).

5. Silko writes that one reason Grandma A'mooh was upset with *Stiya* is that she felt it was a "libelous portrayal of Pueblo life and people. There was a particularly mendacious passage concerning the Pueblo practice of drying meat in the sun. The meat was described as bloody and covered with flies. Grandma A'mooh was outraged" (164).

6. My thanks to Barbara Landis for the coined term "Prattism."

References

Adams, David Wallace. *Education for Extinction: American Indians and the Boarding School Experience, 1875–1928.* Lawrence: University Press of Kansas, 1995.

Burgess, Mariana. *Stiya: A Carlisle Indian Girl at Home.* Cambridge: Riverside Press, 1891.

Erdrich, Louise. *Jacklight.* New York: Holt, Rinehart and Winston, 1984.

Landis, Barbara. Carlisle Indian School Research Specialist, Cumberland County Historical Society. E-mail to author, 9 July 1999.

Littlefield, Daniel F., Jr., and James W. Parrins. *American Indian and Alaska Native Newspapers and Periodicals, 1826–1924.* Westport, CT: Greenwood Press, 1984.

Lomawaima, K. Tsianina. *They Called It Prairie Light: The Story of Chilocco Indian School.* Lincoln: University of Nebraska, 1994.

Prucha, Francis Paul, ed. *Americanizing the American Indians: Writings by the "Friends of the Indian," 1880–1900.* Lincoln: University of Nebraska, 1973.

Silko, Leslie. *Yellow Woman and a Beauty of the Spirit: Essays on Native American Life Today.* New York: Simon and Schuster, 1995.

Tapahonso, Luci. *Blue Horses Rush In: Poems and Stories.* Tucson: University of Arizona Press, 1997.

Blood, Rebellion, and Motherhood in the Political Imagination of Indigenous People

2

VICTORIA BOMBERRY

This essay began after I read Carolyn Steedman's *Landscape for a Good Woman* (1994), which is written with a keen awareness of the author's English working-class background and the illegitimacy of her birth. Her metaphorical borderlands are multiple; they intersect class in terms of her rise from a poor working-class background to academic professional, her nationality (the crossing of a real geographical border between England and the United States), and the deeply felt ambivalence of the circumstances of her birth. Although her background and mine could not have been more different at first glance, I am struck by the profound sense of sadness and longing that is her mother's legacy. That emotional presence is felt throughout her extraordinary book. Her mother's outsider status as an unmarried mother fueled her mother's intense craving for legitimacy and the better life it seemed to promise. Later, her longing and envy found expression in the virulent conservative politics in which she took refuge in a desperate attempt at belonging.

Steedman's use of Gloria Anzaldua's concept of borderlands is helpful in clarifying metaphorical and emotional borderlands that are often obscured by positionality, whether you are a woman of color or a woman from the working class like Steedman. Anzaldua's concept is sometimes reduced to a version of being caught between two cultures. This fails to capture the dynamic interplay between cultures, subjectivity, and the agency required to successfully negotiate a complex set of circumstances located in ethnicity, race, class, gender, nationality, and sexuality. Caught between two cultures implies a kind of paralysis and an inability to act in any meaningful way in either culture. Anzaldua defines borderlands in the following passage from the preface of her book:

> Borderlands are physically present wherever two or more cultures edge each other, where people of different races occupy the same territory, where under, lower,

middle and upper classes touch, where the space between two individuals shrinks with intimacy. (not numbered)

The tentativeness of this definition belies systems of interchange that are present, ongoing, and always contingent. Paradoxically, Anzaldua's borders appear hard, restrictive, and extremely successful at excluding, filtering, and discarding the other while simultaneously attempting to recover the indigenous. Mary Louise Pratt's "contact zone" makes these complex sets of circumstances visible as well as points out the geographical locations and historical and temporal elements on which they depend.

> [Contact zone] refer[s] to the space of colonial encounters, the space in which peoples geographically and historically separated come into contact with each other and establish ongoing relations, usually involving conditions of coercion, radical inequality, and intractable conflict. (6)

I believe that in "intractable conflict" are the seeds of profound transformation. The narrative of conflict and rebellion is necessary not only for the maintenance of oppositional points of view but also for the processes of transformation. Since Pratt's introduction of the term, there has been a tendency on the part of some scholars to speak of the contact zone as a heady euphoric utopia. While they are extremely productive, contact zones are also a source of great pain and disappointment. They create opportunities for forging alliances that would otherwise be impossible, but sometimes at great costs. I use the term *borderlands* to refer to spaces that are both metaphorical and real, permeable, and emotionally charged and that contain the potentiality of radical transformations of consciousness. Both time and geography play an enormous part in understanding the narrative contained in this essay.

I also examine the idea of a "good woman," a category that might change in the particulars but can be restrictive and destructive to womanhood across cultures when there is inequality between men and women. For many indigenous women, the colonial project resulted in a steady erosion of status and rights and, at times, an overt attack on womanhood and motherhood.

As I delved deeper into each of these issues, I had no idea how difficult it would be to put on paper the thoughts and feelings that surfaced when I examined my life and the lives of my grandmother and mother. I mention this to prepare those of you who undertake this kind of work for emotions ranging from delight in finding the patterns in our lives and gratitude to our many grandmothers and mothers to rage and what seems inconsolable grief. This is also a response to those who say we cannot do good work because we are "too close" to the "objects" of our studies. We must do this work because we are involved in a constant battle to be seen and heard as indigenous women. Indigenous men describing women's lives in the political sphere too easily subsume our stories within what they perceive as a more important battle for recognition of indigenous rights. Our stories cannot be implied in a larger story of our people, nor can we be simply portrayed as selfless, strong women without losing the very real experiences of indigenous women in all parts of our lives, including the political.

I am the daughter of a Muscogee, Choctaw, Chickasaw woman; I am the granddaughter of a Muscogee woman. We are bound to one another and to the historical circumstances into which we were each born. Our life stories reflect these at various turns along our paths. We are, after all, emotional beings who feel the losses and exclusions all over again when we enter the rocky terrain of the borderlands of our pasts and presents. Even though I was captivated by the way stories get told across generations when you reside in the borderlands, I was not prepared for the pain that resurfaced and ebbed over the course of writing this essay. Through this process, I had to become more conscious of how suppressed histories and secret stories work on and through us. Steedman asserts the force of secret stories:

> Real secrets, real events that are concealed by some members of a family, may be matters of legal impropriety and thus connected to the social world outside the household; but such secrets can also produce myths of origin that serve both to reveal and conceal what is actually hidden from view. (66)

I found that the fear of speaking our truth formed a countercurrent in all that I remembered. Unlike the established norms that the very existence of Steedman's family origins transgressed, our family secret stories revealed a time, a specific location, and people who were locked in deadly conflict. There were opposing norms with no sure outcomes.

Going over violent events that happened and are still happening to our people (read "our people" as an attempt in a thin abstraction to place distance between myself and that violence, to not feel it, to detach), I was forced to see that violence as real, happening to my own family whom I love dearly. I was enraged; I felt powerless; I felt ashamed; I felt guilty. I was in abysmal pain, as if my blood were thickly congested and had lost all its life-giving properties. I found that the only way through it was to look to my grandmother's stories, or what I have come to understand and know as women's talk, for relief, for a course of action, for understanding—an insight or clue to our individual and social being. I found myself compelled to make sense of the "contact zone" that Oklahoma was at the turn of the century.

I have come to realize that my grandmother used personal "secret stories" to transmit what I perceived as a child to be only family history. Yet, when I turned seventeen, my grandmother told me the beginning of a story that awakened me in a way I had never experienced. Her secret stories became a method of explaining the overtly political parts of our lives. They demonstrated how circumscribed that political life had become over the years. Our speech had been gradually confined to the household, held by a generation that had been unable to integrate the stories into the lives of their children. She began to tell me about the Crazy Snake Rebellion from her childhood memories, and I realized at once that she was narrating not only our family history but also a history of resistance and the subsequent "death" of the Muscogee Nation at the dawn of Oklahoma statehood. She was providing a cultural, political, and historical context that she had always denied to me. She only began the story then. I learned of her childhood role of carrying food to a cave where the wounded Chitto Harjo (Crazy Snake) lay in hiding from the government troops. She was seven years old at the time.

Her story shaped my politics in my own search for a new articulation of Indian nationhood during the 1970s and through the 1980s. The Snake resisters had two goals that resonated with the aims of progressive factions within Indian Country: (1) the recognition and enforcement of the 1832 treaty promising that the Creek Nation would not be infringed upon again and (2) the return to tribal government, which was being dissolved as a result of statehood—the Dawes and Curtis Acts broke up the communally held land. The Snakes refused to sign up for allotments and gathered to choose the leaders of the traditional council. During her storytelling, I saw her piece together various textures, which were highly nuanced. In what others might term fragmentary and nostalgic in the academic terms of today, I recognized a way of teaching that spoke to my own development as an indigenous woman. My telling you this now intertwines my grandmother's life and mine by compressing and lengthening time, and I hope you understand that it speaks of my different understanding of events at different moments, in what I now believe is the approach my grandmother employed.

The Story of Chitto Harjo

"One night I heard menfolks talking outside the old house." My grandmother motioned toward the dirt road that led to her parents' house. Although it had slowly fallen into disrepair and finally ruin after Great Aunt Selina died, I could still see it whole in the darkness through Grandma's eyes as she talked. "I was just a little girl. I could hear those menfolks bringing someone into the house, cvr-ke [papa] and all of them who were with him. There was blood everywhere and I didn't know what happened. I was scared. No one saw me watching them bring him in. I saw it was Chitto Harjo; he was shot. [long pause] You know, Crazy Snake." Her English softened the sound of Crazy Snake. She looked at me from the corner of her eye, knowing I couldn't know who he was unless she told me, at the same time impatient with me for not knowing. The tension that surrounded the silences in our history caught the pain and held it. Every time my grandmother breached the silence it was deliberate, a gift that could wound as well as help me understand what had made us who we are. Did she believe it was still dangerous to be Indian sixty-five years after Chitto Harjo was shot?

I could see that she knew she was telling me something for the first time and I had to pay attention. No, I didn't know Chitto Harjo, even though by then I was a young woman. I was careful not to say anything because of her look that said watch and listen. "They doctored him there at the old house. Cvr-ke [papa] had to get him out quick and hide him. E-he [yes], he hid him in that cave. Every day after that I took him food. I was just a little girl then. Okis [I am the one telling you this]." She spoke formally to me. That was all she told me then.

We sat quietly as usual on the porch, less than a quarter mile from the old house near the place Chitto Harjo lay bleeding. The spot has become for our family as real as if a bronze marker stood there. Chitto Harjo's blood brands the red earth that peeks through the rocky, cedar-strewn floor of the land. The stones near the old house still bear the names of my mother and her three sisters. They scratched their names in the boulders when they were about the same age my grandmother was when she took food to Chitto Harjo. Near those imprinted with their names are other stones where you can see footprints—marks of ancestors of that land, the strong medicine of remembrance.

When speaking of things that had to do with the government, my grandmother always adopted a tone of bitter resignation. That tone fell away, and all I remember is hearing the desperation of people who wanted to remain Muscogee in Muscogee Land. I heard women's voices. I heard men's voices. I heard the sounds of horses and guns and saw the oozing wound of Chitto Harjo. In the twilight of the cave a dream was dying. We had dreamed together; dreamed ourselves whole, dark, and beautiful in an abundant, undivided Muscogee Land. We had welcomed African, Alabama, Coushatta, and a score of small remnant nations to share in that communal dream while we still resided in the Southeast. The dream had been revived after the bitter removals and resettlement in Indian Territory. Muscogee orators wooed the people of Indian Territory with the utopian vision of Indian statehood, where equality and mutual responsibility were the ideals that governed the nation. Now the lifeblood of the dream was failing, replaced by greed for the oil-rich land.

A few years earlier Eufaula Harjo, speaking at the ceremonials in the Creek town of Tulsa, said, "The mountains and hills, that you see, are your backbone, and the gullies and the creeks, which are between the hills and the mountains, are your heart veins"; Angie Debo, the historian who wrote extensively of the Five Nations, remarks that when the land was divided the Indians knew the horror of

050412

dismemberment (*Road*, 4). Rather than a one-to-one correspondence that would romantically link Indianness with nature, the land corresponds to the political body. Even the idea of nation that was a European invention is pushed aside in thinking about the relationship of people to land and to one another.

The Muscogee had already lived through the violent separation from the aboriginal homeland. Now the political body was dismembered and scattered in the same way that the physical body of the great Aymara leader Tupac Katari was quartered and scattered by the Spanish in the sixteenth century in what is now Bolivia. The myth of Inca Rey, in which the body of the Inca king miraculously becomes whole again, speaks to the desire of and belief in some future reunification of the people. No corresponding myth was elaborated in Muscogee Land; however, the yearning for self-government and self-determination was kept alive by the Snakes and revived again at the end of the century.

In its place, the myth of blood quantum became the grounds for understanding relationships within the new state. The introduction of blood quantum was forced on native people during the Dawes Act (1898) in Oklahoma. Over the next several years, Native people were forced to register and to complete a family tree that established the amount of Indian blood of each person. This became the basis for the redistribution of land in the state. The fresh memory of the horror of cultural dismemberment in the first years of the twentieth century set terror loose in Muscogee Land once again. Thinking through terror forced remembrance underground. The secret stories concealed the thinking of full-bloods from a public that had grown hostile and race conscious. The utopian ideals that fueled the Indian political imagination and articulated a place outside the imperialist myth were aborted. The dream of an Indian nation where, to borrow from Michael Taussig, Indian, African, and white could give birth to a New World would lay dormant for years to come (5).

In the preceding years, statehood was bitterly and violently contested by the tribes whose nation status was in jeopardy. On July 14, 1905, representatives of all the tribes in Indian Territory met in Muskogee, Oklahoma, to adopt a constitution for a state that was to be called Sequoyah. It was a remarkable feat of organizing and unifying vastly different tribes and tribal factions, who had been locked in bitter civil wars forty years earlier, under a unified banner of a new Indian nation—a testimony to the skillful diplomacy of Indian leaders and organizers. Unfortunately, by 1906 the United States had divided and allotted all the land to individual family members, and new boundaries were drawn along racial lines. Indian Territory and Oklahoma Territory were joined, becoming the forty-sixth state on November 16, 1907. The governments of the Indian nations were disbanded, and what had been a native-controlled school system was appropriated by the new state.

As a child attending public school, I studied the heroics of white settlers lined up on the borders of the Territory waiting for the signal, ready to urge their wagons and horses onward. Stakes and markers in hand, these eager colonizers charged onto the land in a series of land rushes, the most dramatic of which occurred in 1889. The signifier "Indian" was taken out of the territory, reinforcing the notion of the wild frontier in need of taming. Wild and civilized were locked in strict opposition in the historical narrative and acted out on the land. The land was claimed, physically and often violently, the stakes driven deep into the earth. The murder of whole Indian families was frequent, yet the historical narrative presented the land rush as laying claim to empty, fertile territory. Readily forgotten are the murders, the usurpation and violent erasure of native peoples.

I can look back now and see why the pictures accompanying the official history in my schoolbooks were so profoundly disturbing. They depicted determined, rugged white men digging their spurs or cracking their whips deep into animal flesh, driven by a violent desire to possess a land that did not belong to them. Glorifying those who jumped the gun in a mad rush of greed and envy, the nickname the Sooner State seemed at best a cynical joke at the native peoples' expense. It was a lesson full of sorrow for me and the other Indian students in the class. We were silent, contained by the four walls of the classroom: the institutional green of the bottom half of the wall met the yellowing white upper half of the wall. I became a master of stillness. I stared at the line that circled the entire classroom where the two colors met, which mimicked the sharp division within the classroom.

The combat over that story never occurred in the classroom; we stored our anger and let it loose on the playground. The pushing and shoving and the intense athletic prowess were all part and parcel of the inability to speak in the classroom. Our bodies spoke what our voices could not.

During music class, our voices joined with the other children's in renditions of Rogers and Hammerstein's Broadway hit and 1954 Academy Award—winning film *Oklahoma!* The musical locates the dramatic conflict in forging unity in an emergent state in the relationship between the fresh-faced cowboy and the staid, reasonable farm girl. It offers an easy solution for the resentments generated by the Oklahoma land rush. The only categories of inhabitants of the territory, in the Rogers and Hammerstein musical, are the cowboy and farmer whose differences actually amount to nothing more than a matter of taste, according to the pair of songwriters. They succinctly demonstrate this in the chorus of the song "The Farmer and the Cowman."

> The farmer and the cowman should be friends,
> Oh, the farmer and the cowman should be friends.
> One man likes to push a plough, the other likes to chase a cow,

> But that's no reason why they can't be friends.
> Territory folks should stick together,
> Territory folks should be pals.
> Cowboys dance with farmer's daughters,
> Farmers dance with the ranchers' gals.

The opposing poles are first homogenized in the chorus by the exclusive tag "Territory folks," then consolidated by the exchange of women at the country dance that will culminate with the pairing of the cowman's and farmer's children. The unspoken battle between progress represented by the farmer and the wild retrogression represented by the cowboy is simply dissolved. For Anglo-Americans, the Biblical story of Cain and Abel is innocently resolved. Predictably, the word *Indian*, which should precede Territory, never makes it onto the lyrics sheet. For a child, absence and erasure is the most insidious weapon education deploys. The seemingly innocent songs, sung by schoolchildren, especially the deracinated *Oklahoma!* in the multi-racial, multi-ethnic state whose name inspired it, are a gross albeit unconscious violation.

Fortunately, the native children in our class knew that *Oklahoma* is a Choctaw word for "red people"; we never questioned its meaning. It was a name that everyone recognized as "Indian." The Choctaw-speaking Reverend Allen Wright coined the term, which certainly had a better ring to it than the I. T. (Indian Territory) scrawled on nineteenth-century maps. Non-native children would pronounce with wide-eyed authority, almost in whispers, "It means home of the red man!" as if anything louder might disturb the ghostly presence of officialdom that the classroom represented to us. The ubiquitous exclamation point in *Oklahoma!* is often interpreted as the neverending optimism of the American psyche, but for me it captures the underlying paranoia that accompanies institutionalized silence. That paranoia operates on and through the hegemonic citizen, in this case non-native children, as unnamed fear and perhaps guilt, lurking beneath surface well-being. The border is established and reinforced between normative racial homogeneity and other. Curiously, skin tone had less to do with the barrier than self-identification and class. The silent erasure of the native in *Oklahoma!* (cast in terms of the "empty" home of the red man) creates a black cloud over the narrative that traverses tornado-like throughout the plot and drops down in the elementary music class. There, native opposition consisted of holding on for dear life to a name. Oklahoma! Native "Oklahoma!" is simultaneously a talisman against the erasure of self and a cultural marker of the collectivity of red people.

After so many years, what prompted my grandmother to open the story of the Crazy Snake Rebellion, which was a part of the long struggle against the "death" of the Muscogee Nation? Why did she tell only bits and pieces over a period of many years? How did the safe space from which to speak reveal itself to her? These are only a few of the questions that swirl around me as I remember her words. She was keenly aware of the politics surrounding her, from what she could expect to push for and get from the local county commissioner (particularly around election time), who was in national politics, to who wanted to lease her land and why in any given year. The process of reconstructing the oral history of our family was caught up in all of these considerations. I believe now that the ebbs and flows of what ruled as the common sense of the nation played a role in what she would and would not talk about.

Over a period of fifteen years, my grandmother revealed more of the years that opened the new century. The landscape of stories gradually came into focus, bringing each part of the land into view. Her most personal revelations were always tied to the places in the physical landscape of eastern Oklahoma. Time came loose from its moorings, even though the landscape bore the marks of change. The simple story of her widowhood intensified. In 1924 my grandmother married and gave birth to four girls before she was widowed six years later. That much I had always known, but what I didn't know was the depth of her sorrow when she realized firsthand that motherhood was not immune to assault by the nation-state that grew up around her. The loss of her children to the federally run boarding schools was a chapter that haunted her for the rest of her life.

In the waning years of the twentieth century, I cannot help but compare my life to my grandmother's. As a Native American mother and enrolled member of the rebirthed Muscogee Nation, I also want to think through the meaning of *motherhood* and *nation*. I became a mother in 1980 with the birth of the first of my three sons. It was the year that Ronald Reagan came into the presidency, bringing with him the rhetoric of family values and the seeds of a xenophobic nationalism that bore fruit in the 1990s in the new jingoism and exclusionary practices that are growing daily. Although I am also Choctaw, Chickasaw, and Lenni Lenape, my primary identification has followed customary law. We identify ourselves through our mothers' clans and national affiliations, which means that I am a member of the Raccoon Clan and a citizen of Muscogee Nation. Until a few years ago, I was comfortable with this method of identification, but there was always the nagging feeling that I was forced to give short shrift to a part of my heritage that had determined in large part how I saw the world.

I was uncomfortable with a strain of Native American nationalism that ran parallel to Ronald Reagan's, a vision that grew out of the American Indian Movement in the 1960s. It denied on the one hand that our racially mixed heritages existed but contested on the other the notion of blood quantum in determining cultural identity. My husband, like me, came from a mixed First Nations background. His father was Cayuga from the Six Nations Reserve in Ontario, Canada, and his mother Squamish from North Vancouver, British Columbia. Her family had also intermarried with Hawaiian merchant seamen who had fled Hawaii in the latter half of the nineteenth century. In a climate that denied these vast migrations and mixings and located Indianness in authenticating spaces on reserves and reservations, there was little room for those of us who lived outside that reality. There was a massive push in the language of the Red Power movement to go home again, to reclaim tribal purity and a return to original laws. At the same time, the nationalists ignored or perhaps could not see the new mapping taking place that had its foundations in an earlier version of Indian nationalism that laid claim to the power of a dynamic world. Still, home tugged at the heart.

Two small hills rise from the green rolling farmland near Eufaula, Oklahoma. The tops of the hills are dotted with blackjack oak, cedar, hickory, dogwood, and pine. The winters are generally mild in this part of the state. It is rare for snow to stay on the ground for more than a day. The flowering dogwood seems to bring spring in on its coattails and, along with the beauty, the danger of hibernating snakes who also wake up to the warmth. The summers are so hot and humid that sweat does little to cool the body. The falls are beautiful because of the brightly colored leaves that the cold, crisp air of the fall weather intensifies.

For more than a century, Twin Hills and the surrounding area has been one of the last places identified as a full-blood Muscogee stronghold in McIntosh County. The names are old ones. Eufaula is one of the original *talwas* moved from the aboriginal Muscogee Land 1,500 miles to the east, in what is now Georgia and Alabama. The county is named after William McIntosh, a mixed-blood chief who was one of the signatories of a "treaty" exchanging all of Muscogee Land for a tract in Oklahoma in the first half of the nineteenth century. McIntosh was condemned by the council for his betrayal of the compact between the members of the confederation that prohibited the sale or transfer of Muscogee Land. Anyone violating the compact was condemned to death. Opothle Yahola, the spokesman of the Muscogee Council, warned McIntosh that signing the land away would have fatal consequences. McIntosh escaped the death sentence, but in the next decade more than half the citizens of Muscogee Land perished in the series of harsh removals that followed.

Twin Hills, the descriptive name applied to the two blackjack oak–covered hills when Muscogee people moved their *talwa* to the New Muscogee Nation, now designates prime real estate along the shores of Lake Eufaula. The lake is a vast body of water created by the Corps of Engineers in the 1960s by damming the Canadian River. Anxiety ran high when rumors of the dam began to circulate in the late 1950s. The memory of removal resurfaced as women all over Muscogee Land cried at the thought of disturbing the bodies of the dead. Even worse was the thought that the dead would be forgotten under the waters of the lake. I was a girl then. I remember that bitter, outraged tears flowed among the strong, angry voices of the women. A few years before we had buried my mother near many of our relatives in Eufaula. I felt an intense fear of losing her all over again. I dreaded the loss of the names and stories of relatives who had died before her.

After a while, letters on official government stationery began to arrive in post office boxes in town. Individuals received the standard form letters through the Bureau of Indian Affairs (BIA), notifying them of the intended dam. The official letters outlined the plans and assured people that graves would be protected or moved, well out of the path of the water. The individual letters reminded everyone they were separate and alone, and the letters reinforced the wardship status between the federal government and the Muscogee people.

At that time, Muscogee Nation as a political entity was a shadow, a memory stretching back before statehood. The anxiety of political powerlessness choked any thought of collective opposition. As the women predicted, the dam brought new removals of both the dead and living members of Muscogee Nation. Hushed tones and tears of grief followed a few years later when people received notice of the condemnation of their land. As I remember, the communal cemetery space was the first to go. Bodies were exhumed and moved out of the path of the floodwaters. Over the next few years, families were moved. The places they held in Muscogee Land were enfolded in the story of loss. The lake has existed for more than thirty years now. Drowned blackjack oaks and hickory trees that once struggled for survival against the rising flood have been claimed by the muddy waters of the lake, thoroughly mixed in the sandy silt bottom.

My grandmother's house still sits at the top of one of the hills. She spent her whole life there, with three exceptions. Her first time away was when she went to school at Haskell Institute in Lawrence, Kansas. The second time was when she married my grandfather and moved to Choctaw Nation until he died six years later. The third time was when she went to Los Angeles to work in a munitions factory during World War II.

Angie Debo, the Oklahoman historian, writes that Chitto Harjo was the most eloquent spokesman of the Creek full-bloods. "He lived in a log cabin in the hills along the North Canadian, cultivated five or ten acres of land with a pony, raised cattle and hogs and filled his smokehouse with meat, and sharpened his neighbors' plowshares and beat out silver ornaments on a little forge he had constructed" (*Road*, 310).

My great-grandparents, both full-bloods, lived a life very similar to Chitto Harjo. Although the river is dammed now, the old house and my grandmother's house is located near a fork of the North Canadian River. In front of my grandmother's house are the volunteers that sprouted from the old orchard trees—pear, peach, and pecan—planted by her mother and father. The area is thick with hickory and blackjack oaks, as well as wild berries such as the sweet, juicy kv-co-hul-kv (dew-berries) that grow close to the ground, flower, and bear fruit before the taller, heartier kv-co-hue-ra (blackberries). Smaller trees such as sand plums and elderberry are abundant. The dark purple wild grapes and their smaller cousins, the possum grape, grow up and encircle the bigger trees. Dock, polk salad, and tv-fum-pue-ce (wild onions) bring in the tv-sut-ce (spring) as people excitedly go out and gather the young tender shoots.

My grandmother's home still remains my first home. For my own children, home has become an almost mythic place where the full moon turns night into day.

Language

My grandmother's experience of school was tied to a vision of acquiring language, and with language, the power to negotiate the new reality in which she lived. Although they made a living from the land, the full-blood holdouts from the allotment policy in many cases received the most marginal farmland. The "surplus" land of Muscogee Nation was given to white settlers. My grandmother told me: "I was eighteen years old when I asked cvr-ke [papa] if I could go away to school. I was working in the fields with him when I asked if I could go to Haskell. I didn't speak a word of English and I wanted to learn. Cvr-ke [papa] didn't want me to go, but I was the oldest and he couldn't say no. I boarded the train with other Indian girls on their way to school, some for the first time like me. I was a big girl but I had to learn with all the little kids in the primary grades. Oh, I sho nuff ashamed at first. I couldn't speak a word of English. I met Indians from everywhere at Haskell. When I came back I spoke English better than a white woman. I could hold my own with any of them. Now, my English is broken and I've forgotten so many words that I knew. But they never could cheat me." The remembrance of opposition to the new reality surfaces in her statement. Her school experience was voluntary and was vastly different from what the school experience of her own children was to be. At the same time that my grandmother held onto the intense pride she had of being self-sufficient on her small plot of land and cagey enough not to be cheated, she expressed regret at not holding a job. In her mind, a job equated legitimacy and citizenship, not only in Muscogee Nation but also in the United States. There was a keen ambivalence at play in her desire to be viewed as a wage earner rather than a full-blood living on the land. In the official eyes of the Bureau of Indian Affairs, she lived an antiquated, useless life on "restricted land." These same officials wielded enormous power over her rights to production and reproduction in terms of children and culture.

The war waged by language is dramatically manifest in this single term. From the hegemonic popular viewpoint, "restricted land" appeared to be the unproductive prison that she was confined within, while the bureaucrats of the Bureau of Indian Affairs saw "restricted" in terms of the regulations and paperwork that had to be completed to make that land available for non-native settlers. Fortunately, it is difficult to sell restricted land. However, the land can be effectively alienated from the people who own it, by leasing it to outside parties, if the regulations are followed. In my grandmother's view the land was Muscogee Land, and she as a citizen of that land and a family member had usufruct rights to the land that could be passed from generation to generation.

Through production on the land and the right to reproduce culture, succeeding generations would have knowledge of these rights and enact them. As the hegemonic term *restricted land* took hold, many native people became caught up in a fight for who would control what happened with their "real estate." The single term *restricted land* led to a new way of thinking of Muscogee Land as commodity. For many, the battle shifted from maintaining some form of communal landholding to a battle over sales of a commodity.

In a particularly bitter moment in the 1960s, I remember my grandmother criticizing a new language program, not because Muscogee language was finally to be taught at Haskell in Lawrence, Kansas, but because it was yet another manifestation of white people deciding something about language. "Before [when she was at school] they forbid us to speak Muscogee, and now they say it is good to speak your language. Now, there are words I don't remember. I ask Alice [her sister] and she doesn't remember either." This from a woman who was completely bilingual but could feel the destruction of the nuances of language and memory imposed from outside and the violence done to her and the community. She could see the problems in thinking through native concepts generated by the war the English language waged on our thoughts.

She never believed the pride I felt for her ability to speak our native tongue and English. She had an uncanny ability to maintain and pass on native concepts to me in English. She referred to her English as broken when it was I who felt that my tongue was broken, incapable of speaking what my ears could hear fleetingly, in snatches, bare meaning, words sweet with my desire to know them, to feel them in my mouth and being. I felt the bitter taste of her knowledge that somehow she had been forced to acquiesce to this loss, and now the reinstatement of her language as worthy to be taught within the curriculum of the very school that denied her language to her could only be taken as a cruel insult. It was as if I were a strange young woman sitting at her side who was evidence of her unwitting consent. How would she talk with her own flesh and blood in her old age? Who would understand her? This was always unspoken between us, but we both knew when she spoke to me in Muscogee that my understanding was flawed and incomplete. It lay like a cold stone between us: her refusal to explain when I asked and later my refusal to ask for explanation. I still feel the ache of rejection that the loss of my language engendered. My grandmother belonged to a world that she was sending me from, for what she saw as survival in a different future. As bewildering and frightening as it seemed, I trusted her sending me. There was no choice. The acceptance of the pain in our lives that the stillbirth of the new Indian nation allegorized lay deep in the ground like the water that could never be found on the hill where my grandmother lived.

While acquiring English as a second language gave my grandmother a tool with which to fight back, there was nothing in writing to mirror her reality. I have gone through the literature and found very little written on the Crazy Snake Rebellion. I visited the Muscogee national archives a few years ago, only to be told that the materials would not be available for years. What remains of the story is only a minimum outline and leaves the following question: Who gets to tell the story of rebellion over the years? At the time of the Snake Rebellion, Alex Posey, the mixed-blood writer from Eufaula and employee of the Dawes Commission, commented profusely on the Snakes in articles and poems published throughout Oklahoma in which he alternately praised and condemned the rebels. To Posey, Chitto Harjo was "the last true Creek, perhaps the last to dare declare, 'You have wronged me!'" (Littlefield, 144). By 1902, Posey wrote about the Snakes, "They are the most ignorant among the Indians." When Chitto Harjo and a number of his followers were arrested and sent to jail, Posey jeered: "This ought to be a warning to all Indians to be good." By this time, Posey's own anxiety about progress and Indianness culminated in his disavowal of his earlier portrayal of the rebels as noble savages. Perhaps his collusion with the commission lay the seeds of guilt in his conscience. Did he feel shame for his work with the Dawes Commission that became entangled with shame of the defeat of the Snakes? Posey began to represent himself as more and more apolitical as the years wore on, although he built a personal empire through real estate holdings and the leasing of oil-rich land from the Indians.

Posey died young. He ignored warnings and attempted to cross the swollen floodwaters of the North Canadian River and was swept away in the red waters. At the edge of the town limits, a historical marker bears his likeness and what seems from this vantage point an ironic designation: Creek National Poet.

If the defeat of the Snakes lay heavy on the consciousness of the opposition, how did it affect my grandmother to be represented as the most ignorant of the ignorant, defeated and jeered by literate Indian men in fancy suits, ready to shed their Indianness in favor of a new narrative of progress? The denigrating words must have determined in some way her later responses about the power of language. She spoke of her Aunt S., who went to court to speak on behalf of the imprisoned men. Always a strong woman, the real gift that Aunt S. had was to make her menfolks' presence and persecution known in the courtroom because she could speak the enemy's language. Literacy, in terms of Posey's widely read journalistic endeavors, was proving to be a double-edged sword that was more successful in obliterating rather than preserving indigenous rights. It was women's spoken word that was resistance during this crisis.

This history of women's roles as outspoken advocates for the men is never mentioned in the official histories of the state. In fact, it took Angie Debo, the white Oklahoman historian, decades of struggle to publish her history of Indian-white relations. Debo clearly sympathized with native peoples and was unafraid of naming names. She describes the most vicious swindles perpetrated against native people. In 1970, her book *A History of the Indians of the United States* appeared in print for the first time. Her history contains scathing commentary on the treatment of native peoples and oral histories gathered during the Works Progress Administration (WPA) years of the Depression; however, the Snake Rebellion had a few scant entries. The spoken word, especially women's history, remains the method of transmission.

Motherhood

My grandmother was widowed at an early age, during the height of the Great Depression. Her father and brothers traveled by wagon to Choctaw Nation and brought her house back to Twin Hills board by board. Her house was reassembled there. Her mother and father wanted her near her relatives during these hard times; unfortunately, it wasn't enough to have the closeness of family. While her own experience of Indian boarding school was voluntary, there was little choice when the government men came calling about her own children. They were hard times, and the marginal farmland and closed market refused to give up enough to maintain the family. By that time, native peoples were locked out of the market. They might sell to non-native town dwellers with whom they formed a friendship, even though it was on unequal footing, but otherwise it was hard to live on the land.

The government workers persuaded my grandmother that her girls would be taken care of in the government-sponsored orphanage for Indian children fifty miles away in Tahlequah. Sorrowfully and reluctantly, she gave her permission for her daughters, one after the other, to go to Sequoyah Orphan Training School. The government promised to step in and take the role that her husband's death had left vacant. There was no room in their concept of family for Indian motherhood.

In the summers, the school counselors placed the Indian girls with white families as domestic servants. My grandmother's children were being transformed into good workers while she was cast in the role of the bad woman/mother who could not care for her children properly. I can imagine a checklist of "good woman" characteristics being used at the time with an entry: Instruction in wage labor? "No" checked with a note: lacking in the home. These summer placements caused a rift so deep between her and her two middle daughters that they rarely visited her throughout their adult lives. My grandmother grew ashamed that she couldn't provide them with the material comfort they would have while working as domestics. My aunts were angry and resentful because they thought their mother didn't want them. My aunts' class consciousness was constructed by the dominant narrative, which claimed them as its own. My grandmother remained on the outside, an Indian mother whose children were abducted and held in captivity.

In the 1980s, Beth Brant worked on a publication called *A Gathering of Spirit*. She solicited writings from native women throughout North America, including letters from women in prison, poetry, short stories, excerpts from novels, and interviews. The theme of the discarded mother and kidnapped children runs throughout the book. The fear of rejection and abandonment continues to be present in our stories today, recoded by institutional forces to criminalize and pathologize us and our children. The boarding school system is being replaced by the justice system. We need to warn our children about how they are perceived when they walk down the street, or even when they are in the classroom. The fear that they will be swept away in the tide of epistemic violence haunts us. One of the most telling examples in the anthology is a prison letter to Brant from Rita Silk-Nauni that reads in part:

> I haven't seen my Son for over a year now. Each second I'm away from him the lonely feelings I endure becomes worse. . . . I was on lock from July 9th till a week and a half ago. They put me on lock for defending a young girl that was being used and abused. (93)

That is the fear I carry with me daily. We are mothers in the borderlands. The conflict-ridden vision of Indian womanhood and motherhood is still being contested in the writings of native women. I listen to the stories of my grandmother as I try to untangle our history, to see and feel it. We still have our words, language, memory, and imagination to help us through.

References

Anzaldua, Gloria. *Borderlands/La Frontera*. San Francisco: Aunt Lute Books, 1987.

Brant, Beth. *A Gathering of Spirit*. Ithaca: Firebrand Books, 1988.

Debo, Angie. *A History of the Indians of the United States*. Norman: University of Oklahoma Press, 1970.

————. *The Road to Disappearance*. Norman: University of Oklahoma Press, 1989.

Littlefield, Daniel F. *Alex Posey: Creek Poet, Journalist, and Humorist*. Lincoln: University of Nebraska Press, 1992.

Pratt, Mary Louise. *Imperial Eyes: Travel Writing and Transculturation*. London: Routledge, 1992.

Steedman, Carolyn. *Landscape for a Good Woman: A Story of Two Lives*. London: Virago, 1986.

Taussig, Michael. *Shamanism, Colonialism, and the Wild Man: A Study in Terror and Healing*. Chicago: University of Chicago Press, 1987.

Personalizing Methodology: Narratives of Imprisoned Native Women

3

LUANA ROSS

Many people ask how I developed an interest in criminality, deviance, and imprisoned women. The answer concerns itself with my culture, race/ethnicity, gender, class, and experiences growing up on the Flathead Indian Reservation.[1] I was raised at the Old Agency, across the street from the tribal jail. This tiny, one-room structure was seldom locked. Prisoners were seen walking and visiting around the Agency; no one was alarmed that they were not secured on a twenty-four-hour basis. As a little girl, I regularly ate breakfast—deer meat and hot cakes—with the prisoners at the cook's shack. We listened to the radio, and the prisoners would sing to me.

One day, when I went to the jail to visit, I noticed two teenage girls locked up in a cell. They tearfully explained their grandmother had died, and they would miss the funeral because they were in jail. They asked me to steal the key from the jailer and free them. I complied, and we walked across the field to their grandmother's wake. My mother and grandmother, who were at the house where the wake was held, were surprised to see me. They thought it was humorous that I liberated the girls, although the jailer may have thought otherwise. But then again, this was the Old Agency and he was a Native man, so perhaps he was happy the girls had the chance to pray and sing for their grandmother.

When I was young, my godfather was training to be a Jesuit priest when, due to the illness of his father, he returned to our reservation. He was a wonderfully brilliant man *and* was imprisoned four times. How could this possibly happen to a well-educated, spiritual person? My godfather, Dick McDonald, was not my only relative who was imprisoned; other relatives preceded and followed. It is common for Native people to have either been incarcerated or to have relatives who have been imprisoned in various institutions. Because we are a colonized people, the experiences of prisonization are, unfortunately, all too familiar. Native Americans disappear into Euro-American institutions at alarming rates. People from my reservation seemed to simply vanish and magically return. I did not realize what a "real" prison was and did not give it any thought. I imagined this as normal—that all families had relatives who went away and then returned.

I offer my experiences as a reservation Native woman and sociologist; my personal life intertwines with the research process. I explore the role of my life history in the shaping of the research design and interpretation of data, and I describe the process of gaining entry into a closed, total institution and gathering data. It is important to examine the complexity of everyday life as it intermingles with our scholarly selves. My life, as I live it, guides my selection of research topics, theories used, and interpretation of data. The aim is to give the reader a glimpse of the process of methodology as a highly personal occurrence and the power of culture in my survival as a Native woman. I am keenly aware of the influence of Salish culture in my life and sanity.

Two predominant themes emerge from this essay: closed institutions and various forms of prison—specifically academia and a women's state prison—and the notion of social control. These themes illuminate the interrelationship of nationhood, race/ethnicity, gender, and class that molds our experiences as Native women. There is an institutional foundation for these systems of oppression, and to operate they depend on institutional policies and ideology. Furthermore, the narratives presented are reflective: By examining personal experiences, we gain perspective on societal arrangements.

Research Preparation

When I begin the research on imprisoned women, I know the realities of crime: I have been raped, I have been assaulted, and I have friends and relatives who were murdered. I am no stranger to jails, prisons, and violence when I begin the interviews. I am not, however, prepared for what I find. To visit a friend or relative in prison is very different from experiencing what incarcerated people confront. My relatives who have been imprisoned, similar to my relatives who served in the armed forces during wartime, do not talk about their suffering in prison. We do not ask them to tell us about these things—to do so is considered impolite in my culture. The rule is, if someone freely tells another of his or her experiences, then one listens intently. Otherwise, one does not ask curious questions because others may not be prepared to talk about the past.

I have many questions for my research, which evolves into a dissertation: Why are so many Natives incarcerated? What crimes are they convicted of to warrant such treatment? Do Native women experience prison differently than white women? How does prisonization affect their lives and their families, particularly the children? The study design is qualitative rather than quantitative because I am interested in experiences. A comparison of Native and white women allows me to isolate nationhood, race/ethnicity, and culture as critical factors. I examine the prisonization experience, the form racism takes in prison, and the major concerns of imprisoned mothers by conducting tape-recorded interviews. The interviews are supplemented with nonparticipant observation, reports and letters from the American Civil Liberties Union (ACLU), documents from the Department of Corrections, archival data, prisoners' diaries, and correspondence from the prisoners.

It is important for me, as a Native woman, to conduct research that reflects the experiences of Native women. As a researcher, I want to be sensitive to the implications of gender, race/ethnicity, and nationhood during all phases of the study. Moreover, because I am both a woman and a Native American, I can facilitate a more in-depth definition of the research problem. My gender and race, however, are also problematic. I continually worry, because I am visibly Native, that I will not be received well by the prison staff (who are all white). In addition, because I am a woman I have the same anxieties—that I will not have credibility in the eyes of criminal justice system officials in their male-dominated field.

As a Native woman, I want to conduct research that is emancipatory, for both myself as a researcher and for imprisoned women, by providing an understanding of the social position of women in society as Native women experience it. A technique based on personal accounts elicits a much more profound perspective of the experiences of imprisoned women. By comparing Native and white women, the experiences of these prisoners will illuminate how the social structure operates according to nationhood, race/ethnicity, and culture. I am interested not only in their personal biographies but also in how these are tied to the larger social structure, which is characterized by racist and patriarchal relations.

Research Process

In the midst of family chaos and personal illness, I am committed to the research. As Native women, we have not emerged from colonization unscathed and have our own problems to sort out and endure. My father committed suicide, not long after his lobotomy, when I was six years old. My mother remarried, and my sister, Susie, and I were raped for many years by our stepfather. We are damaged; I survive, while my sister becomes loonier as the years roll by. That I remain functional, as defined by Euro-American society, and Susie does not, distresses me.

My sister sends me letters nearly every day. Concerned about children being raped, she is consumed with this type of violence and regularly accuses various people of being perpetrators. Many times Susie writes of demons and people changing into other people, always an evil transformation; sometimes she writes a sweet, sad memory from our youth. Her letters are disturbing only because she is lost to our family as we knew her. I grieve for a sane, well Susie: the woman with the zany sense of humor who cooked the family dinners.

Susie is confused about how we are related and says her mother's name is Laura, not Opal. Susie insists she's not Indian, although sometimes she will say she's Nez Perce—never Salish or Flathead. By blood, we are Nez Perce; however, we are also Salish and enrolled at Flathead. Susie imagines herself as Jewish and Italian; she writes much about New York City. She charges she's "a doctor on the Astral Plane fixing confused families everywhere." According to Susie, I am confused about my family, and she will heal me. One day she proclaims bodies and brains are being switched in epidemic proportion on our reservation. She knows this because when she woke up one morning she was "stretch marks from head to toe." She screamed, "My god, whose body is this anyway?"

Life is surreal; words cannot describe Susie or the pain my family feels. She lives in another world. In good humor, I imagine it's the Astral Plane, although she talks about living specifically on the planet Uranus. She favors Uranus because "there are no attorneys there." She is a character out of Sherman Alexie's mind, yet she's my sister and more real than any human I've encountered. When I begin my research, everything in my life has become high-pitched.

In December of 1990, I enter the Women's Correctional Center (WCC) in Warm Springs, Montana, prepared to ask inquiring questions and listen to the voices of invisible women, imprisoned women. Warm Springs is "home" to the state mental institution, and the women's prison is located on the same grounds. I remember when Susie was a prisoner there (patient is too kind a word). When we were in high school, we both attempted suicide. My feeble attempt went unnoticed; Susie's dramatic, passionate attempt did not. The judge ordered her to the state's mental institution against our mother's wishes. She is not the only relative who was imprisoned in a mental institution—others preceded and followed.

Although the prison is decorated for Christmas, the reality of oppression in this prison is devastating. The decorations provide a superficially festive atmosphere. Prisoners are especially lonesome on this family holiday. A month later the warden is putting up an American flag, complete with yellow ribbons, outside the prison. He tells me several prisoners have sons and other family members in the war. The prisoners pool their money and buy yellow ribbons to show their support for the troops, not as an endorsement for the war. On this day, the prison is extra clean. A legislator, Ron Marlenee, is expected to visit. I tiptoe down the hall as the prisoners wax floors and complain about having to clean for this "special" visit. The prison, in this old vacant nurses' dormitory, presents a benign appearance.

I stay in a small town, Anaconda, near the women's prison. Native Americans are never comfortable in white towns, and I am no exception. The town reminds me of another white town in Montana where, as an undergraduate, I assisted in the research of rural criminal justice systems. In a cafe/bar—near the women's bathroom—was a sign, "Niggers are proof Indians fuck buffalo." I knew I had to proceed with caution—this is the same feeling I have in Anaconda. It is remote and isolated, the economy depressed. Most of the people, at one time employed by the Anaconda Company, are either unemployed or work at one state institution or the other. Many are guards, as their parents and grandparents were, at the nearby prisons. It is an eerie feeling being surrounded by institutions: the men's prison on one side, the women's prison and state mental institution on the other.

Many prisoners experience assessment as rape, particularly the debasing cavity searches. A friend of mine, an imprisoned Native woman, describes the intake process at the WCC (Ross 1993):

> You are taken into a bathroom and ordered to strip naked. You are searched thoroughly, which also means cavity searches which are at the discretion of the officers. And usually it depends upon how much they have heard about you and if they want to make it hard for you, they will do their humiliating cavity searches. Next is the shower. The shower is turned on and you are ordered into the shower with the guards watching you. You are given the "*solution*" for delousing. You are told where to wash and to wash "*good*," or they will wash you. When the "*fun*" time is over, you are given a gown and put into lockdown. The room will become your life for fourteen days. It has three beds (two single beds and a wooden box used as a bed), toilet, sink, and an old dresser. The room is dark, gloomy, and always cold. The heat is shut off and there are no vents in the room. I remember it was so cold and I had been issued one small pillow, one sheet, one old army blanket. Even so, I was so thankful to have those. I had less when I was drinking around. You are later taken out and your picture is taken for identification purposes. The last process, the best of all this, is you are given your own number.

Prisons are "total," or closed, institutions and consequently are concerned with control over the lives of prisoners. Prisoners have already been branded, labeled as unruly women; after all, they are criminals (Faith 1993). Prisoners are ritualistically dehumanized, regulated, reduced to numbers. Part of the "ceremony" of assessment is to "break a prisoner's spirit" and ready them for "rehabilitation." The assessment concludes with a visit from the psychologist, who asks the prisoners if they realize why they are in prison. I suppose this is the point where prisoners demonstrate remorse for their transgressions. The schoolteacher enters and asks them what educational level they are. Assessment—done coldly and quickly.

On the periphery of the grounds is a relatively new building that houses maximum-security prisoners. All doors are locked, and women are imprisoned in individual cells. The smell of urine throughout the building is overwhelming. Previously this was the forensic ward for the state mental hospital, and guards and prisoners both say the "patients" urinated everywhere. This unit, with its heavy doors, bars, and locked control room, imprisons eleven in maximum security and four in isolation cells. Prisoners here, of course, do the hardest time. Native women are disproportionately imprisoned in maximum security.

Gaining Entry

I initially contact the warden of the prison by telephone. I nervously tell him I am a sociologist employed at one of the state universities and desire to tour the facility. The WCC is never called a prison by prison staff; it is referred to as a "facility" or "center." Likewise, prisoners are "inmates," cells are "rooms," and guards are "officers." Euphemisms run amok. I explain to the warden that I have a great interest in criminology and was employed at the first correctional halfway house in the state. Because I am visibly Native and racial tension runs high in Montana, I expect some initial resistance and skepticism on the part of some institutional personnel with respect to the purpose of the study. I am extremely anxious for the introductory meeting with the warden and consumed with presenting myself as a credible scholar.

The meeting goes well, although I am overcome by the poor conditions of the prison and the number of prisoners I know. At the end of the tour, and at the risk of losing credibility, I tell the warden I have a close relative in the prison and ask if I can see her. He agrees, and I am allowed to visit with my young cousin for several minutes. This is a difficult conversation. It is heart-wrenching to see my little cousin in prison. She repeats, "I'm in prison—I hit rock-bottom. It doesn't get any lower than this." She is deeply ashamed that I see her in such circumstances.

Assuming that the only true way to know how women experience prison is to become a prisoner, I originally want to enter the prison as an inmate—a scheme only the warden would be aware of. After the prison tour, I quickly conclude that it would be insulting and disrespectful to real prisoners to carry out such a ruse. I telephone the warden and ask if I can conduct a study on imprisoned women. I give the warden the letter of invitation to take part in the study and the consent form for his review. The warden posts the letter on the prisoners' bulletin board so anyone interested will have knowledge of the study. The warden states that in the course of the study, if I become aware of escape plans or the use of drugs by prisoners, I need to relay that information to him. I agree, and following Salish propriety, I offer to conduct a free cultural awareness workshop for his staff in return for permission to conduct the study. The warden does not schedule the workshop.

Being a Native woman plays a key role in gaining entry into the prisoner population. Most Native women say they will not give the same information to a white person conducting interviews. I offer the women ten dollars apiece for the interviews. I want to offer more, but the warden tells me the limit they can have in their account is ten dollars. Clearly this is an incentive because most imprisoned women are financially needy. That my cousin is in prison is paramount in the reception I receive from both Native and white women. They appear to trust me more. Several women, both Native and non-Native, comment that the only reason they were interviewed is because they trust my relative, and therefore, I am trustworthy. Their status as co-prisoners overcomes any racial differences, and white prisoners openly talk with me.

Interviews and Observations

A series of constraints are encountered during the initial phase of selecting prisoners to interview. I plan on using a snowball technique, starting with my cousin and spinning off from there. After my first interview, the treatment specialist presents me with a list of incarcerated mothers, Native and white, whom she believes I should interview. I wonder whom she left off the list and why, and I am too intimidated to suggest a different technique. Also, she says I will not be allowed, for my own safety, to interview "dangerous" offenders, with the exception of one Native woman that the treatment specialist thinks will be an "interesting" subject. I take the roster and start interviewing women from my reservation, whom I have known for several decades.

Next, feeling constrained by the situation, I follow the treatment specialist's instructions and proceed down the list of women. After several weeks, I become familiar with women in the halls and request that guards send them to me to be interviewed, although they are not on the list. For example, I hear about a Native woman in isolation and want to interview her. Thus, I purposefully choose women I want to interview. Although the interviews are presenting similar information, I never sense I have reached a saturation point. In fact, I feel as though I want to interview more women, especially prisoners in isolation cells and those designated "dangerous." I view each interview as an individual experience, despite the similarities.

The primary source of data is in-depth interviews. They are loosely structured in an attempt to elicit the women's own narratives. A series of interviews, which range from thirty-five minutes to five hours, are conducted from December 1990 through February 1991. I interview fourteen Native women out of seventeen and thirteen white women out of a total of forty-eight. Limited nonparticipant observation and informal conversations with prisoners and prison staff are utilized to supplement the interviews. Observation and informal conversation provide me with a clearer sense of the social environment of the prison. My observations of prisoner-staff and prisoner-prisoner interaction are especially valuable. In the write-up of the study, I disguise the identities of the women; I alter details that threaten the anonymity of the prisoners. In this small prison, this proves to be a painstaking task.

Institutional personnel are a powerful influence in the lives of prisoners due to their presence on a twenty-four-hour basis; because of this, they provide important information about the prison and prisoners. This tiny prison permits frequent contact between prison staff and prisoners. Prison staff members, in interviews and off-the-record conversations, often make negative remarks to me about various Native and white prisoners.

I suggest to the warden that I interview one particular Native prisoner. He responds she will be a good candidate for an interview because she "represents everything bad in Indian culture." He never says anything similar about white prisoners and white culture. This remark reflects his ignorance and racism, albeit unconscious. How do I reply to this remark? Once again, I graciously offer to conduct a free cultural awareness workshop. Again, the warden never calls or asks about the workshop. Moreover, the warden does not understand Native American religion. When he mentions sweetgrass and the sweat lodge, he does so with suspicion. The guards and many white prisoners refer to Native spirituality as "voodoo." I try to clarify Native ceremonies for the warden. Later, while visiting in the dayroom with prisoners, I tell several Native prisoners about my talk with the warden and his ignorance of Native culture. I suggest to them, as traditional Native women, that they conduct the cultural awareness workshop. After a long and hearty laugh, they explain that because they are prisoners nobody ever believes them, particularly prison staff.

The treatment specialist is an older woman, near retirement age, who smokes incessantly. She appears committed and dedicated to her work with imprisoned women, although she has a demanding workload. She constantly worries about not having a college education and insists her qualifications are her experience (I agree). She is kind, gentle, and powerless in the prison system. I find her helpful and gracious—the prisoners experience her as controlling. I have a difficult time keeping the treatment specialist focused on the questions at hand. She talks for over an hour about her life experiences, and then the chemical dependency counselor enters the room and takes a seat. Her responses are definitely affected, and she is not as open after the counselor enters the room; she frequently asks him his opinion before offering her own. This pattern emerges another time when the warden enters the room. I notice she agrees with everything he says and contradicts what she previously told me. It is possible, especially given her generation and years of work in a male-dominated field, that she defers to men.

The treatment specialist, who theoretically represents the needs of imprisoned mothers, has no knowledge of the Indian Child Welfare Act. When I ask about the act, she says, "That's what we don't know anything about. Well, our county attorney said, 'I don't know anything about that act.' I don't know how to proceed, so for me to fill these papers out is nonsense." I explain the act to the treatment specialist and give her the telephone number of a Native social worker. Her lack of knowledge impairs her work on behalf of imprisoned Native women.

Given the oppressive prison regime, I question the treatment specialist about suicides and suicide attempts. The treatment specialist says in the past five years, only one "serious" suicide attempt occurred because the staff is well trained and "on top of it all." This cannot be true because four women told me about their suicide attempts. Furthermore, any attempt should be viewed as serious. I question how much time the staff really has to notice suicidal behavior; and in many, many ways prison staff are isolated from the prisoners. I dispute how "well trained" the staff are—everything at the WCC is at a crisis stage.

The treatment specialist introduces me to the state social worker. The social worker, a fresh-faced young man, is not a member of the prison staff. He is the county social worker who works with families regarding child placement. A great amount of caution is exercised by the social worker in his responses to my questions. Again, my race is noticed, and he repeatedly mentions, totally unsolicited, all the Native American studies courses he has taken and his familiarity with the Indian Child Welfare Act. This strikes me as odd given that one month prior to this, he told me he had no knowledge of the act. Apparently, he wants to impress me with his knowledge and perhaps is a bit nervous that he does not know more about Native American culture and federal policy.

Before conducting each interview, I give the potential interviewee the letter of invitation to the study. I read through the letter of invitation and the consent form with the prisoners, emphasizing the fact that their identities will be protected. Some women, both Native and white, do not care if their names are used, whereas others are relieved no one can possibly identify them. The prisoners are all eager to talk to me, and I feel as if I have known these women all my life; and, indeed, in a few cases I have known them all my life. In addition to my cousin, several women I know from my reservation are in prison. Although the interviews are easy to conduct because the women readily share their experiences and concerns with me, each evening when I walk out of the prison I am numb—filled with grief and sadness.

The interviews proceed with the gathering of demographic data. I discover that 25 percent of the total women's prison population is Native American, in a state where Native Americans make up 6 percent of the total population. Native women are significantly over-represented (imprisoned Native men in Montana make up 18 percent of the total men's prison population). After this information is collected, I ask a series of questions focusing on the women's incarceration experiences. General lead-in questions are followed by a more in-depth discussion of family information.

When I interview Native women, I ask about cultural barriers they think might be important to the study. I find that issues of racism and culture-bound programs surface much before this point in the interview. Most Native prisoners are well aware of racism within the prison and voluntarily raise the issue throughout the interviews. For instance, although imprisoned Native men in Montana have freely practiced their religion behind bars since 1983, imprisoned Native women are denied religious freedom. This especially angers Native women who rely on their culture to survive the brutal dynamics of prisonization and colonization. Moreover, the prison and the Department of Corrections blatantly ignore the American Indian Religious Freedom Act. Regardless of race/ethnicity, most prisoners initiate discussions of sexism and sexual intimidation by male guards. I am not prepared for the horrendous treatment and social environment these women endure (see Ross 1994, 1998).

Trained thoroughly in mainstream sociology at the University of Oregon, a conservative and racist department (and insecure as a human being, let alone a researcher), I begin the interviews by following textbook advice. My formal education demands that I isolate myself emotionally in the production of good scholarship. Hence, I operate on the notion of objectivity and initially avoid emotions and answering questions from the women or giving them information I know will benefit them. After several interviews, I come to my senses and decide I am acting inappropriately as a human being. I freely give out information, particularly facts regarding child-placement matters to white prisoners and information on the Indian Child Welfare Act to non-reservation prisoners. Initially, I avoid describing the specific focus of the study until after the interview. Once again, I am afraid of introducing bias by directing the interview. I feel as though I am using these women for my own gain, for a dissertation. I grow uncomfortable.

The notion of objectivity is widely and openly disputed by scholars from many disciplines. The idea that a researcher can remain objective and free of bias is preposterous. The reality, of course, is that everyone has a point of view, a bias. It is, however, critical to be conscious of our various viewpoints and accept what we see. If researchers want to know about women's lives, then we must let them articulate. Native women need to tell their own stories with their own voices. I thoroughly reassure myself that I am proceeding correctly.

The asking of personal questions is particularly problematic when interviewing Native women. Culturally, one does not ask such questions as "Why are you in prison?" or "Where are your children?" Embarrassed, I preface these questions with "I know this may sound nosy, but . . ." This seems to put both of us at ease, given I am clearly breaking a cultural rule. All the Native women are interested in my study, and this decreases my anxiety about asking questions that may be too curious. Furthermore, all the Native women want to know what reservation I am from and if I know certain people (and I usually do). This informal conversation contributes to the trust and flow of the interview.

When I engage in a dialogue, the women participate more and, subsequently, give me more information about themselves and their families. I uncover this while interviewing Native prisoners. It is culturally inappropriate to simply ask questions and not engage in a dialogue. Moreover, when I use this technique with white prisoners, it proves beneficial to the interview process. Even though the dialogue between the women and me appears to enhance the process, I continue to worry that my involvement is creating a bias. My insecurity arouses suspicion that my research is not scientific. I begin reading literature on feminist methodology (e.g., Nielsen 1990). I set aside my worries and learn that what seems natural to me is now in print and, therefore, credible.

The prisoners' attitudes toward the study surprise me. They are stunned anyone can possibly care about them and truly want to hear their stories. One prisoner, a white woman, reveals she is pleased that I care about white women, too, and am not just interviewing Native women. Although I am comfortable with the interviews, in some cases I am apprehensive. Prior to interviewing prisoners, the treatment specialist many times briefs me on a particular woman. The treatment specialist warns me about several women, whom she characterizes as dangerous, manipulative, slow, or "borderline mentally retarded—we tested her." One particular woman, according to the treatment specialist, is prone to bursts of anger when she does not understand something. I am absolutely anxiety-ridden when I meet her and present a letter of invitation and consent form. I start to read over the material with her—slowly and deliberately, pronouncing each word loudly, as though she is deaf. It is not long before I feel idiotic and continue as though she is a normal person.

I find only one woman to be anything like the treatment specialist described. This white woman, whom the treatment specialist does not warn me about, openly expresses her distaste for Native Americans. Unquestionably, this causes anxiety on my part, and I am thankful when the interview is completed. Only one woman on the treatment specialist's list refuses to be interviewed—a Native woman who is heavily medicated (Thorazine) and simply does not want to subject herself to an interview. She would approach me in the hall and tell me with glazed-over eyes that she wants to be interviewed, but "I can't—not now. Maybe another time, OK?" Other prisoners say this woman has been broken by the prison regime. Part of the breaking process is the overuse of mind-altering drugs and lengthy time in maximum security. She had her share of both.

The image of the "savage Indian" thrives in the WCC. Many white prisoners are afraid of Native prisoners. And, this very image may be the reason why prison staff use heavy control mechanisms with Native prisoners: much use of medication and lockup in maximum security. They are all afraid of "the Indians." Perhaps that is why prisoners are not allowed to see *Soldier Blue*. According to the prisoners, the warden is afraid Native prisoners will riot if they see this film ("squaws on the warpath"). Also, he is concerned about the violence in the film, although the prisoners just saw *Platoon*. The prison is a weird, sick place. I wonder how the guards can possibly work in such a diabolic institution.

One interview with a Native woman in an isolation cell poses a special problem. The warden insists I interview her through a small slot in the door of her cell. I try his method, and we both have to stand stooped over. After several minutes of stooping, I request that I interview her outside her cell in a vacant room. We talk for several hours, with guards posted outside the door because she is considered dangerous. She is initially apprehensive concerning me and the study. As we progress, she relaxes—I will never forget the interview. The remorse she shows regarding her "crime" is haunting. She was convicted of killing her mother, although she does not remember committing the crime. She is heavily medicated most of the time. Elder women from her reservation tell me it was the white man who hung out with her mother, not the daughter, who committed the murder.

On several occasions, the warden invites me to dine with the prisoners in the general-population building. One lunch that I am treated to consists of old, dry fish and overcooked rice with black specks. Hardly anyone eats the lunch—they fill up on bread and margarine. I naturally sit with my cousin and am very comfortable. At the lunch, we sit with two other prisoners. An older white prisoner objects to the conversation when my cousin and I talk about racist white people from our reservation. My cousin gives her "the hate stare," and we continue our conversation.

I complete most of the interviews with the white women and over half of the Native women, then I realize the rest of my "sample" are locked up in the maximum-security unit. The interviews in maximum security are difficult, at best, to conduct. For instance, although I am allowed to interview in the dining hall with some privacy, the women continually look over their shoulders during the interview. I assume this behavior is a survival mechanism because all the women in this building admit they do not trust anyone inside the prison. Although the guards cannot hear our conversations, we are always within their view and are, indeed, watched.

Similar to those in general population, the interviews are disrupted many times. The only available space is the dining room, and several times we are interrupted either for the serving of food or the cleaning of the room. Another time a guard comes in to get some food. The prisoner says he is mixing a drug in with the applesauce for a prisoner in isolation. They do this to ensure the prisoner does not "tongue her meds." She says the mixing of food and drugs is a common practice in prison. The woman I am interviewing is greatly bothered by his presence. These disruptions interfere with our conversation; in one case, the interview promptly ends at the suggestion of the prisoner.

Another difficulty in maximum security is maintaining the concentration of the conversation on parenting issues and their needs as imprisoned mothers. All the women immediately begin discussing the injustice of lockup in the maximum-security unit. I assume, because of their particularly oppressive conditions, they want to talk about why they are in the maximum-security unit, rather than parenting issues. The interview schedule is thus cast aside, and I let the women lead the conversation. I listen intently and naively try to pull the focus back to the study. I feel extremely awkward and soon give up—I listen and offer support. All of these women express the desire that the public know about their particular situation. In one case, a Native woman hauls a stack of documents to the interview. Included in this package are letters to criminal justice officials and attorneys, copies of grievance files, and copies of her write-ups for breaking prison rules. Although these interviews are tedious and much longer than those in the general population, they offer the best insights into the prison's social environment.

Many women in isolation and maximum security are medicated. The overuse of mind-altering drugs, prescribed by a psychiatrist known to the prisoners as "Dr. Feel Good," is staggering (Ross 1994). This is another way the prison controls prisoners: medicate them into conformity. The fact that it is difficult to keep these women focused on issues of mothering is telling in itself. These women are more concerned with their personal survival of prisonization and, therefore, are not afforded the occasion of thinking about and discussing their children. Or, perhaps, these women are too medicated to keep a focus and are not afforded the luxury of concentration.

I interview all the Native women in maximum security and one white woman. The focus, as directed by the women in this unit, is on race/ethnicity, gender, and social control. Out of eleven prisoners in maximum security, six are Native. It is not surprising the subject of parenting behind bars is superseded by more pressing issues. I am overwhelmed by their experiences and consider changing the focus of my dissertation. This topic is not something I can ignore. In this unit, as well as the general-population building, every Native woman raises the issue of racism within the criminal justice system.

In maximum security, while waiting to conduct an interview, I notice a beautiful redheaded woman pacing back and forth in an isolation cell. I ask other prisoners about her. She accused a guard of raping her, and while it is being investigated she is in isolation. I ask about the guard. Prisoners tell me he is on duty—with pay. That's her reward for telling on him. The message is clear to other prisoners: accuse a guard and go to isolation. Clearly, another way to dominate prisoners—it is so obvious.

Another way prisoners are controlled is through their children. Although the formal rules specify otherwise, prison staff deny visits at any time. A Native mother addresses the issue of being in maximum security on a charge she does not consider valid and how the guard on duty affects her visit with her three-year-old son (Ross 1993):

> I was really upset. My whole world had just fallen apart. That weekend was supposed to be the weekend that I had worked four months to achieve for my son to come and spend a weekend with me. The prison staff dropped it; they pulled it. I was in that back area in max and I had to visit him through those bars. I couldn't even touch him; I got him for one hour. My family traveled hundreds of miles to get him here and I get him for one hour. I said to the officer, "Can I just touch his hand?" [The guard said,] "No, you cannot touch him; it's a write-up if you touch him." Now that's ridiculous! (172)

Although visits are an important way to maintain contact with children, some mothers, Native and white, will not allow their children to visit them in prison because they believe it is too hard emotionally on the children. Some mothers talk about the difficulty young children have conceptualizing a prison. One mother tearfully tells me her six-year-old stole a bicycle so he will go to prison. There he will be reunited with his mother.

Discussing the separation from children proves to be emotionally taxing for both me and the women. Some mothers serve their entire sentences without seeing their children; one woman, because of the length of her sentence, will never leave the prison. All of the women cry when they talk about their children, and most women proudly bring pictures of their children to the interview or retrieve them from their cells and show me the pictures after the interview. Women with lengthy sentences, and Native women generally are given longer sentences than white women, have a particularly difficult time with the emotional pain of separation (Ross 1993). One Native woman believes she has been in prison so long she has totally estranged herself from her entire family. This woman worries that, because of the serious crime she was convicted of, others will taunt her son. She said just thinking about what people would say to her son, she "started thinking real crazy." According to her, this drove her to several suicide attempts. She is extremely distraught and on medication most of the time. Her most recent suicide attempt occurs when her confidant, her spiritual mentor, is transferred to maximum security.

Other women are concerned with placement issues. Native mothers believe that nationhood and race/ethnicity are major factors in regard to the quality of care their children receive in various placements. One non-reservation Native woman is distraught over the placement of her son in a white foster home. She remarks,

> the foster home my son's in right now refuses to let him know about his culture. I went to court and requested that my child be placed with American Indians who are spiritually active, because that's my religion and that's his. (Ross 1993, 164)

This mother, as well as other non-reservation Native women, has no knowledge of the Indian Child Welfare Act. Given the long history of federal government removal of Native children from their homes and communities to boarding schools and of state government removal to white foster and adoptive homes, it is understandable Native mothers believe the race/ethnicity of the caretakers is a critical factor in regard to the quality of care the children receive. I give all non-reservation Native mothers information about the act and telephone numbers of contact people. Reservation and off-reservation mothers are well informed about the act.

At this point in the research, I discover the racial category of "Native American" is not working. Issues are far too complicated to reduce interviewees to the stereotypical "white and Native." I superficially divide Native Americans into reservation, non-reservation, and off-reservation. Obvious differences exist between Native prisoners that relate directly to their reservation status (see Ross 1993, 1998).

After interviewing, I leave the prison for the motel. I notice a young blonde guard getting off duty. She is one of the guards who is continually rude and disrespectful, not only to the prisoners but also to me. She yells and sways down the prison hall—feeling powerful with keys jangling from her belt. She jumps into her car—a cheap sports car. It has personalized plates that read "Cuff 'Em." She is a scary woman. The license plate is reminiscent of the handcuff tie-tacks many people working in the criminal justice system favor as an accessory.

Prison Thoughts

The longer I am in prison, the more I find the situation to be black and white— us and them. Have I gone *native* (so to speak)? In graduate school, we were warned this is the worst event that can befall a researcher: showing bias toward interviewees. I find myself strongly identifying with the prisoners. Why? First, there are too many informal and formal prison rules. For example, there is the informal rule that children cannot sit on an imprisoned mother's lap during regular prison visiting hours;

and there is the formal rule that imprisoned mothers who have not taken the parenting course cannot have children for overnight weekend visitation. In addition, too many families are broken as a direct result of incarceration. And, the punishments do not appear to fit the crimes. It is not likely any true rehabilitation can take place in an institution that thrives on control and punishment. The prison system is flawed by design.

My inability to do anything about the injustices I witness and hear from the women is overpowering. How does a researcher respond when a mother tearfully relates the emotional pain she is in because she misses her children? Or, the anguish she feels because her daughter is in the hospital as a result of sexual abuse by a foster parent? Or, when a woman tells you she was raped in jail by the jailer (and raped not once but seven times by the same jailer)? Ninety percent of the women in this prison are victims of sexual abuse. There has been much violence in their lives, and violence remains in their lives. Now it is in the guise of "rehabilitation" and punishment that awaits them because they are unruly women.

What do I say to a prisoner who tells me she "took the fall" for a man she trusted? That the man in her life was the one who really committed the crime, but she pled guilty so he wouldn't do prison time? Or, when a young mother grieves for her baby who just died prior to her incarceration? What do I do when a prisoner looks forward to the interview because she has not had one visitor since she was imprisoned?

Disengaging from the prisoner population proves difficult. After I conduct my last interview, which is in the maximum-security building, the treatment specialist requests I see her before leaving the grounds. After we talk, I gather my belongings. All the women in the general-population building are lined up in the hall for the afternoon count. (Count refers to the process in which prisoners line up outside their cells. The guards then count the prisoners to ensure no one has escaped.) As I leave, I shake their hands on down the line and say my respectful goodbyes. My cousin and I are allowed to hug, and it is with great difficulty and sadness that I leave her and others who must endure and survive a poisonous environment. Given that the setting is a prison, I soon learn incarcerated people have very little control over anything, and this permeates their lives. I am intensely aware of domination and power issues.

I am at the motel, and I telephone home. I tell my youngest son my work will be completed tomorrow and I will be home soon. He is frightened and wants to know if I will be talking to "anyone who hassss toooo gooo tooo the electric chair." I reassure him, "No, but some will be here for one hundred years." He responds, "Nobody lives that long! Oh—they'll die in prison?" "Yes," I answer. He quietly says, "That makes me sad."

The interviews with the imprisoned women are totally overwhelming. I am depressed and find myself offering a variety of things to ease their discomfort: books and videotapes to some, information on the Indian Child Welfare Act to others, and telephone calls to tribal social services and attorneys regarding custody of children. I conduct a book drive in my office building and send books to the prison library. About a month later, I receive a letter from the schoolteacher, the person in charge of receiving books. He requests I not bring any more "trashy, romance novels" to the prison because they "stir the women up." This is another illustration of the control used by the prison. The prisoners are not allowed to make decisions for themselves concerning what they can or cannot read.

I continually think about the women. I am indebted to them for sharing their lives with me. I did not want to leave as others might have—not returning anything to them. Part of the depression comes from interviewing too many women in one day. Due to the short time off from my teaching responsibilities, I would interview two or three women on some days. I would not advise this; with so many horrendous experiences and grief over families, it is too much emotionally for one to absorb. While the prisoners are concerned with their sheer survival, I frivolously worry about burnout and stress.

Other Prisons

Several months after I complete the interviews, I receive a letter from a female researcher. She desires my data from the interviews. According to Native prisoners I have contact with, she wants to interview them; they refuse and instruct her to contact me. Does this woman really believe I will give her the tape-recorded interviews? I am incredulous. I question what kind of scholar this woman is—not ethical or one with high moral standards. Does she realize what she's asking? I look at her letter again to see if she is a naive junior scholar like me. No, she is a senior scholar. Why does she want the information? After all, I promised confidentiality. I curiously ponder how she, as a white woman, would interpret the same data. Academia makes people do strange things. This controlling institution has a woman, with publish or perish burning her brain, hot on my trail to get my original research for her benefit. Would she do anything to change oppressive conditions for Native people? For imprisoned women? I think not. I send her a letter telling her, no, she cannot have the interviews.

Although I am safely away from the prison, back to teaching and writing my dissertation, my life is a shambles. My husband is angry with me because I am writing day and night on the dissertation. I have a deadline to meet and no time for him or family. Finishing the dissertation means I will retain my position at Montana State University. I selfishly concentrate on my career and cross the border into insanity-land. I receive a telephone call asking if I will deliver a keynote on balancing work and family at a state conference on women. I decline, deciding

I don't know a damn thing about the subject matter. I eat very little, barely sleep (who has the time?), and feel ill.

In the next few weeks I am told I have cervical cancer. Internalized oppression, a cervix out of control. Several weeks later I have a hysterectomy. I need several months to heal, but I must also defend my dissertation in several months. By now, my dissertation committee is my mortal enemy; we lock horns over my work, which is qualitative not quantitative. We have basic philosophical differences that escalate. Some members question the objectivity and generalizability of my study. They question whether the prisoners were telling me the "truth." I wonder: What truth? Whose truth? Now I am ill and must ask them for assistance. I explain I need a three-month extension because of the cancer; they are doubtful I will get an extension. People, according to them, are tired of me complaining about my illnesses.

Before my dissertation defense, I am warned by some committee members not to invite family and friends. I was to consider my defense a "working session." I ask the support staff at the U of O if other candidates invite guests to their defense. "Yes," is the reply, "it is considered a celebration." Obviously, not in my case. I am admonished to be prepared to defend my methodology, which is indigenous methodology. I feel small, brown, stupid, ugly. To some committee members, I remain a "dumb Indian." I am raped by the whole sorry process.

On the eve of my defense, in a fit of anxiety, I recall when a professor at the U of O told me my "problem" was I acted too much like an "Indian" and not enough like a sociologist. I will never forget that hideous remark. He followed by saying if I did not "straighten up," I would be forced to teach Ethnic Studies or Native American Studies, as though they are lesser disciplines. He ended his tirade by saying they (he either meant dumb white men or sociologists) would never let me teach sociology, with the implication it was because I act too much like an Indian. It is ironic that this occurred at my oral examination for the specialty area of race/ethnic relations. No wonder I am nervous for the defense of my dissertation.

In a bold act of resistance, I invite all my friends—most of them varying shades of brown—to my defense. Rob Proudfoot, a Seneca and the outside committee member, begins the defense by articulating the importance of my research. He concludes by presenting me with an eagle feather. The defense process is decolonized; some say he did not follow protocol. My status is elevated before I am formally granted the mysterious PhD. A week later, I am given my *true* name, Charging Buffalo Woman, in a dream. I am not a "dumb Indian."

In the winter I move to Berkeley, leaving my husband and boys in Montana, to begin a new position. Faculty at this prestigious university add to a chilly campus climate. I am finally invited to lunch by one of the senior faculty. She belittles me regarding my research on imprisoned women and harangues that I will never get it

published—shoddy methodology, according to her. I leave the Women's Faculty
Club and vomit. Gerald Vizenor, my colleague, hopes I did not pay for the lunch
I left in the bushes.

Several months into my new position, I receive a telephone call from Montana's ACLU. The director wants me to issue a summary of findings from my research. Their office must obtain it immediately as support information for a class
action suit they will file on behalf of women prisoners against the Department of
Corrections. Included in the list of grievances is the denial of religious freedom
for imprisoned Native women. I cast aside writing lectures and revising my dissertation for articles (must get published!) and, in the next few days, summarize
the findings. I deliberately detail the wretched conditions for imprisoned women
and send them to the ACLU. Because the information will soon be public, I send
the summary to the warden, prisoners I interviewed, key political people in the
state, and the Department of Corrections. This action put me squarely at odds
with the department. Not only is the Department of Corrections leery of me, attorneys and political figures do not return telephone calls or answer my letters. I
am seen as a vicious, dangerous woman (I am on the *white list*). I decide I must be
doing a good job. I am Charging Buffalo Woman.

The following summer, I travel to Montana, hoping to conduct more interviews with imprisoned women. The warden will not let me in, although two white
researchers have free access to the prisoners. I call everyone I think may have some
power or connection, but no one can or will help.

The grand opening of the new women's prison will take place in September.
As a member of the prison site selection committee (appointed by the governor
in 1991), I had to get an invitation. I do and travel to Billings with my husband.
I will finally have a chance to greet women I know who are imprisoned. The grand
opening is a gala affair complete with streamers, balloons, speakers, tea, and cake.
The cake is shaped like the new sign in the prison yard. Primary colors are blue
and yellow (Montana state colors, I presume); everything is decorated in these colors. I uncomfortably notice that I am the only Native not locked up. One of the
speakers, a learned political official, is talking about women and criminality. I am
busy greeting the prisoners who are brought out for dignitaries to ogle. I tune in
to the speaker—he is lecturing on "women and mortality." He repeats the phrase
"women and mortality." I listen closely and decide he means "morality." I laugh
and find comfort in humor—it is a most bizarre event.

Archival Research

As I continue my research, I want to present colonialism as a process (not an
event) and tie the loss of sovereignty to Native criminality. As a sociologist, rather

than reconstructing past events, I am interested in historical data that will enable me to examine social structures. Because I cannot get into the prison, I concentrate my efforts on archival work. Who, I wonder, was the first imprisoned Native woman in Montana? According to the Montana Historical Society archives, it was Madeline Trottier, Cree from northern Montana, imprisoned in 1897 for rape. She was described as a "half-breed Indian," twenty-seven years old. She had no previous convictions and served four years and three months of a six-year sentence. I search the old newspapers and find an article in the *River Press*, February 10, 1897. The newspaper reported that R. Trottier (her husband) was in jail for rape and was accompanied by "a female prisoner, who was charged with being an accessory to the crime." Madeline's crime was being at the crime scene when her husband committed the rape. The victim was a "half-breed girl." The same newspaper on March 10, 1897, reported that the district court went into the evening hours to dispose of the Trottier case. Madeline Trottier and her husband were both convicted of rape. He received a thirty-year sentence and Madeline Trottier, who pled guilty, a six-year sentence.

I locate several documents that relate to Madeline Trottier in "Letters From the Governor." On November 10, 1899, the warden sent the governor a letter regarding the prison's only female prisoners: Madeline Trottier and Ella St. Clair. By this time, Madeline Trottier had been in prison nearly three years. The warden, aware that Madeline Trottier did not commit a crime, begged the governor to release these women. He asked for a pardon "on grounds of humanity" because they were the only women imprisoned with 325 men. When the women were taken outside for fresh air, the men were locked in their cells, making daily exercise impossible. Referring to Madeline Trottier as "an ignorant Indian" and citing that prisonization is more difficult for women than for men, the warden wrote:

> One year in the women's quarters is certainly worse than five years to the men. Ella St. Clair has become very much discouraged and we have had hard work to keep her from suicide. Madeline Trottier is an Indian woman and can only speak a few words of English and for that reason the two women are not even company for each other. To be perfectly frank about it the situation of these two women is nothing short of horrible and we are powerless to alleviate their position. It certainly seems to us that the five years and more than Ella St. Clair has been here is more than sufficient. The Trottier woman, if she be guilty of the crime for which she is imprisoned, is entitled to some leniency from the fact that she is an ignorant Indian and at the best is not expected to have the highest ideas of morals. . . . We hope that we can prevail upon you to pardon these people and if you consent to do so, why not do it to become effective say on Thanksgiving Day? (Conley 1899)

In a racist reply, the governor succinctly denied the pardon: "When a pardon is granted to a prisoner from Northern Montana, the people there pretend to be indignant, and while I would like to do some thing in these cases, I do not feel that I can at the present time." These documents, of course, are indicative of racism, prison conditions, and Native-white interaction, particularly in northern Montana where indigenous people were fiercely resisting colonization. I contemplate how St. Clair and Trottier survived prisonization and lived the remainder of their lives.

I search the Montana Territorial Prison archives and discover pictures and descriptions of relatives. This is where I unearth my uncle, Marion Deschamps. Received at the penitentiary on May 8, 1946, he was fifty-eight years old. My uncle was given a four-year sentence for grand larceny (no previous convictions). The history of the crime read that he stole a 1941 Chevrolet pickup at Polson. He was described as being in good health, Catholic, fifth-grade education, occupation as farmer/rancher, and "dark complected." The longest section on the description sheet was "marks and scars":

> mole in center of back. Vaccination. Crooked and scarred left ring finger. Scar left forehead. Scar left hairline. Scar left temple. Scar bridge of nose. Scar left lip and chin. 6" knife scar on neck. 2 broken ribs. M D - D C tattooed on left forearm.[2]

Although he was described as one tough hombre, in his mug shot he looks as kind and handsome as I remember. My mother says my uncle did not steal the pickup. His partner did, and he was unaware of the theft as they drove the back roads on the reservation near Post Creek.

Back to Reality

I move to Aptos to write my book on imprisoned Native women (I am busy gathering tenure points). Every time I relocate, which is often, Susie becomes confused about the various Luanas in her memory. I finally receive a letter from Susie, and she says Mom received a book in the mail from someone named Luana Ross. She wonders who this woman is and "is she my sister, too?" Susie constantly worries about people being "impostors." She writes she will accept that her sister Luana lives in Aptos, although she ends the sentence with a question mark. My elder sister asks if I am in California looking for our father and warns me to "be careful" in the search. She writes: "He just died. Suicide I don't believe. Not my father. If he were alive, he'd return. He wasn't unkind. If there are 2, they are both dead. I'm certain." She recalls our mother when our father died: "I remember how sad and Catholic and kind she was. That's her right there, but she's not Catholic and I find that unusual. She was always Catholic. I wonder why?" I continue to write about the horrors of imprisoned women, while Susie writes of "vicious coyote women who snap into other languages."

I receive a telephone call from an ex-counselor of Alternatives, the women's pre-release center. Cindy informs me that the governor has issued a get-tough policy regarding criminals. Responding to public outcry, the governor will not allow violent criminals into the state's pre-release centers. Because Native women are more likely than white women to be directly or indirectly involved in violent crimes, such as killing an abusive spouse, this will heavily impact them. They will serve longer sentences and do harder time than white women. Two friends of mine are immediately transferred back to prison. One woman is considered by state officials as the "most dangerous" female criminal in Montana. I find her soft, spiritual, wise. I wonder what public is crying over these "violent" women—same ol' powerful rednecks. The *San Francisco Chronicle* (March 27, 1995) reported that in Montana, a bill was proposed that would classify gay adults as *violent criminals*. Violence is, once again, defined by Euro-America.

Methodology and Everyday Life

We need to deconstruct old, tired methodologies. As researchers we have an obligation to rework methodologies with various worldviews and unequal power structures in mind. Mainstream Euro-American sociology creates "scientific" descriptions through "objective" generalizations and employs "universal" theories in the search for the "truth"—mysterious concepts. This procedure bears no resemblance to reality. Truths, I believe, are evidenced by allowing invisible groups to describe their experiences.

Descriptions of experiences are uncovered in qualitative, not quantitative, methodology. Donald Green (1991, 253) comments that "more qualitative research is needed to contribute to our knowledge of American Indian criminality." However, he also cites and seemingly agrees with Inverarity, Lauderdale, and Feld, who declare that quantitative research is advantageous because it offers the benefit of "impos[ing] some constraints on *overly creative imaginations*" (emphasis added). This is precisely the kind of reasoning that renders voices of Native people hidden, invisible. Obviously, qualitative work is not seen as "scholarly" or rigorous enough by some researchers to devote any time to it as a serious methodology. However, without qualitative research, we have investigations devoid of context, experience, humanity, and imagination; it is an overly creative imagination that leads to concept building. I propose that we need both qualitative and quantitative methodologies to fully develop theories that may prove helpful in the explanation of the social position of Native Americans and women.

As researchers, we must be compassionate and sensitive to decently interpret experiences; we cannot pretend to remain objective. When I interview people, I communicate in a meaningful, sincere manner. I share myself and my life—I am not simply "gathering data." Moreover, the people I interview are not objects—I see them as real people. The goal of my research is to implement social change by taking their voices, their experiences, back to Native communities and policy-making officials.

As Native women, we can define experiences of oppression emotionally and intellectually. At the risk of being labeled an essentialist (academic suicide), I believe that Native women are in a position to better understand and interpret Native women's experiences. I experience oppression as I research systems of oppression. The personal, indeed, is the political. Social institutions, powerful forces in daily life, are influenced by systems of race/ethnicity, gender, and class. I am cognizant of the various ways in which Native women are imprisoned and violated by social institutions. I wish to demonstrate the inherent prohibitive conditions in Euro-American social institutions, whether in a prison, an insane asylum, a boarding school, academia, or a family. I am not saying my experiences with family and academia are the same as those imprisoned in "real" prisons, such as the Women's Correctional Center. That would be ludicrous. I am, however, acutely conscious of the connections as I labor on issues regarding imprisoned Native women.

When I interview imprisoned women, I am mindful that I could be in their prison and they in mine. As Native women, we live life precariously. Gloria Wells Norlin served prison time for a crime she did not commit (see Ross 1998). Several Native women I know are still in prison because they, like Madeline Trottier, were at the scene of a brutal crime. Another friend is imprisoned, similar to countless other women, for murdering her husband after years of emotional and physical abuse.

Oppression is multifaceted and multilayered; not only is it complex, it also is unyielding. As Native women, we are subjected to institutional violence that shapes itself in various ways. Acts of violence against Native women are manifestations of a racialized patriarchy and have the power to eliminate the desire for survival. Many Native women, indeed, do not survive the violence. Some go crazy, as my sister Susie did, while others exist in a depression they cannot—or dare not—name.[3] It is important to challenge the oppression that all Native women face; we cannot afford to be silent.

Notes

1. I wrote this essay in 1994, and it was my first attempt at conceptualizing indigenous methodology.

2. State of Montana, Prison Convict Register, 1878–1977. Territorial Prison Museum, Deer Lodge, Montana.

3. Unfortunately, especially for her two children, my sister is now imprisoned in the State Mental Institution in Warm Springs, Montana.

References

Conley, Frank. *Montana Governors' Papers.* Letter from Frank Conley to Governor White, 10 November 1899. MC 35a, Box 31, Folder 3. Montana Historical Society Archives, Helena.

Faith, Karlene. *Unruly Women: The Politics of Confinement and Resistance.* Vancouver, BC: Press Gang Publishers, 1993.

Green, Donald E. "American Indian Criminality: What Do We Really Know?" In *American Indians: Social Justice and Public Policy,* edited by D. E. Green and T. V. Tonnesen. Milwaukee: University of Wisconsin Institute on Race and Ethnicity, 1991.

Inverarity, James M., Pat Lauderdale, and Barry C. Feld. *Law and Society: Sociological Perspectives on Criminal Law.* Boston: Little, Brown, 1983.

Nielsen, Joyce McCarl, ed. *Feminist Research Methods: Exemplary Readings in the Social Sciences.* Boulder, CO: Westview, 1990.

Ross, Luana. "Major Concerns of Imprisoned American Indian and White Mothers." In *Gender: Multi-Cultural Perspectives,* edited by J. T. Gonzalez-Calvo. Dubuque, IA: Kendall/Hunt, 1993.

———. "Race, Gender, and Social Control: Voices of Imprisoned Native American and White Women." *Wicazo Sa Review* 10, no. 2 (1994): 17–39.

———. *Inventing the Savage: The Social Construction of Native American Criminality.* Austin: University of Texas Press, 1998.

Rape and the War against Native Women

4

ANDREA SMITH

In Indian Country, there is a growing "wellness" movement, largely spearheaded by women, that stresses healing from personal and historic abuse, both on the individual and the community level. This wellness movement is based on the fact that Native peoples' history of colonization has been marked on our bodies. In order to heal from personal abuse, such as sexual abuse, we must also heal from the historic abuse of every massacre, every broken treaty, that our people have suffered. As Cecelia Fire Thunder states:

> We also have to recognize and understand that we carry the pain of our grandmothers, mothers, and the generation that came before us. We carry in our heart the pain of all our ancestors and we carry in our hearts the unresolved grief [and] the loss of our way of life. . . . There is no way we can move forward and be stronger nations without recognizing the trauma and pain that took place within our nations, our families, and within ourselves.[1]

One of the barriers, however, to healing from violence in Native communities is the reluctance to openly address violence against Native women. Native women who are survivors of violence often find themselves caught between the tendency within Native communities to remain silent about sexual and domestic violence in order to maintain a united front against racism and colonialism and the insistence on the part of the white-dominated antiviolence movement that survivors cannot heal from violence unless they leave their communities. The reason Native women are constantly marginalized in male-dominated discourses about racism and colonialism and in white-dominated discourses about sexism is the inability of both discourses to address the inextricable relationship between gender violence and colonialism. That is, the issue is not simply that violence against women happens during colonization but that the colonial process is itself structured by sexual violence. It is not possible for Native nations to decolonize themselves until they address gender violence because it is through this kind of violence that colonization has been successful. It is partly because the history of colonization of Native people is interrelated with colonizers' assaults upon Indian bodies. It is through the constant assaults upon our bodily integrity that colonizers have attempted to eradicate our sense of Indian identity.

As a multitude of scholars such as Robert Allen Warrior, Albert Cave, H. C. Porter, and others have demonstrated, Christian colonizers[2] often envisioned Native peoples as Canaanites, worthy of mass destruction as they went about the task of creating a "New Israel."[3] What makes Canaanites supposedly worthy of destruction in the biblical narrative and Indian peoples supposedly worthy of destruction in the eyes of their colonizers is that they both personify sexual sin. In the Bible, Canaanites commit acts of sexual perversion in Sodom (Gen. 19:1–29), are the descendants of the unsavory relations between Lot and his daughters (Gen. 19:30–38), are the descendants of the sexually perverse Ham (Gen. 9:22–27), and prostitute themselves in service of their gods (Gen. 28:21–22; Deut. 28:18; 1 Kings 14:24; 2 Kings 23:7; Hos. 4:13; Amos 2:7).

Similarly, Native peoples, in the eyes of the colonizers, are marked by their sexual perversity.[4] Alexander Whitaker, a minister in Virginia, wrote in 1613, "They live naked in bodie, as if their shame of their sinne deserved no covering: Their names are as naked as their bodie: They esteem it a virtue to lie, deceive and steale as their master the divell teacheth them."[5] Furthermore, according to Bernardino de Minaya, "Their [the Indians'] marriages are not a sacrament but a sacrilege. They are idolatrous, libidinous, and commit sodomy. Their chief desire is to eat, drink, worship heathen idols, and commit bestial obscenities.[6]

Because they personify sexual sin, Indian bodies are inherently "dirty." As white Californians described in the 1860s, Native people were "the dirtiest lot of human beings on earth."[7] They wore "filthy rags, with their persons unwashed, hair uncombed and swarming with vermin."[8] The following 1885 Procter & Gamble ad for Ivory Soap also illustrates this equation between Indian bodies and dirt.

> We were once factious, fierce and wild,
> In peaceful arts unreconciled,
> Our blankets smeared with grease and stains
> From buffalo meat and settlers' veins.
> Through summer's dust and heat content,
> From moon to moon unwashed we went,
> But IVORY SOAP came like a ray
> Of light across our darkened way

And now we're civil, kind and good
And keep the laws as people should,
We wear our linen, lawn and lace
As well as folks with paler face
And now I take, where'er we go,
This cake of IVORY SOAP to show
What civilized my squaw and me
And made us clean and fair to see[9]

Because Indian bodies are "dirty," they are considered sexually violable and "rapable." That is, in patriarchal thinking, only a body that is "pure" can be violated. The rape of bodies that are considered inherently impure or dirty simply does not count. For instance, prostitutes have almost an impossible time being believed if they are raped because the dominant society considers the prostitute's body undeserving of integrity and violable at all times. Similarly, the history of mutilation of Indian bodies, both living and dead, makes it clear to Indian people that they are not entitled to bodily integrity. Andrew Jackson, for instance, ordered the mutilation of approximately 800 Muscogee Indian corpses, cutting off their noses and slicing long strips of flesh from their bodies to make bridle reins.[10] Tecumseh's skin was flayed and made into razor straps.[11] A soldier cut off the testicles of White Antelope to make a tobacco pouch.[12] Colonel John Chivington led an attack against the Cheyenne and Arapahoe in which nearly all the victims were scalped; their fingers, arms, and ears were amputated to obtain jewelry; and their private parts were cut out to be exhibited before the public in Denver.[13]

In the history of massacres against Indian people, colonizers attempted not only to defeat Indian people but also to eradicate their very identity and humanity. They attempted to transform Indian people from human beings into tobacco pouches, bridle reins, or souvenirs—an object for the consumption of white people. This history reflects a disrespect not only for Native people's bodies but also for the integrity of all creation, the two being integrally related. That is, Native people were viewed as rapable because they resemble animals rather than humans. Unlike Native people, who do not view the bodies of animals as rapable either, colonizers often senselessly annihilated both animals and Indian people in order to establish their common identity as expendable. During the Washita massacre, for example, Captain Frederick W. Benteen reported that Colonel Custer "exhibits his close sharpshooting and terrifies the crowd of frightened, captured squaws and papooses by dropping the straggling ponies in death near them. . . . Not even do the poor dogs of the Indians escape his eye and aim, as they drop dead or limp howling away."[14] Whereas Native people view animals as created beings deserving of bodily integrity, Bernard Sheehan notes that Europeans at that time often viewed animals as guises for Satan.[15] As one Humboldt County newspaper stated in 1853, "We can never rest in security until the redskins are treated like the other wild beasts of the forest."[16] Of course, if whites had treated Native people with the same respect that Native people have traditionally treated animals, Native people would not have suffered genocide. Thus, ironically, while Native people often view their identities as inseparable from the rest of creation, and hence the rest of creation deserves their respect, colonizers also viewed Indian identity as inseparably linked to that of animal and plant life, and hence deserving of destruction and mutilation.

Today, this mentality continues in new forms. One example is the controversial 1992 hepatitis B trial vaccine program conducted among Alaska Native children. In this experiment, almost all Alaska Native children were given experimental vaccines without their consent. Dr. William Jordan of the U.S. Department of Health has noted that virtually all field trials for new vaccines in the United States are first tested on indigenous people in Alaska, and most of the vaccines do absolutely nothing to prevent disease.[17] As Mary Ann Mills and Bernadine Atcheson (Traditional Dena'ina) point out, this constant influx of vaccines into Native communities is a constant assault on their immune systems. They are particularly concerned about this hepatitis B vaccine because they contend it might have been tainted with HIV. They note that even Merck Sharp & Dohme seems to acknowledge that the vaccine contained the virus when it states in the *Physicians' Desk Reference* (PDR) that "clinical trials of HEPTAVAX-B provide no evidence to suggest transmission of . . . AIDS by this vaccine, even when the vaccine has been used routinely in infants in Alaska."[18] According to Mills and Atcheson, alarming cases of AIDS soon broke out after these experiments, mostly among women and children, and now some villages are going to lose one-third of their population to AIDS.[19]

The equation between indigenous people and laboratory animals is evident in the minds of medical colonizers. The PDR manual notes that Merck Sharp & Dohme experimented both on "chimpanzees and . . . Alaska Native children."[20] Mills and Atcheson question why these drugs are being tested on Native people *or* chimpanzees when Alaska Native people did not have a high rate of hepatitis B to begin with.[21] Furthermore, they question the precepts of Western medicine, which senselessly dissects, vivisects, and experiments on both animals and human beings when, as they argue, much healthier preventative and holistic indigenous forms of medicine are available. This Western medical model has not raised the life expectancy of indigenous people past the age of forty-seven. States Mills, "Today we rely on our elders and our traditional healers. We have asked them if they were ever as sick as their grandchildren or great-grandchildren are today. Their reply was no; they are much healthier than their children are today."[22]

Through this colonization and abuse of their bodies, Indian people learn to internalize self-hatred. Body image is integrally related to self-esteem.[23] When one's body is not respected, one begins to hate oneself. Thus, it is not a surprise that Indian people who have survived sexual abuse say they do not want to be Indian. Anne, a Native boarding school student, reflects on this process:

> You better not touch yourself. . . . If I looked at somebody . . . lust, sex, and I got scared of those sexual feelings. And I did not know how to handle them. . . . What really confused me was if intercourse was sin, why are people born?. . . It took me a really long time to get over the fact that . . . I've sinned: I had a child.[24]

As her words indicate, when the bodies of Indian people are inherently sinful and dirty, it becomes a sin just to be Indian. Each instance of abuse we suffer is just another reminder that, as Chrystos articulates, "If you don't make something pretty / they can hang on their walls or wear around their necks / you might as well be dead."[25]

While the bodies of both Indian men and women have been marked by abuse, Inés Hernández-Avila (Nez Perce) notes that the bodies of Native women have been particularly targeted for abuse because of their capacity to give birth. "It is because of a Native American woman's sex that she is hunted down and slaughtered, in fact, singled out, because she has the potential through childbirth to assure the continuance of the people."[26] David Stannard points out that control over women's reproductive abilities and destruction of women and children are essential in destroying a people. If the women of a nation are not disproportionately killed, then that nation's population will not be severely affected. He says that Native women and children were targeted for wholesale killing in order to destroy the Indian nations. This is why colonizers such as Andrew Jackson recommended that troops systematically kill Indian women and children after massacres in order to complete extermination.[27] Similarly, Methodist minister Colonel John Chivington's policy was to "kill and scalp all little and big" because "nits make lice."[28]

Because Native women had the power to maintain Indian nations in the face of genocide, they were dangerous to the colonial world order. Also, because Indian nations were for the most part not patriarchal and afforded women great esteem, Indian women represented a threat to colonial patriarchy as they belied the notion that patriarchy is somehow inevitable. Consequently, colonizers expressed constant outrage that Native women were not tied to monogamous marriages and held "the marriage ceremony in utter disregard,"[29] were free to express their sexuality, had "no respect for . . . virginity,"[30] and loved themselves. They did not see themselves as "fallen" women as they should have. Their sexual power was threatening to white men; consequently, they sought to control it.

When I was in the boat I captured a beautiful Carib woman. . . . I conceived desire to take pleasure. . . . I took a rope and thrashed her well, for which she raised
such unheard screams that you would not have believed your ears. Finally we came
to an agreement in such a manner that I can tell you that she seemed to have been
brought up in a school of harlots.[31]

Two of the best looking of the squaws were lying in such a position, and from the
appearance of the genital organs and of their wounds, there can be no doubt that
they were first ravished and then shot dead. Nearly all of the dead were mutilated.[32]

One woman, big with child, rushed into the church, clasping the altar and crying
for mercy for herself and unborn babe. She was followed, and fell pierced with a
dozen lances. . . . the child was torn alive from the yet palpitating body of its
mother, first plunged into the holy water to be baptized, and immediately its
brains were dashed out against a wall.[33]

The Christians attacked them with buffets and beatings. . . . Then they behaved
with such temerity and shamelessness that the most powerful ruler of the island
had to see his own wife raped by a Christian officer.[34]

I heard one man say that he had cut a woman's private parts out, and had them for
exhibition on a stick. I heard another man say that he had cut the fingers off of
an Indian, to get the rings off his hand. I also heard of numerous instances in
which men had cut out the private parts of females, and stretched them over their
saddle-bows and some of them over their hats.[35]

American Horse said of the massacre at Wounded Knee:

The fact of the killing of the women, and more especially the killing of the young
boys and girls who are to make up the future strength of the Indian people is the
saddest part of the whole affair and we feel it very sorely.[36]

Ironically, while enslaving women's bodies, colonizers argued that they were actually somehow freeing Native women from the "oppression" they supposedly
faced in Native nations. Thomas Jefferson argued that Native women "are sub-
mitted to unjust drudgery. This I believe is the case with every barbarous people.
. . . It is civilization alone which replaces women in the enjoyment of their equality."[37] The *Mariposa Gazette* similarly noted that when Indian women were safely under the control of white men, they "are neat, and tidy, and industrious, and soon
learn to discharge domestic duties properly and creditably."[38] In 1862, a Native
man in Conrow Valley was killed and scalped, his head twisted off, with his killers

saying, "You will not kill any more women and children."[39] Apparently, Native women can only be free while under the dominion of white men, and both Native and white women need to be protected from Indian men rather than from white men.

While the era of Indian massacres in their more explicit form is over in North America, in Latin America, the wholesale rape and mutilation of indigenous women's bodies continues. During the 1982 massacre of Mayan people in Rio Negro (Guatemala), 177 women and children were killed; the young women were raped in front of their mothers, and the mothers were killed in front of their children. The younger children were then tied at the ankles and dashed against the rocks until their skulls were broken. This massacre was funded by the U.S. government.[40] While many white feminists are correctly outraged by the rapes in Bosnia, organizing to hold a war crimes tribunal against the Serbs, one wonders why the mass rapes in Guatemala or elsewhere against indigenous people in Latin America has not sparked the same outrage. In fact, feminist legal scholar Catherine MacKinnon argues that in Bosnia "the world has *never* seen sex used this consciously, this cynically, this elaborately, this openly, this systematically . . . as a means of destroying a whole people."[41] She seems to forget that she lives on this land only because millions of Native people were raped, sexually mutilated, and murdered. Is perhaps mass rape against European women genocide while mass rape against indigenous women is business as usual? In even the white feminist imagination, are Native women's bodies more rapable than white women's bodies?

In North America, while there does not seem to be the same wholesale massacres of Indian people as in Latin America, colonizers will revert back to old habits in times of aggravated conflict. In 1976, Anna Mae Aquash (Micmac), who had been fighting U.S. policies against Native people as a member of the American Indian Movement (AIM), was found dead—apparently raped. Her killer was never brought to justice, but it is believed that she was killed either by the FBI or as a result of being badjacketed by the FBI as an informant. After her death, the FBI cut off her hands. Later, when the FBI pressured Myrtle Poor Bear into testifying against political prisoner Leonard Peltier, they threatened that she would end up just like Anna Mae if she did not comply.[42] In the 1980s when I served as a nonviolent witness for the Chippewa spearfishers, who were being harassed by white racist mobs, one white harasser carried a sign saying "Save a fish; spear a pregnant squaw."[43] Even after 500 years, in the eyes of the colonizers, Native women's bodies are still rapable. During the 1990 Mohawk crisis in Oka, a white mob surrounded the ambulance of a Native woman who was attempting to leave the Mohawk reservation because she was hemorrhaging after having given birth. She was forced to "spread her legs" to prove she had given birth. The police at the scene refused to intervene. An Indian man was arrested for "wearing a disguise" (he was wearing jeans), and he was brutally beaten, his testicles crushed. Two women from Chicago WARN (Women of All Red Nations, the organization I belong to) went to Oka to videotape the crisis. They were arrested and held in custody for eleven hours without being charged and were told they could not go to the bathroom unless the male police officers could watch. The place they were held was covered with pornographic magazines.[44]

This colonial desire to subjugate Indian women's bodies was quite apparent when, in 1982, Stuart Kasten marketed a new video game, "Custer's Revenge," in which players get points each time they, in the form of Custer, rape an Indian woman. The slogan of the game is "When you score, you score." He describes the game as "a fun sequence where the woman is enjoying a sexual act willingly." According to the promotional material,

> You are General Custer. Your dander's up, your pistol's wavin'. You've hog-tied a ravishing Indian maiden and have a chance to rewrite history and even up an old score. Now, the Indian maiden's hands may be tied, but she's not about to take it lying down, by George! Help is on the way. If you're to get revenge you'll have to rise to the challenge, dodge a tribe of flying arrows and protect your flanks against some downright mean and prickly cactus. But if you can stand pat and last past the strings and arrows—You can stand last. Remember? Revenge is sweet.[45]

Just as historically white colonizers who raped Indian women claimed that the real rapist was the Indian man, today white men who rape and murder Indian women often make this same claim. In Minneapolis, a white man, Jesse Coulter, raped, murdered, and mutilated several Indian women. He claimed to be Indian, adopting the name Jesse Sittingcrow and emblazoning an AIM tattoo on his arm.[46] This is not to suggest that Indian men do not rape now. After years of colonialism and boarding school experience, violence has also been internalized within Indian communities. However, this view of the Indian man as the "true" rapist obscures who has the real power in this racist and patriarchal society.

Also, just as colonizers in the past targeted Native women for destruction because of their ability to give birth, colonizers today continue their attacks on the reproductive capabilities of Native women. Dr. Connie Uri, a Cherokee/Choctaw doctor, first uncovered sterilization abuses of Native women when a Native woman requested from her a "womb transplant." Dr. Uri discovered that this woman had undergone a hysterectomy for sterilization purposes but was told the procedure was reversible. The doctor began investigating sterilization abuses, which led Senator James Abourezk to request a study on IHS (Indian Health Services) sterilization policies. The General Accounting Office released a study in November 1976 indicating that Native women were being sterilized without informed consent. Dr. Uri conducted further investigations, leading her to estimate that 25 percent of all Native women of childbearing age had been sterilized without their informed consent, with sterilization rates as high as 80 percent on some reservations.[47]

While sterilization abuse has been curbed somewhat with the institution of informed consent policies, it has reappeared in the form of dangerous contraceptives such as Norplant and Depo-Provera.[48] These are both extremely risky forms of long-acting hormonal contraceptives that have been pushed on Indian women. Depo-Provera, a known carcinogen that has been condemned as an inappropriate form of birth control by several national women's health organizations,[49] was routinely administered to Indian women through IHS before it was approved by the FDA in 1992.[50] There are no studies on the long-term effects of Norplant, and the side effects (constant bleeding—sometimes for over ninety days—tumors, kidney problems, strokes, heart attacks, sterility) are so extreme that approximately 30 percent of women on Norplant want the device taken out in the first year, with the majority requesting it be removed within two years, even though it is supposed to remain implanted in a woman's arm for five years.[51] To date, more than 2,300 women suffering from 125 side effects related to Norplant have joined a class action suit against Wyeth Pharmaceuticals, the manufacturer of the product.[52] The Native American Women's Health Education Resource Center conducted a survey of IHS policies regarding Norplant and Depo-Provera and found that Native women were not given adequate counseling about the side effects and contraindications.[53]

Native women (as well as other women of color) are seen by colonizers as wombs gone amok who threaten the racist world order. In 1979, it was discovered that seven in ten U.S. hospitals that performed voluntary sterilizations for Medicaid recipients violated the 1974 DHEW guidelines by disregarding sterilization consent procedures and by sterilizing women through "elective" hysterectomies.[54] One recently declassified federal document, National Security Study Memorandum 200, revealed that even in 1976 the U.S. government regarded the growth of the nonwhite population as a threat to national security.[55] As one doctor stated in *Contemporary Ob/Gyn*:

> People pollute, and too many people crowded too close together cause many of our social and economic problems. These in turn are aggravated by involuntary and irresponsible parenthood....We also have obligations to the society of which we are part. The welfare mess, as it has been called, cries out for solutions, one of which is fertility control.[56]

Consequently, Native women and women of color, because of their ability to reproduce, are "overpopulating the world" and pose "the single greatest threat to the health of the planet."[57] Consequently, Native women and women of color deserve no bodily integrity—any form of dangerous contraception is appropriate for them so long as it stops them from reproducing.[58]

Finally, completing the destruction of a people involves destroying the integrity of their culture and spirituality, which forms the matrix of Native women's resistance to sexual colonization. Native counselors generally agree that a strong cultural and spiritual identity is essential if Native people are to heal from abuse. This is because a Native woman's return to wellness entails healing from not only any personal abuse she has suffered but also from the patterned history of abuse against her family, her nation, and the environment in which she lives.[59] Because Indian spiritual traditions are holistic, they are able to restore survivors of abuse to the community, to restore their bodies to wholeness. That is why the most effective programs for healing revolve around reviving indigenous spiritual traditions.

In the colonial discourse, however, Native spiritual traditions become yet another site for the commodification of Indian women's bodies. As part of the genocidal process, Indian cultures no longer offer the means of restoring wholeness but become objects of consumerism for the dominant culture. Haunani-Kay Trask, Native Hawaiian activist, describes this process as "cultural prostitution."

> "Prostitution" in this context refers to the entire institution which defines a woman (and by extension the "female") as an object of degraded and victimized sexual value for use and exchange through the medium of money. . . . My purpose is not to exact detail or fashion a model but to convey the utter degradation of our culture and our people under corporate tourism by employing "prostitution" as an analytical category. . . .
>
> The point, of course, is that everything in Hawai'i can be yours, that is, you the tourist, the non-native, the visitor. The place, the people, the culture, even our identity as a "Native" people is for sale. Thus, Hawai'i, like a lovely woman, is there for the taking.[60]

Thus, this "New Age" appropriation of Indian spirituality represents yet another form of sexual abuse for Indian women, hindering its ability to help women heal from abuse. Columnist Andy Rooney exemplifies this dominant ideology when he argues that Native spiritual traditions involve "ritualistic dances with strong sexual overtones [that are] demeaning to Indian women and degrading to Indian children."[61] Along similar lines, Mark and Dan Jury produced a film called *Dances Sacred and Profane*, which advertised that it "climaxes with the first-ever filming of the Indian Sundance ceremony."[62] This so-called ceremony consisted of a white man, hanging from meat hooks from a tree, praying to the "Great White Spirit" and was then followed by C. C. Sadist, a group that performs sadomasochistic acts for entertainment. Similarly, "plastic medicine men" are often notorious for sexually abusing their clients in fake Indian ceremonies. Jeffrey Wall was recently sentenced for sexually abusing three girls while claiming this abuse was part of American Indian spiritual rituals that he was conducting as a supposed Indian medicine man.[63] David "Two Wolves" Smith and Alan "Spotted Wolfe" Champney were also charged for sexually abusing girls during supposed "cleansing" ceremonies.[64] That so many people do not question that sexual fondling would be part of Indian ceremonies, to the point where legitimate spiritual leaders are forced to issue statements such as "No ceremony requires anyone to be naked or fondled during the ceremony,"[65] signifies the extent to which the colonial discourse attempts to shift the meaning of Indian spirituality from something healing to something abusive.

Nevertheless, as mentioned earlier, Native women resist these attacks upon their bodies and souls and the sexually abusive representations of their cultures through the promotion of wellness. The University of Oklahoma sponsors two national wellness and women conferences each year, which more than 2,000 Indian women attend (it also sponsors smaller gatherings for Native men). These conferences help women begin their healing journeys from various forms of abuse and teach them to become enablers for community healing. The Indigenous Women's Network also sponsors gatherings that tie together the healing of individuals and communities from the trauma of this nation's history. At the 1994 conference, each of the four days had a different focus: individual healing, family healing, community healing, and political struggles in North America and the world.

I belonged to a wellness and women circle where Native women share their stories and learn from each other as they travel on the road toward wellness. At one circle, where we discussed the effect of hormonal contraceptives on our bodies, women talked about the devastating effects these hormones were having on their bodies, but the response of their medical providers was simply to give them more hormones. We began to see that we do not need to rely on the "experts" who have their own agendas; we need to trust our bodies, which colonizers have attempted to alienate from us. Our colonizers have attempted to destroy our sense of identity by teaching us self-hatred and self-alienation. But through such wellness movements, we learn to reconnect, to heal from historical and personal abuse, and to reclaim our power to resist colonization.

Notes

1. Cecelia Fire Thunder, "We Are Breaking a Cycle," *Indigenous Woman* II (1995): 3.

2. I shall not discuss how Jewish traditions have interpreted the Canaanite narratives, nor whether there even was a wholesale conquest of the Canaanites, which many scholars doubt. I am describing how the Christian appropriation of Canaanite narratives has impacted Native people; I make no claims either for or against Jewish colonialism.

3. Albert Cave, "Canaanites in a Promised Land," *American Indian Quarterly* (Fall 1988): 277–297; H. C. Porter, *The Inconstant Savage* (London: Gerald Duckworth, 1979), pp. 91–115; Ronald Sanders, *Lost Tribes and Promised Lands* (Boston: Little, Brown, 1978), pp. 46, 181, 292; Djelal Kadir, *Columbus and the Ends of the Earth* (Berkeley: University of California Press, 1992), p. 129.

4. Richard Hill, "Savage Splendor: Sex, Lies and Stereotypes," *Turtle Quarterly* (Spring/Summer 1991): 19.

5. Robert Berkoher, *The White Man's Indian* (New York: Vintage, 1978), p. 19.

6. David Stannard, *American Holocaust* (Oxford: Oxford University Press, 1992), p. 211.

7. Charles Loring Brace (1869), quoted in James Rawls, *Indians of California: The Changing Image* (Norman: University of Oklahoma, 1984), p. 195.

8. Hinton Rowan Helper (1855), quoted in Rawls, *Indians of California*, p. 195.

9. Andre Lopez, *Pagans in Our Midst* (Mohawk Nation: Akwesasne Notes), p. 119. It should be noted, as Paula Gunn Allen points out, that Native people in fact bathed much more frequently than did Europeans; see Paula Gunn Allen, *The Sacred Hoop* (Boston: Beacon, 1986), p. 217.

10. Stannard, *American Holocaust*, p. 121.

11. William James, *A Full and Correct Account of the Military Occurrences of the Late War between Great Britain and the United States of America* (London: printed by the author, 1818), Vol. 1, pp. 293–96, in *Who's the Savage?* ed. David Wrone and Russel Nelson (Malabar: Robert Krieger, 1982), p. 82.

12. U.S. Congress. Senate, Special Committee Appointed under Joint Resolution of March 3, 1865. *Condition of the Indian Tribes*, 39th Congress, Second Session, Senate Report 156, Washington, DC, 1867, pp. 95–96, quoted in *Who's the Savage?* p. 113.

13. John Terrell, *Land Grab* (New York: Dial Press, 1972), p. 13.

14. Terrell, *Land Grab*, p. 12.

15. Bernard Sheehan, *Savagism and Civility* (Cambridge: Cambridge University Press, 1980).

16. Rawls, *Indians of California*, p. 200.

17. Traditional Dena'ina, *Summary Packet on Hepatitis B Vaccinations* (Sterling, AK, November 9, 1992).

18. *Physicians' Desk Reference* (PDR) (Oradell, NJ: Medical Economics, 1991), pp. 1292–93.

19. Traditional Dena'ina, *Hepatitis B*.

20. PDR, pp. 1292–93.

21. Traditional Dena'ina, *Hepatitis B*.

22. Mary Ann Mills (speech delivered at a WARN Forum, Chicago, IL, September 1993).

23. For further discussion on the relationship between bodily abuse and self-esteem, see Ellen Bass and Laura Davis, *The Courage to Heal* (New York: Harper and Row, 1988), pp. 207–22, and Bonnie Burstow, *Radical Feminist Therapy* (London: Sage, 1992), pp. 187–234.

24. Celia Haig-Brown, *Resistance and Renewal* (Vancouver: Tilacum, 1988), p. 108.

25. Chrystos, "The Old Indian Granny," in *Fugitive Colors* (Cleveland: Cleveland State University Press, 1995), p. 41.

26. Inés Hernández-Avila, "In Praise of Insubordination, or What Makes a Good Woman Go Bad?" in *Transforming a Rape Culture*, ed. Emilie Buchwald, Pamela R. Fletcher, and Martha Roth (Minneapolis: Milkweed, 1993), p. 386.

27. Stannard, *American Holocaust*, p. 121.

28. Stannard, *American Holocaust*, p. 131.

29. *Cattaraugus Republican*, 11 February 1897, in Lopez, *Pagans in Our Midst*, p. 9.

30. Dominican monk Thomas Ortiz, quoted in Kirkpatrick Sale, *The Conquest of Paradise* (New York: Penguin, 1990), p. 201.

31. From Cuneo, an Italian nobleman, quoted in Sale, *Conquest of Paradise*, p. 140.

32. U.S. Commissioner of Indian Affairs, *Annual Report for 1871* (Washington, DC: Government Printing Office, 1871), pp. 487–88, cited in *Who's the Savage?* p. 123.

33. Le Roy R. Hafen, ed. *Ruxton of the Rockies* (Norman: University of Oklahoma Press, 1950), pp. 46–149, cited in *Who's the Savage*, p. 97.

34. Bartolome de Las Casas, *The Devastation of the Indies*, trans. Herma Briffault (Baltimore: Johns Hopkins University Press, 1992), p. 33.

35. Lieutenant James D. Cannon, quoted in "Report of the Secretary of War," 39th Congress, Second Session, Senate Executive Document 26, Washington, DC, 1867, printed in *The Sand Creek Massacre: A Documentary History* (New York: Sol Lewis, 1973), pp. 129–30.

36. James Mooney, "The Ghost Dance Religion and the Sioux Outbreak of 1890." In *Fourteenth Annual Report of the United States Bureau of Ethnology* (Washington DC: U.S. Government Printing Office, 1896), p. 885, quoted in Stannard, *American Holocaust*, p. 127.

37. Roy Harvey Pearce, *Savagism and Civilization* (Baltimore: Johns Hopkins University Press, 1965), p. 93.

38. Robert Heizer, ed., *The Destruction of California Indians* (Lincoln: University of Nebraska Press, 1993), p. 284.

39. Rawls, *Indians in California*, p. 182.

40. Information gathered by the Guatemalan Forensic Anthropology Team and posted by Stefan Schmitt, online at garnet.acns.fsu.edu/~sss4407/RioNeg.htm.

41. Catherine MacKinnon, "Turning Rape into Pornography: Postmodern Genocide," *Ms. Magazine* 4, no. 1: 27 (emphasis mine).

42. Johanna Brand, *The Life and Death of Anna Mae Aquash* (Toronto: Lorimer), pp. 28, 140.

43. "Up Front," *Perspectives: The Civil Rights Quarterly* 14, no. 3 (Fall 1982).

44. Personal conversations with author (Summer 1990).

45. Promotional material from Public Relations: Mahoney/Wasserman & Associates, Los Angeles, CA, n.d.

46. Mark Brunswick and Paul Klauda, "Possible Suspect in Serial Killings Jailed in N. Mexico," *Minneapolis Star and Tribune*, 28 May 1987, 1A.

47. See "The Threat of Life," *WARN Report*, pp. 13–16 (available through WARN, 4511 N. Hermitage, Chicago, IL 60640); Brint Dillingham, "Indian Women and IHS Sterilization Practices," *American Indian Journal* (January 1977): 27–28; Brint Dillingham, "Sterilization of Native Americans," *American Indian Journal* (July 1977): 16–19; Pat Bellanger,

"Native American Women, Forced Sterilization, and the Family," in *Every Woman Has a Story*, ed. Gaya Wadnizak Ellis (Minneapolis: Midwest Villages & Voices, 1982), pp. 30–35; "Oklahoma: Sterilization of Native Women Charged to I.H.S." *Akwesasne Notes* (Mid Winter, 1989): 30.

48. For a description of the hazards of Depo-Provera, see Stephen Minkin, "Depo-Provera: A Critical Analysis," Institute for Food and Development Policy, San Francisco. He concludes that "the continued use of Depo-Provera for birth control is unjustified and unethical." For more information on the effects of Norplant, see *Womanist Health Newsletter*, Issue on Norplant, available through Women's Health Education Project, 3435 N. Sheffield, #205, Chicago, IL 60660.

49. For a statement on Depo-Provera from the National Black Women's Health Project, National Latina Health Organization, Native American Women's Health Education Resource Center, National Women's Health Network, and Women's Economic Agenda Project, contact NAWHERC, PO Box 572, Lake Andes, SD 57356-0572.

50. "Taking the Shot," series of articles from *Arizona Republic* (November 1986).

51. Debra Hanania-Freeman, "Norplant: Freedom of Choice or a Plan for Genocide?" *EIR* 14 (May 1993): 20.

52. Kathleen Plant, "Mandatory Norplant Is Not the Answer," *Chicago Sun-Times*, 2 November 1994, p. 46.

53. "A Study of the Use of Depo-Provera and Norplant by the Indian Health Services" from Native American Women's Health Education Resource Center, South Dakota, 1993.

54. "Survey Finds Seven in 10 Hospitals Violate DHEW Guidelines on Informed Consent for Sterilization," *Family Planning Perspectives* 11, no. 6 (Nov/Dec 1979): 366; Claudia Dreifus, "Sterilizing the Poor," *Seizing Our Bodies*, ed. and intro. by Claudia Dreifus (New York: Vintage Books, 1977), pp. 105–20.

55. Debra Hanania-Freeman, "Norplant," p. 20.

56. *Akwesasne Notes*, p. 11.

57. Population Institute, *Annual Report*, 1991. See also Zero Population Growth, fund-raising appeal, undated; "Population Stabilization: The Real Solution," pamphlet from the Los Angeles chapter of the Sierra Club—Population Committee; and Population Institute fund-raising appeal, which states that the population growth is the root cause of poverty, hunger, and environmental destruction.

58. For a more detailed discussion of the population control movement and its impact on communities of color, see Andy Smith, "Women of Color and Reproductive Choice: Combating the Population Paradigm," *Journal of Feminist Studies in Religion* (Spring 1996).

59. Justine Smith (Cherokee), personal conversation, 17 February 1994.

60. Haunani-Kay Trask, *From a Native Daughter: Colonialism & Sovereignty in Hawai'i* (Maine: Common Courage Press, 1993), pp. 185–94.

61. Andy Rooney, "Indians Have Worse Problems," *Chicago Tribune*, 4 March 1992.

62. Jim Lockhart, "AIM Protests Film's Spiritual Misrepresentation," *News from Indian Country* (Late September 1994): 10.

63. "Shaman Sentenced for Sex Abuse," *News from Indian Country* (Mid June 1996): 2A.

64. David Melmer, "Sexual Assault," *Indian Country Today* 15 (30 April–7 May 1996): 1.

65. Michael Pace, in David Melmer, "Sexual Assault," *Indian Country Today* 15 (30 April–7 May 1996): 1.

The Big Pipe Case

ELIZABETH COOK-LYNN

"It is true," says an old Dakota legend, "that women have always had a very hard time. Their richness and joy is in having many children and numerous relatives."

What mainstream America may know about Sioux Indians is that they name Civil War captains "Dances with Wolves." What social scientists and politicians know stems from their relentless gathering of dismal statistics concerning poverty, alcoholism, early death, and fetal alcohol syndrome in tribal childbearing.[1] Probably one of the things that the American public most needs to know is that the enforced movement toward modernity for Indians is embedded in a legal world which can best be described as a confusing and vast folly emerging from the nineteenth century Major Crimes Act, and that for no one has this folly been more profoundly dangerous than for the women of the tribes, who were, literally and figuratively, stripped of their authority in tribal life.

The modern attack on the civil and tribal rights of Indian women of child-bearing age on reservation homelands suggests that life for them is not only "hard," as the legend says, but that modern change has often resulted in staggering, violent, misogynistic practices previously unknown to the tribes. As alcohol and native women have interacted with the imported legal system of the white man, the once honored women of tribal societies have become scapegoats for the failed system. As the U. S. government has taken legal charge of Indian lives, the results of its work in a specific, exemplary case are worth contemplating.

In 1989, a grand jury issued an indictment of a teenage, alcoholic Indian mother in South Dakota who, denied abortion services, gave birth to her third infant. It was charged that the Indian mother neglected and "assaulted her with intent to commit serious bodily injury" by breastfeeding the infant while under the influence, thereby committing a felony.[2]

The court, without a jury trial, sentenced her to almost four years in a federal penitentiary at Lexington, Kentucky. Shortly thereafter, the tribal court terminated her parental rights to this child and two previous children. The court believes it has "done the right thing."

"Do not forget," admonished the U. S. Attorney for South Dakota at that time, Philip Hogen, "a lot of caring people got involved. They investigated the conditions in the home. They went to the authorities and they got that child out of there and she is now in foster care. And Sadie Big Pipe [not her real name] who will soon be two years old, is going to live. . . I hope that you are not going to forget that there were courageous, caring people involved here, and that they did exactly the right thing."

The early details of the entire episode might, for some, seem to bear out Mr. Hogen's position. When tribal police were called to the Big Pipe home at Lower Brule that spring day, they saw a nearly starved infant and a drunken mother. They went to the tribal judge and, with the help of social workers, the Community Health Representative (CHR), and others, removed the nursing child from the home and took her to the only hospital in the area, some twenty miles off the reservation in Chamberlain, South Dakota.

The child had a bad diaper rash, a virus that caused ulcers on her legs, and an alcohol level in her blood measured at .02. The infant, then nine weeks old, weighed 5 pounds and 4 ounces. While no infant should ever ingest alcohol, many medical assessments of this level suggest that it is, perhaps, not in every case "medically consequential."

The mother's blood alcohol levels, on the other hand, measured at different intervals over the next two weeks as she was incarcerated and released, were .10, .12, and .30 (.10 being legally intoxicated and unable to drive a car). These levels suggest that the mother's condition was worsening, and many medical persons believe them to be dangerous. Some say that at a level of .25 some people lose consciousness, and at .50, death may occur. Yet, Marie Big Pipe was never hospitalized, nor was she sent to a detoxification center during this entire episode.

Within days, the South Dakota State Department of Social Services took custody of the child. The action was called a "rescue" in formal reports. Because Marie Big Pipe was indigent, the federal courts appointed an attorney for her and then released her on condition that she "refrain from the use of alcohol" and "enroll in an out patient alcohol treatment center." Ten days later, the court revoked the release when Marie was arrested on charges of intoxication in violation of the bond.

Another ten days passed before a hearing was scheduled, during which time the court stated that the teenaged mother "[had] a serious history of alcohol abuse and [was] unable to control her use of alcohol without an inpatient treatment program; that currently there [were] no inpatient facilities capable of providing placement; and that she [was] unlikely to abide by any terms and conditions of release to assure her court appearance." The court ordered that she be held in custody and that a jury trial be scheduled for two weeks later.

Marie's attorney from Chamberlain, the second lawyer on the case, who was appointed by the court when the previously appointed lawyer from Gregory, several hours' drive away from the reservation, withdrew, filed a futile motion to dismiss. His argument was that the heart of the matter was the legal definition of "assault with intent to commit serious bodily injury" as only involving beatings and did not apply to nursing babies and their alcoholic mothers. Basically, he said, the issue was whether her actions constituted "neglect," a misdemeanor; or assault with "intent" to commit serious bodily injury," a felony.

Black's Law Dictionary defines assault as "any willful attempt or threat to inflict injury upon the person of another when coupled with an apparent present ability to do so, and any intentional display of force such as would give the victim reason to fear or expect immediate bodily harm . . . an assault may be committed without actually touching, or striking, or doing bodily harm, to the person of another." Neglect, as defined in *Black's*, "may mean to omit, fail or forbear to do a thing which can be done, but it may also import an absence of care or attention in the doing or omission of a given act. And it may mean a designed refusal or unwillingness to perform one's duty."

The U. S. Attorney in his opposition to the motion to dismiss argued that Marie's "decision not to care for the baby is an intentional act of omission which is sufficient under the circumstances of this case to constitute an assault." He went on to say that "her act of giving the infant alcoholic beverages or allowing alcohol to enter the baby's system is sufficient to constitute an assault against the child." The motion to dismiss was denied. Marie's health problems were criminalized, her parental actions defined as crimes, and her family forever destroyed.

A jury was never impaneled, and five months later a federal judge quietly sent Marie Big Pipe to the Kentucky prison for nearly four years. There was no outcry, not from the attorney who handled her case, nor from the Indian community of relatives and friends, nor from Marie herself.

Twisted History Declares Women a Threat

The principal effects of overt federal legal action to condemn Indian parenthood and take Indian children away from Indian parents have been the subject of controversy in native communities for a century, during which time Indian children were routinely snatched from dysfunctional tribal families by state agencies and other concerned parties. Finally, in defense of themselves, the tribes fought for the 1978 Indian Child Welfare Act, saw it passed, and convinced themselves that help was on its way. The irony of the usurpation of this legislation in specific cases such as Marie Big Pipe's is a cruel one. No matter what the tribes assert in theory, they are faced with a paternalizing federal mandate.

One of the convincing arguments against criminalizing an Indian parent's action and terminating forever the rights of recalcitrant parents was articulated in the mid-1970s by Ramona Bennett, chairwoman of the Puyallup Tribe of Washington State:

> The alienations of Indian children from their parents can become a serious mental health problem. If you lose your child you are dead; you are never going to get rehabilitated or you are never going to get well. If there are problems, once the children are gone, the whole family unit is never going to get well.

If this is true, who will help Marie Big Pipe get well? If she does not get well, what is the future for any of us?

To suggest that an ill parent (an alcoholic parent) should be made a criminal and that her children should be forever removed from her presence, violates one of the principles of Chairwoman Bennett's brilliant and useful discussion, twenty years ago, on the welfare of Indian children. The effort to get tribal jurisdiction over tribal children was not made so that objectionable parents, particularly mothers, could forever be banished from tribal life through criminalization and incarceration.

Every Indian parent will tell you that the welfare of tribal children is dependent upon the welfare of tribal parents, not the state or federal government Foster care, placement, termination of parental rights, pre-adoptive placement, and adoptive placement, while now in the hands of the tribal officials since the passage of the Indian Child Welfare Act in 1978, were never meant to become instruments destructive to families. How has this all happened? Why? Who is responsible?

A Little Background

From about 1944 through 1964, the United States government, using its powers of eminent domain, seized thousands of acres of Lakota/Dakota, treaty-protected reservation lands in the northern plains to bring domestic electricity and agricultural irrigation to the region. In the process, Indian communities (including the Lower Brule reservation, which is the home of Marie Big Pipe and her relatives) were destroyed by flooding. As if nothing could stop the mid-century rush for hydropower, communities of the Missouri River tribes of the Sioux were uprooted and moved, and it has taken decades to even begin to heal the wounds. Traditional governing groups steeped in long sustained cultural values were fragmented, economic systems and reservation infrastructures were destroyed, as they had been in the late 1800s. Churches, cemeteries, governmental, medical, and educational facilities were flooded out, moved out, and never replaced.

The South Dakota Indian reservations called Crow Creek and Lower Brule, across the river from each other, the smallest groups of the Sioux Nation and the setting for events in this article, were particularly devastated. As the physical landscape was torn apart, so was the fabric of the social and cultural life of the tribes. *Termination* was the word which described the federal policy toward these communities and these people.

Accompanying the physical devastation on the reservations was the backlash of paternalism, racism, and misogyny by the nearby white populations and the federal government, which now claimed supremacy and domination over these reservation lands and resources. Decades later, the Sioux Nation and most other native communities are still fighting an undeclared war for their sovereign rights against an ineffectual and stifling, paternalistic bureaucracy. And Sioux women, exemplars of their own tribal histories, are subjected to an incapacitating colonial tyranny.

There is evidence that women, thought by the tribes to be the backbone of native society and the bearers of sacred children and repositors of cultural values, are now thought to pose a significant threat to tribal survival. Indeed, the intrusive federal government now interprets the law on Indian reservations in ways which sanction indicting alcoholic, childbearing Indian woman as though they alone are responsible for the fragmentation of the social fabric of Indian lives. As infants with fetal alcohol syndrome (FAS) and fetal alcohol effect (FAE) are born in increasing numbers, it is said that women's recalcitrant behavior (consuming alcohol and other drugs during pregnancy and nursing) needs to be legally criminalized by the federal system to make it a felony for a woman to commit such acts.

The collaboration of tribal, federal, and state law enforcement agencies in recent times, particularly, has done little to support Indian values or put any value on the Indian family. In fact, many Indian women's groups believe it does the opposite by solidifying non-Indian values and perpetuating the separation of family. What the imposed laws have finally done is to declare that what used to be a tribal societal problem, that is, a failure to protect women and children from harm, is now solely a woman's failure, a woman's despair, a woman's fault, a woman's crime. Young Indian women, many with minimal education and weakened familial support systems, have been subjected to closer scrutiny by social services and the court system than ever before. They have become objects of scorn, singled out for a particular kind of punishment dictated by their alcoholism, drug use, and promiscuity. They are seen as a root cause of the rise in infant mortality, abuse, and fetal deformity.

The white man's law and the tribe's adoption of Anglo government have removed the traditional forms of punishment and control for criminal acts. As tribal police, court systems, state social service agencies, and Christian conservatives replace traditional tribal ideas and systems of control, the legal focus on the young, childbearing Indian woman as culprit and criminal has been of major concern to women's groups.

In prior days, while childbearing was considered women's business, it was not thought to be separated from the natural and ethical responsibilities of males. Therefore, men who caused stress in the community or risked the survival of the tribe by dishonoring women were held accountable by the people. They could not carry the sacred pipe, nor could they hold positions of status. They were often physically attacked by the woman's male relatives and driven from tribal life. These particular controls in tribal society often no longer apply. In many tribal communities, such men who are known to degrade women and abandon children, now hold positions of power, even sometimes sitting at the tribal council tables. They are directors of tribal programs, and they often participate unmolested in sacred ceremonies. Many others who may not purposefully or intentionally degrade women often remain silent about the atrocities and hypocrisies they see in their communities. In the process of their public lives they assist in transferring to women the responsibility for the social ills of the tribes.

Such contradictions may occur, some suggest, because the historical influence of Christian religions and Anglo law in native communities has made it possible for individuals to abandon long-held views concerning marriage patterns and tribal arrangements for childbearing and parental responsibilities. Interracial marriages and illicit sexual relationships, denied the sanction of the tribes and families, often ignore the particular responsibilities prescribed for both males and females in traditional societies. Failures in these duties were dealt swift and severe punishment, but seldom was male honor in matters of marriage and sex abandoned as routinely as it is today. Young women, while held accountable for their actions, were seldom the only ones condemned in matters of this kind as they are today.

If the Marie Big Pipe case is any indication of law enforcement and justice on the reservation, it is a sad portrayal of the failure of the system and the subsequent loss of a woman's human and civil rights, and obviously of her treaty rights as well. The complex issue of Indian sovereignty, that is, the "power of self governance and the inherent right to control their internal affairs," while beyond the scope of this article, is as much a subject of this discussion as is a woman's right to protection by the law.

Federal Authority Criminalizes the Disease of Alcoholism

In South Dakota, two sovereign entities have criminal jurisdiction over crimes committed on reservations: the Indian nation and the federal government. Who has jurisdiction depends on various factors, such as the severity or degree of the crime, the location, who committed the crime, and against whom.

Indian jurisdiction has been steadily eroded by Congress through the Major Crimes Act (18 U.S.C. 1153), which transferred jurisdiction over major crimes committed on reservations to the federal government. This act was passed by Congress in 1885 as a result of public reaction to the U.S. Supreme Court's holding that federal courts lacked jurisdiction over a Sioux Indian who had already been punished by his tribe (the Sicangu) for the killing of another Indian (the now famous ex-parte Crow Dog case). The Act is now seen by many as a major incursion into traditional tribal powers.

Fourteen enumerated crimes (originally there were only seven) are now under the provision of this federal jurisdiction. The charge of assault, the definition of which has been broadened and redefined through the appeals process, is now used by the courts and social agencies on reservations to redefine a woman's health issues in terms of criminal behavior.

If such federal litigation as has been allowed in the Big Pipe case occurs because of the federal government's notion of its own superiority, it may also be the function of a deep-seated mysogyny that white feminists say is at the core of American society. In either case, it pits mother against child in a way that is unbearable to thinking American Indians. Yet, almost everybody is too stunned by the rising statistics of bitter violence in Indian communities, substance abuse, divorce, family violence, murder, crimes of brother against brother, cruelty toward women and the elderly, child abuse and neglect, and wife beating, to defy the idea that making criminals out of young, childbearing Indian women and applying for federal funds to build "shelters" are viable solutions.

In such an outrageously dangerous world, it is thought, there has to be someone to blame. Quickly, easily, thoughtlessly, the blame is directed toward a defenseless victim who is said to be victimizing others, and Marie Big Pipe becomes everyone's target. This is nothing new in America, known for its culture of quick and easy solutions, but it is something new to many Indians whose societies have often cherished the idea that for the weak, the young, the aged, ill, and orphaned, there has been special tribal caretaking obligation.

Indian America knows that Marie Big Pipe, ill and weak, too young to help herself, was neither to blame nor blameless. More than anything, Indian America knows that *she, too, is its daughter, neither criminal nor saint.*

The Big Pipe case is one of thousands in America today, many of which occur on reservations, that represents an outrageous violation of human rights for those who come from tribal societies in which the child is a sacred gift and motherhood a cultural ideal to be protected as the quintessential survival mechanism of an ethical society. It makes a mockery of the 1948 Universal Declaration of Human

Rights, which states that "Motherhood and Childhood (not just childhood) are entitled to special care and assistance."

America Defends Itself against Marie Big Pipe

It is interesting to note that U. S. federal attorneys have discretion in which cases they will try, that they pick and choose the cases which will justify their time and purpose. It is probably no accident that federal authorities, with either the acquiescence of or a directive from tribal authorities, decided upon the criminality of Marie Big Pipe's actions for reasons well articulated in the early findings. The child abuse or neglect charge could have been brought by the tribal authorities, because it is still within their jurisdiction to prosecute misdemeanor charges, but it was rejected in favor of the federal "assault resulting in serious bodily harm" charge available from the federal arsenal of legal remedies.

This decision-making process probably deserves further discussion, which should center upon whether the law provides appropriate remedy to Indian communities beset with poverty, social ills, inadequate education, health, housing, and legal facilities, to say nothing of constant harassment concerning jurisdictional issues from federal, state, and county governments. (In South Dakota, the tribes confront steady efforts by the courts to overturn settled law in everything from hunting to casino gaming issues, often with the blessing of the state and federal legislators.)

For whom should the law provide extraordinary protection under these particular conditions, and what is the role to be played by the courts? Unfortunately, tribal courts have no jurisdiction over many offenses committed on their homelands. Even when they do have jurisdictional decisions to make, however, they often fail to rise to the occasion.

In the Big Pipe case, former U. S. Attorney Phil Hogen says, "There is no ideal federal statute for this kind of offense or crime of omission, though it was, of course, a classic case of child abuse/neglect. The assault resulting in serious bodily injury is the charge that most nearly fit."

Most nearly fit? This is a clear failure of the courts and the lawyers in Indian Country to take to a jury not only a challenge to the feminization of the "assault" charge which some believe has been the result of more than a decade of conservative, right-wing thinking, but also a challenge to any argument over whether alcoholism is a crime or a disease. If alcoholism is a disease rather than a crime, as defined by the federal government (and by the American Medical Association since 1956), why didn't this case reflect that description? While there is no question Marie's infant was not receiving love and care and nourishment from her mother, whose responsibility it was to see that she came to no harm, there is no evidence that this neglectful, ill, addicted mother could be described as incorrigible, nor genetically defective, evil, vengeful, nor criminally violent for the purpose of domination or control, nor any of the other more egregious or radical definitions of criminality. Even a doctor's deposition, presented in her defense, indicated that there was no evidence of "malicious, evil intent" on her part.

The Indian Public Health facility, the institution in charge of health care for her people, and to which she turned for help, provides some assistance in birth control but denies access to abortion services and probably fails in its counseling of young women of childbearing age. At this time, there is little or no sex education in most federal and tribal schools.

Needless to say, the oppressive Christian religious presences on reservations, the churches, the schools (which exert considerable influence in Indian communities), the dismissal of traditional native female guidance and medical advice by existing, reservation-based institutions—all these combined to stifle Marie Big Pipe's natural inclination to do what she knew was best for her in this instance.

Drinking heavily at the time, depressed, apathetic, and in serious ill health, she knew she wanted an abortion but did not have the confidence, the personal knowledge, nor the financial means to seek out abortion services on her own. Medical practitioners know that when a woman's *choice* to bear children is removed in cases like this, suicide can be the next logical step. Alcohol may have been Marie's method of suicide or, at the very least, self-obliteration if one wants to make a case for willful behavior. Abortion services, including counseling on options, are legally outlawed in reservation hospitals, and there are no hospital facilities at all on the Crow Creek and Lower Brule Sioux reservations, an area of several hundred thousand acres.

There is only one abortion clinic in South Dakota, located in Sioux Falls, several hours' drive from the Lower Brule reservation. Its physician, Dr. Buck Williams, OB/GYN, has appeared on national television saying he fears for his life as the result of threats from antiabortion factions in the state. Dr. Williams says he wears a bulletproof vest and carries a gun. Pro-lifers in the state have threatened to "cut off my fingers," he has said.

Interviews with Marie reveal a troubled young woman burdened by an inadequate education and unable to make choices (her schooling at a local Catholic boarding school was ended at seventh grade). Her mention of the sexual abuse and repeated rapes she endured over a long period of her young life at home and at the boarding school were never taken seriously by any of her mostly male interviewers.

Not taking any of these matters under advisement, handling the case as though it were without context, failing to take the responsibility to alleviate the suffering of both victims in this case, the United States' denial of the motion to dismiss argued that Marie Big Pipe's "decision not to care for the baby was an intentional act of omission, which is sufficient under the circumstances of this case to constitute an assault. Furthermore, her act of giving the infant alcoholic beverages or allowing alcohol to enter the baby's system is sufficient to constitute an assault against the child."

It argued further that Marie's actions "were more than neglect. She intentionally decided to starve the child so that she would not be around to further 'mess up her life.'"

This argument was based upon a narrative written by a white male agent of the FBI who interrogated her months after she was arrested. This interview, conducted in the presence of a white female social worker from the South Dakota Department of Social Services in Pierre, was in the eyes of the judge particularly damning. The FBI agent wrote,

> Big Pipe stated that she felt that Sadie was the source of all her problems. She did not want to have her and tried everything she could think of to induce an abortion while she was carrying her. She continued to drink all during the pregnancy, she would do situps, and jump up and down in an effort to induce an abortion. She even investigated having a surgical abortion performed but was unable to find any agency that would pay for it so she did not have it done. She still wanted to have an abortion performed on herself after the three-month limit but could find no one to help or to pay for it. She felt that the pregnancy "screwed up" her good life with her new boyfriend. He would not accept the pregnancy or the baby since it would not be his. Even after the baby was born she didn't want it and could barely bring herself to touch it or care for it. It made her mad and angry because she had "messed up [her] life." Her older daughter didn't like her either and did not want her around. Marie cares a great deal for this older daughter's feelings and felt bad for her being against the baby but understood how she felt, she had ruined her life, too.

The government, in its prosecution of Marie Big Pipe, referred to a newspaper article from July 1989 which reported a mother in New York who abandoned her baby in the woods and was charged with first-degree assault and first-degree reckless endangerment. The government pressed this parallel, though its speciousness was readily apparent since Marie had not abandoned her baby. Indeed, Marie said she tried not to nurse the infant while she was under the influence of alcohol but the infant refused to take the bottle with its prepared formula. Because a jury was not impaneled to hear the discussion of all relevant inquiry, and the question of "intent" was never fully explored, the case clearly was stacked against the defendant.

By the end of five months of local incarceration, Marie's will to continue her "not guilty" stance had worn down completely. She finally signed a statement, which her lawyer claims she had written and understood:

My attorney has explained my . . . rights . . . and explained the facts of this incident and what impact they will have upon a jury. He also explained that whether I assaulted my daughter by neglecting her is a unique case and presents a fairly significant factual issue for the jury. Even if [sic] would lose this case by a jury verdict, the issue of assault by neglect presents a strong appealable issue.

My attorney has further explained that this will not be an easy case to win, because of the emotional impact of a malnourished child.

I have decided to plead guilty to the charge lodged against me. I do so with the understanding that I waive my right to appeal the issue of assault/neglect and all other constitutional rights I have. I chose to plead guilty because of the possibility of a jury conviction, the trauma of a jury trial, and the desire to avoid having this entire matter aired to the court.

In subsequent writings that seem particularly poignant, Marie said her counsel "would urge that any sentence I receive will be served in the Springfield Correction Institution in Springfield, South Dakota." She also said that she wanted to get her baby back and take care of her. The honorable Chief Judge of the U. S. District Court, Donald J. Porter, would have none of it, of course, and sentenced her to "hard time."

Marie Big Pipe is home now, after more than two years in a federal prison. She was on probation until 1996. Her grandmother says, "She done her time and she just wants to put it behind her." Many people connected with the case refuse to discuss it publicly.

Damaged Tribal Families

One of the pragmatic realities for contemporary Indians in the defense of themselves is that, too often, lawyers who are supposedly defending them on their homelands, overwhelmed with the complexity surrounding issues of jurisdiction and structure, just "carry the brief," or plea-bargain the cases before them. These lawyers rarely vigorously defend their clients by establishing precedents, which might prove useful to the development of a civilized legal system on Indian homelands in America.

By simply plea-bargaining in this case, Marie Big Pipe's lawyer failed to persuade her that they should proceed with a jury trial or look at the legal issues this case presented. He says he responded in accordance with "his client's wishes" and did not take it to a jury because, he says, his client was reluctant to have the matter aired before the jury.

This rationale seems unconvincing, since we have here a woman with a minimal education who relied on her attorney. He should have taken this case to the jury and called for a reassessment of the new legal definitions by which the illnesses of

Indian women and their loss of human and reproductive rights continue to be criminalized. As is generally true of Indians with court-appointed attorneys, Marie just didn't get good legal advice. Her quick and painful legal history, then, and the inglorious and corrupt history of the white man's law as it has been applied to indigenous peoples, are inextricably tied.

In the sense that justice is rarely separated from political and legislative processes, neither is it separate from the national ideologies which are expressed therein. Today's politics of the war upon women everywhere (works like Brownmiller's *Against Our Wills*, and Jane Mayer and Jill Abramson's *Strange Justice*) and the suppression of Indian women's rights—reproductive rights in particular—is not unconnected to the suppression of the rights of the indigenes historically. The historical fear that federal power will somehow suffer and that America will suffer damage if tribal government and courts reflect tribal cultural ideals which suggest that *Lakota womanhood is sacred* seems to prevail.

Law is not beyond context, and no one can ignore the effects of historical oppression. Some believe it all seemed to happen quickly and inadvertently. In 1885, a rider to an Indian General Appropriations Act, which seemed to some to be just an unimportant paragraph, soon became the basis for the oppressive Major Crimes Act mentioned earlier in this article. My view of it all is much more cynical because of the consequences. This quick and inadvertent action divested the tribes of virtually any legal and moral jurisdiction over their lives, and it was the beginning of a fearsome justice on Indian lands. It became the law's answer to the political questions posed by "vanishing American" theories resulting in assimilation and genocide. It became the major political tool used in the destruction of long-standing, humane Native American ethical and legal systems.

It is argued by some Native American scholars that the responsibilities inherent in ethical childbearing issues were always in the hands of women, never in legal nor in male societies. Today, on Indian reservations, you can find women's organizations fighting to regain the reproductive rights that they say were once theirs in sympathetic and comforting tribal societies. Responsible men and women of the tribes are working toward developing culturally based systems through which their social lives may be improved. Their antagonists, however, the paternalistically driven federal institutions which have for so long fought for power over tribal infrastructures, are still in place.

The principal effect of the nineteenth-century, white-male-sponsored Major Crimes Act was to permit prosecution of Indians by reference to selected federal criminal statutes applicable on federal reservations. Seven crimes were originally covered. To make sure that no illegal acts escaped punishment, however, the U. S. Congress, only four years after assuming that jurisdiction, passed the Assimilative Crimes Act in 1889, which allowed the government to take on cases for the states. This act includes the following language:

Whoever is guilty of an act or omission which although not made punishable by any enactment of Congress, would be punishable if committed or omitted within the jurisdiction of State, Territory Possession, or District in which such place is situated . . . shall be guilty of a like offense and subject to a like punishment.

What this has meant in Indian country is that when local, state, and regional laws cannot apply, the federal government can "assimilate" them, in other words, assume control, and this often results in making state criminal laws applicable on Indian land, in violation of cultural belief systems or anything else. It is, perhaps, redundant to say that all of this congressional activity was undertaken in violation of the 1868 treaty between the Sioux Nation and the United States, which defends as one of its principles the upholding of tribal sovereignty.

By a series of amendments, then, and through case law, the former list of seven major crimes has been expanded to the present fourteen: murder, manslaughter, kidnapping, rape, carnal knowledge by a man of any female not his wife or sixteen years of age, assault with the intent to commit rape, incest, assault with the intent to commit murder, assault with a dangerous weapon, assault resulting in serious bodily harm, arson, burglary, robbery, and larceny.

All of these crimes have been removed over the years from tribal juris Native diction by white American politicians and lawyers, the U.S. Congress, and the courts. These imponderable forces have often conspired with malice aforethought, in my view, to colonize and suppress a sovereign nation of people, and even now, with this distortion of American democracy exposed, everyone, lawyers and victims alike, continues to turn away.

The expanded definitions of *assault, abuse,* and *neglect* are used now to punish childbearing Indian women suffering from alcoholism as a result of that historical jurisdictional *fait accompli* before the turn of the century when Indians had absolutely no access to the U. S. courts.

In spite of these new definitions, which must be deplored, there is still the question of a jury trial. What happened to the idea of "a jury of your peers" as a facet of justice on Indian reservations? In the Big Pipe case, held in the Ninth District, a jury trial might have made a difference not only for Marie but also for all of us. In one of its lucid moments in 1973, the U.S. Supreme Court rendered a decision (*Keeble v. United States,* 412 USA 204) which said that an Indian is entitled to an *instruction on a lesser included offense* because he or she is entitled to be tried "in the same manner" as a non-Indian under 18 USCA x 3242. While this is not a perfect solution to sovereignty issues, an argument to a jury of her "peers" might have been convincing and might have given the courts a chance to make distinctions between criminal actions and health issues. This maneuver might have put matters back in community hands where native belief systems could have been a part of the solution mechanism. Without the protection of a jury trial, a judge (*al-*

ways white and male in South Dakota) may simply refuse to consider other objections and responses.

If Marie had been tried and convicted of "simple assault," she would have been subject to a $500 fine and six months in tribal jail. Under other, more humane, systems of justice, she might even have undergone extensive medical treatment. She might have been appropriately assisted toward rehabilitation, and her family might have remained intact, her parental rights sustained. Tribal courts are, today, taking these matters under legal discussion, suggesting that the usurpation of tribal court authority in these cases is unconstitutional and that the infusion of massive federal funds into the tribal court systems for training and education would strengthen the integrity of their own communities.

Even with a jury trial, however, as juries are now constituted, there is no assurance that Marie would have been treated fairly. It appears that Indians in positions of power on reservations (mostly male) are themselves Christian religious leaders holding rigid, fundamentalist views, or they are police and social workers trained to defend the status quo, educated in the long-standing and destructive theories of race and law perpetuated in American educational systems. They often "go with the flow," say the lawyers and others who deal with these juries and tribal power systems. They vote with the majority when they vote. They often, as do most Americans, and midwesterners in general, have simplistic attitudes toward complex social and legal problems. Be that as it may, the impact of removing moral and legal jurisdiction from tribal control and placing it in the hands of "exterior," or "white men's," legal and legislative systems has been a disaster.

Most Indian individuals caught up in criminal charges learn that the legal system to which they are subjected is illogical, inconsistent, counterproductive and, often, anti-Indian and racist. Speeding or driving under the influence of alcohol on the reservation roads, for example, may get you arrested by the tribal police, or the state patrol, or a county sheriff, or no one at all, depending upon which of the latest jurisdictional battles has been won or lost. But one thing can be predicted: If you are a childbearing, Indian woman, you will merit the special attention of the federal court system.

In fantasies of a perfect world, idealized models exist in which justice never fails, and people always get what they deserve. The reality is that for all of us in this world, and for American Indians in particular, there is a complex mixture of social, political, institutional, experiential, and personal factors from which courts pick and choose, lawyers argue, and judges rule.

There is, clearly, much work to be done by both whites and Indians before justice can prevail. Only one thing, say tribal leaders, scholars, and politicians, can rid Indians of this chaotic and destructive legal situation: a clear recognition of the sovereign nature of America's Indian nations which means, in practical terms, land reform, cultural revitalization, and the legal, financial, educational, and economic control of our own resources. Most of all, it means the reform of a colonial system of law long despised by the people. The U. S. Congress, its president, and its courts are beginning to understand the need for true home rule on Indian lands, but no one should believe that the antagonists aren't still in place.

Notes

1. This piece, subtitled "Criminalization of Alcoholism: A Native Feminist View," first appeared as a newspaper series in *Indian Country Today*, Rapid City, South Dakota, as a four-part series in 1993. Dianne Zephier-Bird, a young Sioux attorney, collaborated on this writing, and the events described are on public record. Some names have been changed to respect privacy.

2. I first heard about this case from a relative and talked to many people before I wrote this article. I wish to publicly thank my friend and collaborator, Dianne Zephier, who helped me work out the legal issues in this story. The fictitious name of Big Pipe comes from the fictive world described in some of my stories (*The Power of Horses*) and in my novel (*From the River's Edge*) published in the early 1990s by Arcade, Little/Brown. In actuality, the teenaged victim in this story comes from a very well-known and important family on the Crow Creek and Lower Brule Reservations in South Dakota. What this has meant to us as a tribal people is that if it could happen to her, it could happen to any one of us or our daughters. The Indian Child Welfare Act was passed on November 8, 1978.

Toward a Decolonization of the Mind and Text: 6
Leslie Marmon Silko's *Ceremony*

GLORIA BIRD

I chose to be a writer in girlhood because books rescued me. They were the places where I could bring the broken bits and pieces of myself and put them together again, the places where I could dream about alternative realities, possible futures. They let me know firsthand that if the mind was to be the site of resistance, only the imagination could make it so. To imagine, then, was a way to begin the process of transforming reality. All that we cannot imagine will never come into being.

—BELL HOOKS, "NARRATIVES OF STRUGGLE"

I cannot help but to view the world around me as evidence that we are living within the results of our colonization: that the image of "The End of the Trail" is popular back home on the reservation reminds me every time I see that image on a beaded bag or a bandana, and when that image is given a prominent place on a wall, that we as a people buy into the notion of ourselves as 'vanishing'. That image of ourselves as 'dying' pervades not only the ways we have all been taught from the outside in to view ourselves as Othered and vanishing, but can also be viewed as the successful colonization of our minds. What I am attempting, in both my own creative work and as an educator, is to find ways of undoing this process, a way of decolonizing the mind.[1]

This is no easy task. In what may appear to be a contradiction, I catch myself thinking in my mother's colonized version of reality: that once the old people are gone, the songs, the stories, the knowledge will be lost. But in fact, is this necessarily true? I keep an old Kootenai stickgame song lodged in the recesses of my mind. It was taught to me by my mother, though not directly, but in the repetitious hearing of the song on long road trips, a song I know that is *not mine* to sing.

I know that the man to whom this particular song belonged had died previous to my learning. And I do not know how to play stickgame, the game of bones, though I grew up with its sounds that carry long distances, like memory: the excited voices of people singing in unison, the piercing beating on the stickgame poles.[2] No one walks between the two parallel poles, one for each side. I find myself in a cultural double-bind, unable to vocalize the song that is lodged in memory as a part of my heritage but is not mine to sing. And I have never walked the road leading through the heart of the gambling spirit.

I must recognize that I am also the product of colonization in that I speak only English, though my mother is multilingual. In my childhood memories, I have always tread softly around the world of my people, reverently illiterate, though this has not been a conscious choice. Recently, my mother confided to me that in school she was made to learn Latin, and she speaks Spanish. Among the dialects of the Salishan languages she speaks, she knows words that are so old that there is no one who now knows their meanings, which is not to say that the language is dying. It is changing in the way of languages, words fall into disuse or become archaic. Internalizing the colonizer's terms regarding the axiom of our Otherness and obvious difference, she spoke Indian around me only when she wanted to exclude me. I acknowledge how I am the product of my mother's successful colonization and have spent my life trying to ease the guilt of stolen tongues—or so I have thought. It seems I have lived under the weight of meaninglessness, the nadir of making meaning, attempting to find a way in the only language I know to reconnect something, as if to jar the English language from the illusion of its impotence.

In Leslie Marmon Silko's *Ceremony*,[3] there is a moment in which the main character, Tayo, is confronted by the "older language" of his people when the medicine man Ku'oosh comes to see him. Tayo, we are told,

> had to strain to catch the meaning, dense with place names he had never heard. His language was childish, interspersed with English words, and he could feel shame tightening his throat. (Silko, 34)

Tayo's knowledge of and relationship to the older language is taxed in that he can only speak in broken Indian, a condition that creates in him an extreme self-consciousness. I read this as a moment of liberating recognition. Only in the moments when we are able to *name* the source of our deepest pain can we truly be said to be free of the burdens they represent.

As I read this passage, I am reminded of gatherings at my grandparents' house. One of my relatives' favorite pastimes was to argue endlessly on the meanings of Salish words and phrases, on the origination or context in which they were spoken. Tayo, at least, had a rudimentary understanding of his Keresan language. I, on the other hand, seemed always to hover on the periphery of my native world where my relatives spoke to one another in our language that created a world that did not include me. I strained to hear through what, to me, were the nonsensical guttural vocalizations that I have always been positive my own tongue could not imitate, and I have drawn comfort from the cadence and rhythms of the language always spoken at important events and gatherings. Although I have not inherited that system of making meaning, at an early age, I inadvertently received an appreciation *for* language.

For me, the way has been fraught with contradictions all of which can be traced back to issues of colonization. As a writer, I find much use in critical self-examination believing as hooks has written that, "All that we cannot imagine will never come into being."[4] A critical self-examination places one in the social, historical, cultural crux in relationship to the onslaught of colonization upon one's family, tribe or group. It is a departure from and unmasking of the constructs that have draped us since the colonization of this continent. This kind of unmasking of what has led to this point in time permeates every facet of my life including the way in which I read Native American texts. I have found it useful, for my purposes, to read *Ceremony* in the context of the process of colonization and have come to the conclusion that *Ceremony* operates as a work of critical fiction[5] to not only address issues of our colonization but to identify those instances where we have taken over the process of colonization to interiorize both the stereotypes and oppression. Most importantly, *Ceremony* is able to take us through the issues of colonization to identify both the instances of continued colonization of the mind and to simultaneously secure our liberation from the colonizer's mental bondage.

In dealing with Native American literature as a process of critical self-examination,[6] at least in this country, there are no models that discuss the effects of colonization upon the literature in terms of internalization of stereotypes and oppression *as a subject* of critical discourse.[7] My questions are, how has colonization impacted upon the psyche of the people and how has that manifested itself in the literature? What part do we play in perpetuating the old used-up paradigms? At what point do we internalize or reify the damaging representations of ourselves that have been imposed upon us? What is invested in the romanticism of the past and who does it serve? In the search for answers to these and other questions, I have found the essays of bell hooks, as well as other African-American and African critics and writers[8] to both parallel and highlight a similarity of purpose.

In hook's essay "Narratives of Struggle,"[9] for instance, she discusses the potential for the creation of what she terms "critical fictions." She tells us that critical fictions are those that "emerge when the imagination is free to wander, explore, question, transgress" (*CF*, 55). She speaks of the imagination's capacity for employing subversive methods that operate on many levels to engage readers:

> Many new critical fictions disrupt conventional ways of thinking about the imagination and imaginative work, offering fictions that demand careful scrutiny, that resist passive readership. Consciously opposing the notion of literature as escapist entertainment, these fictions confront and challenge. Often language is the central field of contestation. The way writers use language often determines whether or not oppositional critical approaches in fiction or theory subvert, decenter, or challenge existing hegemonic discourses. Styles of language pointedly identify specific audiences both as subjects of the text and as that audience one addresses more intimately . . . Yet to address more intimately is not to exclude; rather, *it alters the terms of inclusion.* [Italics mine] (*CF*, 56)

From hook's definition, it is possible to envision an alternative for the discussion of contemporary Native American literature. I find the potential for "altering the terms of inclusion" particularly compelling in the literary strategies that formerly have been thought of as exclusive are posed in a different light. The possibilities for subverting conventional forms begin to take shape as well. Speaking of Toni Morrison's *The Bluest Eye*, hooks makes the observation that, "Readers must learn to 'see' the world differently if they want to understand this work. This is the fundamental challenge of critical fictions" (*CF*, 57). She might have been speaking as well of *Ceremony*.

Issues of language, its purpose and usefulness to not only communicate, but also to create, are areas that are confronted by Silko in *Ceremony*. I would like to turn to a discussion of some of the strategies employed by Silko to further discussion of the novel as a work of critical fiction and of the ways in which Silko simultaneously challenges "existing hegemonic discourse" and "alters the terms of inclusion." Perhaps what I attempt here is to metaphorically walk that road leading through the heart of the gambling spirit, betting on pieces of my life in the hopes of coming out whole on the other side.

The ideological function of colonialist discourse serves to continue the paradigm of the native as Other by imbibing that Otherness within the tropes of moral and metaphysical difference. Thus, the institutionalization of natives as "wild" equated with both "savage" and "evil" are fixed representations whose underlying purpose serves to bolster the political aims of the colonialists.

In the process of colonization, we are in what is termed "the hegemonic phase." In the words of Abdul Jan Mohammed,[10] "in the hegemonic phase (or neocolonialism) the natives accept a version of the colonizers' entire system of values, attitudes, morality, institutions and more important, *mode of production*" [Italics mine] (AJM, 81). It is this last that I am most interested in as far as what I have formerly termed as critical self-evaluation that can be applied as a way of reading Native American literature: in citing the instances of the internalization and reification of representations of ourselves in colonialist terms, of which we may not even be aware, or conversely, how in becoming aware, the door is then opened to employment of subversive strategies to undermine and challenge accepted paradigms.

The potential for the strategy of decentering the story is to challenge the reader to view reality through the perceptions of the native Other. The motivation behind the employment of this strategy is to challenge the site of privilege of hegemonic discourse, though of course the employment of this narrative strategy does not presuppose a work of critical fiction. As native writers, we are, after all, walking the tightrope between the processes of colonization and the simultaneous process of our own decolonization.

The novel *Ceremony* employs the narrative strategy of decentering the story by collapsing the element of time in the novel. The strategy of decentering the story occurs in Silko's provision of two parallel storylines that, by the end of the novel, merge. A distinctive feature of the novel is that Tayo's story is set against a mythic mirror that provides the connection between the worlds that are ongoingly constructed in the novel as well as providing for the construction of the novel itself. Thus, Tayo is able to maintain that, "Everywhere he looked, he saw a world made of stories . . . It was a world alive, always changing and moving; and if you knew where to look, you could see it" (Silko, 95). But it is Tayo's part and connection to this world that provides the focus of the novel as he moves out of his war sickness toward a completion of the ceremony that frees him from it.

The affinity of human-to-human and human-to-land are the axiomatically constructed patterns that dominate the textual landscape of *Ceremony*. That these patterns in turn inform one's sense of both time and space suggests what I would characterize as a *mythic edge*, that is, a textual terrain with the capacity of encompassing time and space in a simultaneous present, past and future that is played out in the relationships of the human-to-human and human-to-land dynamic with all of the possibilities inherent in native mythologies. Tayo moves back and forth in time that is not only a human sense of time, but also includes as well the mythic time. "Years and months had become weak, and people could push against them and wander back and forth in time. Maybe it had always been this way and he was only seeing it for the first time" (Silko, 18). This narrative strategy coupled with Silko's tendency to write in fragments underscores the connectedness of all things, how each depends upon something else.

Early in the novel, as Tayo makes a distinction between types of rain, he compares the jungle rain to the rain with which he is most familiar. He tells us that the jungle rain "was not the rain he and Josiah had prayed for, this was not the green foliage they sought out in sandy canyons as a sign of spring" (Silko, 11). As he speaks, he recalls what Josiah had taught him about rain, "Nothing is all good or all bad either; *it all depended*" [Italics, mine] (Silko, 11). The subordinate clause is dependent on the sentence in the same way that meaning is also dependent on the story that is to follow. The drought begins even before Tayo's return from the war, but he believes it is the result of his curse of the rain (Silko, 195). The dependency of the people on the rain becomes Tayo's dilemma as he searches for the countermovement to the first, the curse, and then to the witchery itself once he discovers it to be the real cause of the drought.

It is Silko's use of language in the text that exemplifies the way in which language is used to maintain all of the relationships in the novel. It is a finely tuned mechanism by which Silko employs the major trope of Native American literature, which is the interconnectedness of all things—of people to land, of stories to people, of people to people—within the deep structure of *Ceremony*. The interdependence of parts to the whole is one of the pivotal characteristics of the plot upon which Tayo's ultimate dilemma hinges.

Silko frequently relies upon the construction of spoken speech, writing in fragments that reinforce the dependency of parts to the whole, such as when Ku'oosh tells Tayo, "You don't understand, do you? It is important to all of us. Not only for your sake, but for this fragile world" (Silko, 36). This structure is not, however, reserved only for spoken speech in which fragments might occur naturally. Sentences often begin with conjunctions: "But the old man would not have believed white warfare" (Silko, 36); "But the cave was deeper than the sound" (Silko, 35); "And always they had been fooling themselves, and they knew it" (Silko, 191); and, "But the last time he remembered the white walls and the rows of cribs" (Silko, 110). *Everything* depends upon something else. Our ability as readers to enter as participants of the story ultimately relies upon our ability to make those connections, to forego on an intuitive level the constricting notions we have of language and its use. We must also be willing to attempt to, in the words of bell hooks, "see the world differently."

Language and its use is addressed when Ku'oosh, the medicine man, comes to see Tayo,

> [Ku'oosh] spoke softly, using the old dialect full of sentences that were involuted with explanations of their own origins, as if nothing the old man said were his own but all had been said before and he was only there to repeat it . . . [He tells Tayo,] "but you know the world is fragile." The word he chose to express 'fragile' was filled with the intricacies of a continuing process, and with a strength inherent in spider webs woven across paths through sand hills where early in the morning the sun becomes entangled in each filament of web. It took a long time to explain the fragility and intricacy because no word exists alone, and the reason for choosing each word had to be explained with a story about why it must be said this certain way. (Silko 34–5)

This passage expresses a different value system regarding language and the responsibility required in its use. Not even a single word stands alone, as Silko has said, "[W]ords are always with other words, and the other words are almost always in a story of some sort.[11] Implicit in a word's meaning is a view of the world in which language exists less as simply a vehicle for communication but more as a bridge linking human-to-story. In an act of faith as we suspend our disbelief to enter into the textual landscape of *Ceremony* we are transformed. The way we perceive of our world and language's capacity for recreating reality as antagonistic desires is countered.

The world of *Ceremony* is socially constructed in Tayo's relationship to the older spoken Indian language and also in the intricate explanation by Ku'oosh of a single word. The ongoing process that maintains the socially constructed world is reinforced and herein Silko moves us out of the realm of hegemonic discourse. The value system that prefers the native language over English is validated. Interestingly, this does not serve to simply invert the paradigm; it also "alters the terms of inclusion." This is not, after all, a native language text accessible to only those who speak a particular native language, but is given novelistic form in a work written in English that is available to all who speak this language.

I would like to return again to the ideas of examining Native American texts in the context of the process of colonization, and how this process has impacted upon our lives. In *Ceremony*, Silko employs the strategy of representing her characters in confrontation with the world of the colonialist. The tension created between the characters of Tayo and Auntie in *Ceremony* provides the impetus for the confrontational aspects of colonization in the novel.

The way in which Silko addresses the collision of native beliefs with Catholicism, for instance, is direct. Taking on Christianity, Silko tells us,

> Christianity separated the people from themselves; it tried to crush the single clan name, encouraging each person to stand alone, because Jesus Christ would save only the individual soul; Jesus Christ was not like the Mother who loved and cared for them as her children, as her family. (Silko 68)

Silko names for us what the problems are. Auntie in the novel is a pathetic character caught in that conflict between Catholicism and her social reality. Tayo tell us that she "had gone to church alone, for as long as [he] could remember (Silko, 77). That she is confused by a religion that runs counter to the communal nature of the community does not escape his attention, however, and leads him to speculate; he "wondered if she liked it that way, going to church by herself, where she could show the people that she was a devout Christian and not immoral or pagan like the rest of the family. When it came to saving her own soul, she wanted to be careful that there were no mistakes" (Silko, 77). In a community that relies on participation, the individual operating for individual purposes can only lead to conflict.

In spite of Auntie's Christianity, she has little compassion for Tayo. The fact that he is half white produces the tension between Tayo and his acceptance by her. She reluctantly takes him into her household and proceeds to try to keep him away from her own son, Rocky. Tayo tells us that she "had always been careful that Rocky didn't call Tayo 'brother,' and when other people mistakenly called them brothers, she was quick to correct the error... 'that's Laura's boy. You know the one.' She had a way of saying it, a tone of voice which bitterly told the story, and the disgrace she and the family had suffered" (Silko, 65). Auntie's rejection of Tayo is based on the perceived shame that Laura brought to the family. Her shame is directly related to her Christian morality that aids in severing the human-to-human relationships. We learn through Tayo's perceptions of the ways in which Auntie reinforces her denial of his relationship to herself; she "wanted [him] close enough to feel excluded, to be aware of the distance between them" (Silko, 67). She would use Tayo's close physical proximity to reinforce to him all that he was not.

Tayo's knowledge of what motivates her mistreatment of him comes with an understanding of his half-breed status, an alterity that she creates, and in turn becomes the victim of, thus he is able to conclude,

> An old sensitivity has descended in her, surviving thousands of years from the oldest times, when the people shared a single clan name and they told each other who they were . . . the people shared the same consciousness . . . The sensitivity remained: the ability to feel what the others were feeling in the belly and chest; words were not necessary, but the messages the people felt were confused now. (Silko, 68)

It is the clan relationship that binds Auntie to the people.

Silko's strategy is to present simultaneously both Tayo's and Auntie's biographical connection to the tribal historicity, and she tells us what those connections are,

> When Little Sister had started drinking wine and riding in cars with white men and Mexicans, the people could not define their feeling about her . . . they were losing her they were losing part of themselves . . . [and] the people wanted her back . . . [W]hen they failed, the humiliation fell on all of them; what happened to the girl did not happen to her alone, it happened to all of them. (Silko, 68–9)

What Auntie is unable to do is to successfully disengage herself from her relationships so antithetical is that notion to the society she lives in. She is, therefore, "trapped," as Tayo perceives: 1) Auntie finds herself captive of the negativity of her own making; 2) she can never separate herself from her community just as she can never separate herself from her relationship to either Laura or Tayo; and most importantly, 3) she is still a part of that community. These are all startling and liberating revelations that aid Tayo in reclaiming himself.

Tayo is not the sole character of the novel who is interracially mixed; all of the characters who aid him are interracially mixed. The characters of Night Swan and Betonie provide Tayo with important knowledge he will need to survive the world in which he lives. Night Swan, for example, tells him that "Indians or Mexicans or whites—most people are afraid of change. They think that if their children have the same color of skin, the same color of eyes, that nothing is changing . . . They blame us, the ones who look different. That way they don't have to think about what has happened inside themselves" (Silko, 100). Silko is addressing the Othering mechanism as it is employed by colonialist literature to maintain the construction of the social world as well as the discourse. This scene speaks to the issue of internalizing the typifications by which Tayo knows himself, that is, that the color of his skin and eyes alone cannot determine who he is. Night Swan offers him a way out of self-inflicted metaphysical alterity.

Betonie also encourages Tayo's awareness of himself and in the healing cere-mony frees Tayo from a self-destructive self-hate that are the internalization and reification of typifications. By way of speaking to the healing ceremony that be-comes the pivotal and essential motivation for the novel, it might be most useful for this discussion to address the ways in which Betonie facilitates Tayo's accept-ance of the parts of himself both Indian and white. When Tayo confides in Be-tonie, "my mother went with white men" (Silko, 128), he is caught in the conflict between what he has been told about himself—what Auntie has told him, that his birth has brought shame to the family and his people—and what he needs to be-lieve that is positive about himself in order to allow for self-acceptance and heal-ing. Betonie answers him, "nothing is that simple, . . . you don't write off all the white people, just like you don't trust all the Indians" (Silko, 128). Here, the con-struct of the noble/ignoble savage is irretrievably denied; Indians become simply human with human frailties.

As if to exemplify this contradiction in Tayo, Silko immediately presents him in a conflict of value systems. Tayo is deceived by his perception of the poverty of Betonie's hogan as he views his surroundings through both the eyes of the colo-nized at what has been "lost," and through the eyes of the colonizer at what he judges to be Betonie's material lack, "all of it seemed suddenly so pitiful and small compared to the world he knew the white people had" (Silko, 127). As Betonie completes the ceremony, Tayo offers him money in payment, but he rejects it. In doing so, Betonie's action exemplifies an alternative value system, one in which cur-rency has no value, and in which the act of healing is priceless.

That Silko directs her criticism at colonization is apparent in her commentary. In the same way that Silko tells us what the problem with Christianity is, she also tells us what is wrong with colonialist teachings at school and the damage they in-flict. Laura, she says, might not have been lost "if the girl had not been ashamed of herself. Shamed by what they taught her in school about the deplorable ways of the Indian people" (Silko, 68). She points to the problems of combating the internalization of stereotypes, telling us that Laura "hated the people at home when white people talked about their peculiarities; but she always hated herself more because she still thought about them" (Silko, 69). Ironically, it is the educational system that teaches native peoples to deny themselves. Tayo is employed to reject the internalization of these typifications as he frees his cattle from a white man's land all the while debating whether he could label the man a "thief." He acknowledges that, "he had learned the lie by heart—the lie which they had wanted him to learn: only brown-skinned people were thieves; white people didn't steal" (Silko, 191). Silko is at once bringing the problems to our attention and undermining them. Identifying the source of the "lie" is the liberating gesture by which Tayo is then free from its hold over him.

Tayo begins to understand how those images damage, and he recognizes how those around him have been deceived by them. Though he "wanted to scream at Indians like Harley and Helen Jean and Emo" and all of the "people [who] had been taught to despise themselves," he comes to the realization that "they were wrong" (Silko, 204). The rejection of colonialist indoctrination is a major leap toward decolonization.

The factionalization of the community is brought on by contact with the world outside, and in *Ceremony*, Silko consistently undermines the fixity of the process of colonization by naming those moments when Indian people turn upon themselves, looking beyond the speculative assignments of metaphors to their original constructions. She deals with the sociological aftermath of colonization and is able to then move beyond the psychic ills of the moment. That movement is, of course, a decolonization of the mind. Silko accomplishes this by constructing a native world in which Christianity subverts native community life. This world is one in which adopting and assimilating the values of the society outside of the Indian community has damaging repercussions in that the internalization of self-hate on the personal level implicates the well-being of the collective whole. She bolsters the community's self-determined image to counter colonialist typifications offering a surrogate/healing shift in Tayo as he discovers that "he had never been crazy. He had only seen and heard the world as it always was: no boundaries, only transitions through all distances and time" (Silko, 246). In my reading of *Ceremony*, this novel offers us a model for a possible future mapped out in a textual terrain.

We are all the products of colonization. Five hundred years after the colonization of this continent, promoting the ideas of native people as Other, perpetuating as we parrot Othering language when we speak of ourselves, are instances of the internalization of oppression—it is, in fact, to speak the language of the oppressed.

Native people's stories, histories, very beings are inheritors all of a legacy of pain and disinheritance, but to speak of colonization only in those terms is to stay within the realm of creating boundaries between *us* and *them*, to stay locked into a static system with no resolution—that can in fact subvert the healing/shift that is necessary in the process of decolonization. In using the language of the oppressed, we repeat the same patterns of our initial siege. Each time we use the term "the dominant culture" or speak of ourselves as "minorities," we are perpetuating notions of our own inferiority and domination. In order to move out of the colonizing instances of interiorized oppression, we first must identify those moments in which we reinforce those useless paradigms and search for new approaches to the way we speak of ourselves in relation to our histories and stories. To imagine a future.

In reading *Ceremony* in terms of a critical self-evaluation and as critical fiction, I find a model for challenging hegemonic discourse. Tayo, as all of us are, is living with the results of colonization. His story is bound up in the challenging of the social, political, moral, ideological motivations that underlie colonization. This model has been useful to me in my own creative work, and in teaching.

As an educator of Native American students,[12] and in struggling with the particular issues of teaching my students to conform to the standards of conventional rhetorical forms, I am pained at a deep level of (self) recognition, to find that my students, educated in an unsympathetic system, have learned the "big lie" well, and that they speak in a passive, absent language when they speak about themselves. What I recognize in my students' timidity to claim the English language is my own struggle to learn to speak.

Where I come from, as I suspect of anywhere else in Indian Country, the ability to speak is valued and is essential to those times when we are called upon to speak for the dead and for the living, those moments when speaking from the heart is a manifestation of our continuation and is an empowering enactment. Often times, at these formal occasions of both stress and joy, we hear our native languages spoken. Thus, my memories of wakes, funerals, marriages, giveaways, ceremonies and namegivings are remembered as emotional moments that inscribed both feelings of inclusion and participation—and paradoxically, of estrangement and exclusion in not speaking my native language.

As a child, my mother at times would good-naturedly tease me about my Indian accent and mispronunciation of English words—she who was gifted with a knowledge of languages, but who had chosen not to teach her children a native language. I should add that my mother is of an era in which pride in one's heritage was not a given as it is now, and Indian people confronted blatant prejudice in Washington State. Though I did not recognize that I spoke with an accent, I became withdrawn and silent. Before I had spent my first day in school, I was already conditioned to feel ashamed. I had learned at an early age how my own words could be used against me, and I learned the power of both silence and of silencing. The struggle to come to voice has been hard won and the irony is that I now make my living by words and speech.

Later, while in BIA boarding schools, I first noted the phrases that we used as high school students, the passive language that we passed off as speech-making practice to pacify our white teachers and administrators, such as, "My aim is to preserve my heritage." Empty noncommittal language that reeks of internalized oppressions. This claim that presupposes that our *heritage* is in danger of being lost is preposterous, and reinscribes the notion that we are dying. It also suggests to me a buying in of the ambitions and desires which we are continually exposed to, and claim as our own. How well we learn to reinscribe our own domination by our own tongues!

Have things changed all that much? What my students have successfully learned is to speak passively, as if they were not merely separated by miles, but somehow both separated and separate from their cultures and histories.[13] In place of the empowering aspects of speech from their communities, they have learned instead to speak of themselves as *objects*, to avoid the first person and the subjective,[14] as if this were possible in the first instance. In effect, they deny themselves. They are the example of successful colonization.

At every opportunity, I have attempted to raise their awareness of the language and nudge them from complacency. I ask them, who better to write their stories than themselves? (Do we need, after all, another as-told-to life story?) The novel, *Ceremony*, provides a model for opening the discussion to relevant issues that native students must grapple with, and in particular, the issues that deal with identity and acceptance, of identifying instances of internalized stereotypes and oppression, and a way of tracing back issues of colonization to their source, giving *name* to the inherited legacy of pain. The act of naming facilitates a much needed healing/shift that paves the way toward a decolonization of the mind.

I mistakenly assumed that native people approached language differently because they knew of the potential of language to *create* or *make happen*. I now realize that Western culture has known all along of language's capacity to create. The attempts at crushing native languages was motivated by the threat that native languages posed. Native languages were potentially dangerous because through them we would know ourselves and our world with certainty. Yet as English speakers neither are we—as we have been taught—standing at the crossroads between two cultures making attempts at mediating our cultures, as if this were our purpose and function. Instead, we are at the pivotal moment in the act of creating a reality of *encoded*, not "borrowed," language. Here is the potential site of resistance, which can be the final liberating gesture of our decolonization. That is, provided we can *name* this moment and in that recognition throw open the doors to not just envisioning, but creating a future in which we are not draped by colonial constructs.

Notes

1. Wa Thiong'o Ngugi, *Decolonizing the Mind: The Politics of Language in African Literature*. (London: James Currey Ltd., 1986).

2. Stickgame teams used long poles for drumming on with sticks that created a high pitched rythm, but now, small hand drums have replaced the poles.

3. Leslie Marmon Silko, *Ceremony*. (New York: Penguin, 1997).

4. bell hooks, "Narratives of Struggle," *Critical Fictions: The Politics of Imaginative Writing*. Ed. Pilomena Mariani. (Washington: Bay Press, 1991), p. 55.

5. Ibid., pp. 55–61. This collection drew its name from hooks' essay.

6. Toni Morrison. *playing in the dark*. (Cambridge: Harvard University Press, 1992). In *playing in the dark*, Morrison takes the trope of 'whiteness' as a representation of all that is 'good' and turns it around, rendering it powerless and impotent as an image, whereas the trope of 'darkness' retains all of its human contradictions.

7. Although there are numerous books and articles on westward expansion and how puritanism and conquest have shaped this continent, these writings stay within the realm of conquest offering historical documentation. For the purposes of interpreting the historical aspects of colonization and enlightening those otherwise unaware, they are useful. Native people, however, know the methods of colonization and oppression firsthand, and the real work of decolonizing the mind requires a counter-history in the first instance, the one that is unwritten.

8. Influential scholars, writers, and thinkers to my writing journey have been Audre Lorde, June Jordon, Henry Louis Gates, Jr., Toni Morrison, Abdul Jan Mohammed, Chinua Achebe, Wa Thiong'o Ngugi, and Aime Cesaire.

9. hooks, pp. 55–61.

10. Abdul Jan Mohammed, "The Economy of the Manichean Allegory: The Function of Racial Difference in Colonialist Literature," *'Race,' Writing and Difference*, Ed. Henry Louis Gates, Jr. (Illinois: University of Chicago Press, 1985), pp. 78–106.

11. Leslie Marmon Silko, Leslie Fiedler, and Houston Baker, Jr., Eds., "Language and Literature from a Pueblo Indian Perspective," *English Literature: Selected Papers from the English Institute*. (Baltimore and London: The Johns Hopkins University Press, 1981), pp. 54–57.

12. At the time of this original writing, the author taught English Composition and Native American Literature at the Institute of American Indian Arts in Santa Fe, New Mexico.

13. Greg Sarris, *Keeping Slug Woman Alive: A Holistic Approach to American Indian Texts*. (Berkeley: University of California Press, 1993).

14. Ibid. I am greatly indebted to Greg Sarris for his influence on my thought and writing, and whose ideas have greatly influenced me. See Sarris' "Storytelling in the Classroom: Crossing Vexed Chasms," pp. 149–68.

Native InFormation

7

JOANNE BARKER AND TERESIA TEAIWA

THIS IS NOT A TREATY!

> I HAVE NOT SIGNED A TREATY
> WITH THE U.S. GOVERNMENT
> nor has my father nor his father
> nor any grandmothers
> We don't recognize these names on old sorry paper
> Therefore we declare the United States a crazy person . . .
> No this U.S. is not a good idea We declare you terminated
> You've had your fun now go home we're tired We signed
> no treaty WHAT are you still doing here Go somewhere else &
> build a McDonald's We revoke your immigration papers . . .[1]

CHRYSTOS *NOT VANISHING*

THIS IS NOT A TREATY! We're not interested in making any treaties, smoking any peace-pipes, or shaking anyone's hand across conference tables or over long-burning firepits. We're not here to negotiate. We're not here to sign our names on "old sorry paper." And we're certainly not here to amuse. We quite frankly don't believe in treaties, treaty discourse, treaty politics, or (rather) in people who never intended to honor their treaties with indigenous peoples in the first place. We're tired of walking on the long trail of broken promises and well-known betrayals, especially as it leads to a people who claim that the word is sacred, even an embodiment of their god, the flesh of their beliefs, the beginning of time. We've learned from this history of making treaties—governments going back on their word after they've gotten indigenous peoples to move off lands valued only for material resources—and we're simply not interested in play-ing this game with anyone, any longer.

We understand that our ancestors initially entered into contractual relations with European settlers because they expected the colonizers to keep their word—to keep their place. It wasn't naiveté, it was trust. After all, inter-tribal discussions existed and worked quite well to the benefit of those who participated. But Euro-pean settlers entered into such relationships with the "uncivilized Indian" because they anticipated that the Native would eventually disappear and thereby render treaties irrelevant. *Who would have ever thought that such an uncivilized race of barbarians would endure, let alone live to protest when assurances created in treaties were reneged upon?* But indigenous peoples have survived. And they've learned English. And they're protesting in courts for governments to be held responsible to the agreements that they have made in their treaties. And colonizers, waiting for the Native to perish, actively, and in various ways, circulate narratives of the Vanishing Indian in order to maintain the myth of the inevitability of the Native's disappearance.

THIS IS NOT A TREATY! Because we refuse to disappear into those narratives. Indigenous peoples understand that there is no difference between the telling and the material. They understand how we all, in fact, live inside and through the nar-ratives we tell and that the importance in telling stories is inseparable from the identity, community, and history they compose and the spiritual, economic and political realities on which they depend and which they subvert or preserve. Treaties tell a real and particular story, a story of disparate expectations and ir-reconcilable differences between indigenous peoples who believe in keeping prom-ises made and colonizers who wait for the Natives' disappearance. And so, THIS IS NOT A TREATY! And neither is it an entreaty.

Our aim is to interrupt the ways in which the narratives of the Vanishing Indian have intersected with our respective identities, communities, and histories as two mixed-bloods of American Indian and Pacific Islander ancestry. We do so in order to interfere with the logics and persistence of these narratives as we have encountered them within the academic spaces in which we have been and are located as Indian and Native. Our aim is to do so through a different kind of fictional production than merely telling you the usual story of our disappointment with the "white man's be-trayal," and so speaking for all native peoples everywhere, re-creating ourselves as a representational "we." We do so because of the consequences we see these narratives having for us here: one, as Indian/Native we are made to represent an identity-as-authenticity of which we are not quite convinced; and two, even as we are present in the academy, we can only signify absence, the absence to which we have been reduced by the narratives of the Vanishing Indian. Neither of these consequences are accept-able and both of these consequences we attribute to the malleability of the Vanishing Indian narratives for social and political purposes that would want to continue to place indigenous peoples within dramas where they are indeed vanishing—authentic only when absent, romanticized to death. Simply put, we're through with making treaties, telling and participating in stories of our disappearance, creating our absence in its re-telling. We are here to contest. To provoke. To inform. But not to sign up.

And so we begin with our readers. As all good "native informants" do, we assume that our audience is ignorant. We apologize to any of our readers who feel that this is an unfair assumption. But if you are one of those privileged with prior knowledge of the information we divulge, then we're sorry for assuming that your knowledge has been over-determined by the disciplines of History and Anthropology (two disciplines through which colonizingtreatymakers continue to circulate narratives of the Vanishing Indian and against which we write). Situated as our words are, in a collection of essays on women of color in collaboration and conflict, our words are directed to an audience which is both ignorant and "knowledgeable," predictable and unpredictable. *Dear audience:* People of color, women, white men, mixed bloods, and indigenous readers: we realize that for some of you it is an awkward situation being addressed in the same breadth as others. Please forgive us . . . but we know that you will all do what you will with this native information anyway.

* * *

I do not have a reservation to go home to, a "native" language to speak, a uniquely "Indian" religion to practice: the Lenni Lenâpé (Delaware) people do not have a reservation, thanks to the aggressive U.S. land allotment program; it is estimated by the tribal manager that only six members speak the ancient language;[2] and long ago, religious practices (were) reformed (by) Christianity. Five hundred years of physical, social and cultural migrations *have changed what it means for American Indian peoples to have a place to return to (ok, there's a mail order gift shop and the tribal offices in Oklahoma), a language to speak (ok, there are tapes to learn from), and an "Indian" religion to practice (ok, it's my prejudice of Christianity's specific history of colonialism).[3] And then there are the politics of being mixed-blood . . .*

After this, I'm going home. Yup, home in the islands. Lucky me, huh? Like the frigate bird, flying far and wide, but always knowing where to return. The United States of America—this "dream" land—could never be home for me. The blood, sweat, and tears of many ancestors saturate this soil; they give me wings to fly. I'll never forget, but I'll never stay. I belong elsewhere, I long to return elsewhere. I belong to kaainga on Banaba, Tabiteuea, and Rabi—my "native" lands. I long to return to Fiji—my "home" land. Like the frigate bird, flying far and wide, but always knowing where to return. After this, I'm going home. Yup, home in the islands. Lucky me, huh?

* * *

What brings us together? An American Indian and a Pacific Islander. It is often presumed that our reality is most determined by a relationship to "native" land and territory. But we are also subjects of history. Both of us are mixed-bloods and both of us have specific and complicated histories of geographical, cultural, economic and political displacement and mobility. So while we may specify our identities as Delaware and I-Banaba respectively, neither of us grew up in our "native" lands. As "individuals" we have shared our different experiences, ideas, and visions of being "native" through conversations with each other. If all were told in detail, we might be able to explain how history brings us together. But more to the point, we are here.

* * *

Upon entering the hallowed halls of academia, our protagonist, our heroine, Native-in-formation, calls forth the spirit of her ancestor, Vanishing-Indian. "Hey, dude! What's going on?" Vanishing-Indian does not answer. "Dude?" A disembodied voice booms, "Vanishing-Indian does not answer to that name!" "Vanishing-Indian, is that you?" "I am. Ay, I am," the voice reverberates. "Uh-huh . . ." our heroine pauses to consider the situation.

Five hundred years of vanishing Indians. From the unfortunate Taino to the hapless Tasmanians. Five hundred years of vanishing . . . Going, going, gone? (To the highest bidder) Or going, going, still going? (Like the "Energizer" bunny) . . . Five hundred years.

Standing in the middle of the hallowed halls, our protagonist, our heroine, Native-in-formation, watches Professors and Students of Information hurry by. She calls out, "Hello!" The walls echo in response, "Hello-ello-lo-o!" "Hmmm," Native-in-formation says to herself, "You know, that voice sounds familiar." She walks further down the hallowed halls, where she comes upon a statue of Vanishing-Indian standing at the center of a rotunda. "Hello?" No answer. "Well, what the hell am I supposed to say? 'Oh, Great Ancestor hear the pleas of your humble daughter?!' Goddamit Vanishing-Indian! Give me a break!" "Okay, okay! I just wanted to see how creative you could get! Heh, heh." Native-in-formation is stunned: did the statue speak? "Vanishing-Indian?" "Yes." And from the other side of the statue a woman steps forward. She looks familiar. "You're Vanishing-Indian?!" "Mm-hmm." "But what about him?" "He really vanished, girl! And we're all of us always vanishing, I guess. That is if you stick to that particular translation of our name." "What do you mean *our* name?" "Heh-heh," chuckles Vanishing-Indian.

* * *

THIS IS NOT A TREATY! even as we use the written word we refuse to be bound by it. whiteimperialistcolonizers have perjured their own written words ever since they set foot on our shores. they made treaties with us that they would not honor.

and so we learn from this history. THIS IS NOT A TREATY! we make no promises, no deals. these written words do not bind us, they free us; they do not dispossess us, they empower us; what do these written words do for you? this is native information. THIS IS NOT A TREATY!

* * *

Native In Formation

The essential question is *"what counts as Indian?"*

> For Whites, blood is a substance that can be either racially pure or racially polluted. Black blood pollutes White blood absolutely, so that, in the logical extreme, one drop of Black blood makes an otherwise White man Black . . . White ideas about 'Indian blood' are less formalized and clear-cut. . . . It may take only one drop of Black blood to make a person a Negro, but it takes a lot of Indian blood to make a person a 'real' Indian.[4]

As "native" you are expected and required to represent not merely "your people" but the *always already* "Indian" to whom you are constantly speaking and to whom you are constantly referred and of whom you have not participated in the making. You are not convinced of this "Indian's" authenticity but neither is He/She escapable. He/She stands before you. He/She walks with you. He/She interferes with the way of your steps, making you always backtrack, sideways, through the dramas of the Frontier and the stills of Curtis.

CHIEF BRAVE MEDICINE MAN WARRIOR PRINCESS SQUAW FRY BREAD MAKER PAPOOSE CARRIER insists on enclosing you within His/Her reserves of "Indian" identity and "Indian" territory, engendered and racialized as the "primitive-native"[5] Man-Woman, absolutely fixed in a space within and time outside. Just once you'd like to get through a conversation without being coerced into commenting on Geronimo or Pocahontas,[6] the only real "Indians" whose identities you are expected to emulate while *always already* having been occupied by those who have given them their names and so have enclosed (reserved?) what counts as "Indian."

You're really Indian? What's it like to be an Indian? How much Indian are you, anyway? A half? A quarter? What? You know, you don't look anything like an Indian. What kind of fellowship did you say you were on? I don't mean to be rude, but you really don't look anything like an Indian.

For mixed-bloods, the burden of proof is all (y)ours. You had better walk and talk and look and sound "like an Indian" through the *manners and customs* that the whiteeducatedcolonialists have so carefully documented in their anthropological and other literary texts that function like documents of indisputable evidence (field notes) in whose presence you can merely prostrate yourself (for their omniscience) if you ever hope to appease their anger over your being here—there where you have deviated from what counts as "Indian" by speaking, smiling, writing, authoring. You even begin to anticipate the questions and catch yourself making yourself over into *that* "Indian," being (in)formed by His/Her authenticity. And in time, as absurd as it may seem, you actually begin to imagine that people see you as CHIEF BRAVE MEDICINE MAN WARRIOR PRINCESS SQUAW FRY BREAD MAKER PAPOOSE CARRIER and you are *relieved.*

As an undergraduate, I worked as a word processing consultant at the university's Office of the Vice Chancellor for Research, under whose administrative umbrella the Office of Graduate Studies (including Admissions and Fellowshps) were located. I was at work the day that the Office of Graduate Studies at UCSC called to verify whether or not I was really an Indian, assuming I suppose that the graduate office of my undergraduate institution (or my place of employment?) would be able to tell. After receiving the phone call from UCSC, the director of graduate admissions came running up to me with a bright smile on her face, "they're calling to check up on you." It was good news. It wasn't the only place that they had called that morning.

And so we are expected to justify our existence in the locations we have chosen to reside in if they deviate from the "Indian" before us: the Vanishing Indian, the last true informant to knowledge already formed. Or we must remain silent. Or we must confront. Always. The legitimacy of the questions that ask us to validate our authenticity. *Let me see. I think that was 73.89%. No wait. I was never any good with math. I think it's 37.521%. No. That doesn't sound right either. How's ??* Or we must come up with a different set of questions than the ones posed to us, making an other place from which to speak.

We must not allow them to tell us that we don't belong here as though *this* were the location of the sacred and we were the desecrators. We must insist that *they* defend the History that incessantly erases us, displaces us, occupies us, and continues to remove us from the locations which we have chosen to inhabit and in which we have buried our dead. Remember, we can decide what to allow them to see of our worlds. Our dreams. Remember also, they are easily deceived. We must be careful. But this time the decision is ours.

And so I will give you information. Carefully selected information so that you can trust it. And you can learn what it means to be native, and I will be your informant, and you will see who is really being observed and who is really participating—this time around—in what is going to count/be written as Indian. Get out your notebooks. Details are important.

* * *

Native Information:

I was involved in a teaching program for Pacific island mental health workers. Some of the students were Pacific island physicians and some were mental health counselors. They were asked to make presentations to the class about the social and cultural organization of everyday life in their home villages. The teaching faculty of the program was astonished to find that the students would only talk about their social and cultural structures in terms of the established and published ethnographies. The problem for us was that we wanted to have the trainees and ourselves think about the contemporary social interaction in the village, how routine topics in everyday conversation were related—played a part in structuring events—to current mental health problems in the village population, e.g. adolescent suicide, schizophrenia, depression, and violent behavior. Try as we might, we could not get the trainees, or the majority of the faculty, for that matter, to think of village social structure as sequentially produced, moving through time and space as of the symbolic interaction that made structure visible.

What we received were formal reports on kinship systems, land tenure, traditional political structure and religion, mythology, indigenous fishing, agriculture, and transportation technologies. The reports were largely paraphrased versions of recognizable anthropological publications. The publications were often recited verbatim, frequently without attribution. The trainees and many of the faculty were astonished that we were insisting on descriptions of the mundane or ordinary; they could not see anything interesting or "worth telling" (as in tell a story) in everyday life, focusing instead on the monumental, generalized descriptions of the past.[7]

* * *

What is native information anyway?

* * *

ACCOUNTING FOR THE NATIVE. *Question Number 4* on the 1990 Census requested that participants "Fill ONE circle for the race that the person considers himself/herself to be." The options included: White; Black or Negro; Indian (Amer.); Eskimo; Aleut; Asian or Pacific Islander; or, Other race. If participants were Indian (Amer.), they had to write in the "name of the enrolled or principle tribe." If participants were Asian or Pacific Islander, they had to print one group's name. If participants were Other race, then an arrow merely pointed to a blank space in which they were to write down the name of the race to which they identified. *Question Number 7* on the 1990 Census asked, "Is this person of Spanish/Hispanic origin?" Participants were told to "Fill ONE circle for each person." The options were: No (not Spanish/Hispanic); Yes, Mexican, Mexican-Am., Chicano; Yes, Puerto Rican; Yes, Cuban; Yes, other Spanish/Hispanic. If yes, then "Print one group, for example: Argentinean, Columbian, Dominican, Nicaraguan, Salvadoran, Spaniard, and so on."[8]

Table 8.1. 1990 U.S. Census Bureau Results[9]		
ALL PERSONS:	248,709,873	*Not of Hispanic Origin:*
BY RACE:		
White	199,686,070	188,128,296
Black	29,986,060	29,216,293
American Indian, Eskimo, Aleut	1,959,234	1,783,773
Asian or Pacific Islander	7,272,662	6,968,359
Other Race	9,804,847	229,093

Of the 1,959,234 people who identified themselves as Indian (Amer.), Eskimo, or Aleut in the 1990 Census (1,783,773 not of Spanish/Hispanic origin), almost 40% belong to only four tribes: Cherokee, Navajo, Chippewa, and Dakota. The ten largest tribes accounted for 56% of the total indigenous population. Two-thirds of the 542 tribes counted have fewer than 1,000 persons each. (This was the first U.S. Census release of tribal population counts[10] which I imagine have until now resided with Tribal Governments, the Bureau of Indian Affairs, and the Federal Bureau of Investigation.)

* * *

There are over 25,000 islands in the Pacific Ocean. Anthropologists have determined that few of these islands have never been inhabited. The island Pacific is generally recognized as lying within the boundaries marked at its northernmost by the Hawaiian archipelago, by Belau at its westernmost, by New Zealand in the south, and French Polynesia in the east. Since the 1830's the islands have been categorized according to three geo-cultural groupings: Melanesia, Micronesia and Polynesia. There are over 1,228 languages among these groups. In 1986, the total population of the Pacific Islands (excluding Hawai'i and New Zealand) was 4,952,470 (Papua New Guinea accounted for 3,000,000 out of this total). Those Pacific Island groups historically and politically linked to the United States are Belau, the Federated States of Micronesia, the Marshall Islands, the Northern Marianas, Eastern Samoa, Guam, and Hawai'i. *(Wanna know how they got mixed up with the U.S.? Go to the library!)*

* * *

The 1990 United States of America Population Census categorized Pacific Islanders with Asians. *Why are Pacific Islanders and Asians counted together?* The census made a special distinction, however, for Asian Pacific Islanders (API) of "Hispanic origin." In 1990, the total API population in the U.S. was 7,273,662; those not of Hispanic origin totalled 6,968,359. There are more APIs in California than in any other state, but only county-level census reports distinguish between Pacific Islanders and Asians; furthermore, county reports provide statistics for different Pacific Islander ethnic groups. For instance, in Santa Cruz county, which has a total population of 229,734, there were 225 Hawaiians, 433 Samoans, 1 Tongan, and 4 "other Polynesians;" 42 Guamanians, and 11 "other Micronesians;" 13 Melanesians; and 10 "unspecified Pacific Islanders." *What are the political and cultural significances of this relatively small islander presence in the continental U.S.?*

* * *

And then there are the graduate school and fellowship application forms: On the graduate admissions form for UCSC, applicants are asked to fill out an "Ethnic Survey:" "This information is useful to us for statistical purposes but you are not required to provide it." The options for an applicant's ethnic identity are: American Indian/Alaskan Native (with tribal affiliation); Black/African-American; Chicano/Mexican-American; Latino/Other Spanish-American; Philipino/Filipino; Chinese/Chinese-American; East Indian/Pakistani; Japanese/Japanese-American; Korean/Korean-American; Pacific Islander; Other Asian; White/Caucasian; Other, Specify. *Applicants select one.*

* * *

Table 8.2.   1990 Total Percent Distribution Fall Enrollment in Institutions of Higher Education[11]

	ALL STUDENTS	GRADUATE STUDENTS	DOCTOR'S DEGREES CONFERRED FOR ALL FIELDS[12]
Total	100.0	100.0	100.0 (37,980)
White, non-Hispanic	80.2	86.7	67.9 (25,793)
Black, non-Hispanic	9.2	5.9	3.0 (1,145)
Hispanic	5.7	3.2	2.1 (783)
Asian or Pacific Islander	4.2	3.7	3.4 (1,282)
American Indian/Alaskan Native	0.8	0.5	0.3 (102)
Women of Color	11.2	7.6	1,400

* * *

Conversations: We will not analyze the reasons why so few native peoples are in the academy or why so few are graduate students or Ph.D. recipients. Our point is that the relative absence of native peoples from the institutions of "higher education" and the narratives of the Vanishing Indian combine to produce a *very specific* place for natives to occupy—to appear—within the academy. Our work is to simultaneously name that place, identify some of the ways that it is constituted by the Vanishing Indian narratives (and thereby demonstrate its *constructedness*), and finally to reconstruct it. Not merely to produce another place—a "third" place less inhabitable than the first—but to produce our appearance away from the authentic/absent subjectivity created for us by the Vanishing Indian. In other words, to be *in formation/information* is to refuse History's accounts/accounting of us. It is to produce another place that is not a silence made voice, which is a move too familiar to colonial-anthropological forms of knowledge that we refuse to inhabit, but is rather a place in which *we* are the clerks, writers, and curators of our records, artifacts, identities and histories. THIS IS NOT AN (EN)TREATY! This is a conversation, *in spite of* and *because of* our differences and struggles as indigenous peoples and mixed-bloods, in which we engage your participation outside the narratives of the Vanishing Indian as natives who have literally survived.

* * *

In an article on the language and discourse of defense intellectuals, feminist scholar Carol Cohn described the process by which she infiltrated this powerful and dangerous elite culture. Defense intellectuals go about their business in a language which has no reference to human beings, let alone the third world and indigenous peoples on whom weapons are routinely tested. Cohn's task involved listening to, learning to speak, and dialogue in the language of technologic strategy in order to achieve a critical position from which to create alternatives. This path to the "critical" position which Cohn promotes has much in common with an ethnographic project. I find that discomforting because an ethnographer chooses which languages to learn and may leave at any time the places in which those languages predominate. It seems to me that the burden of learning new languages, the languages of the more powerful, is placed every day on the shoulders of the already dispossessed.

If I have a critical positioning, it is not achieved through ethnographic methods. For inherent to the ethnographic position seems to be a fantasy of authority—over language—which allows dialogue. I may have listened to and learned to speak languages to which I am not native, but I doubt that I have achieved the proficiency to "dialogue." Rather, I monologue. I monologue, never quite sure if I understand or am understood. I monologue, you monologue, we monologue . . . and maybe our monologues will coincide. But we have no expectations, make no promises. After all, this is not a treaty, it is native information.

*　*　*

From Epeli Hau'ofa's *Kisses in the Nederends:*[13]

> "Morning, Rita. How are you?"
> "So so. And you?"
> "So so. Where've you been?"
> "From there."
> "And where are you going?"
> "Over there."
> "What for?"
> "Oh, I'm just going to do something. What are you doing?"
> "Just this. How's Oilei?"
> "So so. And how's Tevita?"
> "He's a bit so so."
> "Oh. That's a pity."
> "Yes. . . . I hope Oilei's so so's not too so so. Bye."
> "Yeah, bye."

*　*　*

Most of the time it doesn't matter to me if I'm understood or not. Talking, writing, and being understood can be so banal, familiar and boring sometimes. It can seem so exciting, exotic, and promising to be misunderstood, not to understand. But being obscure is too easy; it takes responsibility and maturity to be clear. Who should rescue all this native information from its obscurity? Who can make the native information clear? You? Me? That man with the notebook? The woman with the camera? Who?

*　*　*

Naming the Place: The Proof of Burden

The Vanishing Indian is not merely a reference to the Warrior on horseback shot by the U.S. soldier or the diseased Indian dying in a teepee on some obscure prairie or the Princess who died from a broken heart in a foreign land. The Vanishing Indian is a more complex *figuring* of Native American peoples that historically, physically and symbolically names and so forms them as *always already* dead while at the same time frozen on a reservation—America's Third World ghetto[14]—drunk and dirty, unemployed and uneducated. This *figuring* has a History not worth repeating; for here, mere episodes provoke:

ANTHROPO-LOGICAL KNOWLEDGE "Into each life, it is said, some rain must fall. Some people have bad horoscopes, others take tips on the stock market . . . But Indians have been cursed above all other people in history. Indians have anthropologists . . . Indians are certain that Columbus brought anthropologists on his ships when he came to the New World. How else could he have made so many wrong deductions about where he was? . . . You may be curious as to why the anthropologist never carries a writing instrument. He never makes a mark because he ALREADY KNOWS what he is going to find. He need not record anything except his daily expenses for the audit, for the anthro found his answer in the books he read the winter before. No, the anthropologist is only out on the reservations to VERIFY what he has suspected all along . . ."[15]

I N D I A N *"Why do you call us Indians?"*[16] The Trivial Pursuit Answer: *The Faulty Geography of Christopher Columbus.* (Who else?) The specific term *Indian* as a designation for the inhabitants of the North Americas begins with Columbus: under the impression that he had landed among the islands off Southeast Asia, he called the peoples he met in Central America *los Indios.* Even after subsequent explorations corrected Columbus' error in geography, the Spanish continued to use the term *Indios* for all peoples "found" to inhabit the "New World." The rest is, as they say, History.

D E L A W A R E The name *Lenni Lenâpé* has been translated and so rendered into various meanings, such as "original people," "men among men," and "men of our kind;" but *len* means "common" and *âpé* means "people." The word *Lenâpé* standing alone can be translated as "common people" and the addition of *Lenni* is a redundancy which reinforces the signification: *Common People.* After the English arrived, the *Lenni Lenâpé* peoples living in the now Delaware and New Jersey areas were given a new name, which was derived from the third Lord de la Warr, Sir Thomas West, who was appointed governor of the English Colony at Jamestown, Virginia, in 1610. One of his followers, Captain Samual Argall,[17] took a voyage up the coast in search of provisions and on his return sailed into a bay that he named in honor of the governor. As time went on, the *Lenni Lenâpé* peoples living on the shores of the "de la Warr Bay" and along the banks of the river that emptied into it became known as the Delaware Indians.[18]

MIGRATION (RECORDED) The Delaware begin moving from the areas of their original settlement to the Susquehanna River area in mid-western Pennsylvania to avoid war with the settlers (1709); the Walking Purchase fraudulently claims lands away from the Delaware for settlement by the British (1737); the remainder of the Delaware move to the Susquehanna River valley under the protection and government of the Six Nations, on the specific lands managed by the Cayuga and Oneida tribes (1742); the Delaware begin moving to the Ohio and Allegheny River valleys in western Pennsylvania in order to exercise self-determination, and eventually align themselves with the Shawnee to do battle against the British settlers (1752); war is declared on the Delaware by the Pennsylvania government (1756); the Ohio River valley Delawares are massacred for "crimes" their warriors allegedly committed against the British settlers (1756); the Delawares are moved by the U.S. government from Ohio to Indiana Territory[19] (by 1800); the St. Marys Treaty with the U.S. government forces the Delaware to move to Missouri Territory (1818–1822); they are further removed to Kansas Territory (1830); through treaty, the Delaware are "officially" merged with the Cherokee Nation, losing all independent rights and sovereignty (1867); the Delaware are forced to cede all lands in Kansas and are moved to Indian Territory in Oklahoma where they purchase lands from the Cherokees (1868) . . .[20] Today, the Delaware Tribe is not recognized as a separate and sovereign nation apart from the Cherokees and is currently negotiating with the Cherokees for support of their legal efforts to obtain separate Federal Recognition.[21]

RESERVATIONS The effects of five hundred years of migration and colonial forms of knowledge have done their well-known violence to native peoples. And yet it is within this History that the paradox is constituted: how can *I* as a mixed-blood *Lenni Lenâpé*/Delaware-Cherokee/European-American return to an "Indian" identity and culture, to a reservation where traditional and spiritual practices are preserved and continued and my native language spoken and nationalism defined and celebrated, and return here to speak from that place when it has been— and I have been—so removed? And how can *I* interrupt, without reservation, the narratives of the Vanishing Indian when my family and tribal history would suggest that, for all probabilities, I am?

Yet, it is from that "impossible" place of foreknowledge and migration that I speak, that I insist on speaking from, as a way of contesting the authentic-as-absent, authentic as particularly seen, Indian within the Grand Narrative: I refuse to disappear/appear as the "heroine" of a Vanishing Indian plot. Rather, I want to claim an alternative for us so that we might speak to one another within the academy outside of the roles as observed/informants and "primitive-native[s]" frozen in some anthropological past from where we cannot speak or write: "always stand[ing] on the other side of the hill, naked and speechless, barely present in [our] absence."[22]

* * *

Table 8.3.   The Native Informant Gives Her Native InFormation

A Family Tree

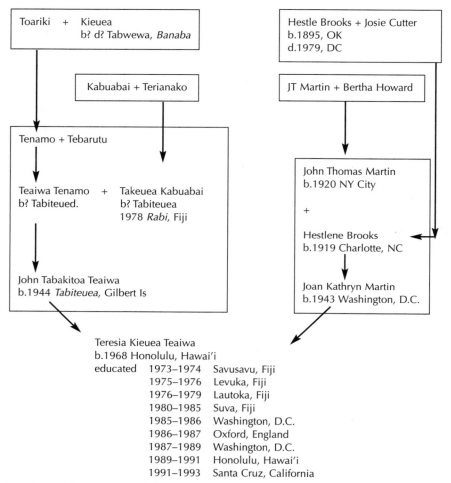

Toariki + Kieuea
          b? d? Tabwewa, *Banaba*

Hestle Brooks + Josie Cutter
b.1895, OK
d.1979, DC

Kabuabai + Terianako

JT Martin + Bertha Howard

Tenamo + Tebarutu

John Thomas Martin
b.1920 NY City

Teaiwa Tenamo + Takeuea Kabuabai
b? Tabiteued.   b? Tabiteuea
                     1978 *Rabi*, Fiji

+

Hestlene Brooks
b.1919 Charlotte, NC

John Tabakitoa Teaiwa
b.1944 *Tabiteuea*, Gilbert Is

Joan Kathryn Martin
b.1943 Washington, D.C.

Teresia Kieuea Teaiwa
b.1968 Honolulu, Hawai'i
educated   1973–1974   Savusavu, Fiji
            1975–1976   Levuka, Fiji
            1976–1979   Lautoka, Fiji
            1980–1985   Suva, Fiji
            1985–1986   Washington, D.C.
            1986–1987   Oxford, England
            1987–1989   Washington, D.C.
            1989–1991   Honolulu, Hawai'i
            1991–1993   Santa Cruz, California

There is no word for—or concept of—being "part" Banaban. Either you are, or you're not. Banaban land tenure, however, is determined ambilineally—that is, through the genealogical lines of both mother and father.

✳ ✳ ✳

A Slice of Life:

May 14, 1993. **7:15** A.M., alarm goes off and I turn on the radio. DJ promotes Discovery Channel's forthcoming series "How the West Was Lost," the American Indian perspective. **7:45** A.M., breakfast of rice and an over-easy egg; cuppa de-caf coffee as I print out a draft of my paper "Between the Traveler and the Native:

The Traveling Native as Informative Figure." **8:30** A.M., deliver the paper to my professor's box. **9:00** A.M., check e-mail: my mom mentions an indigenous women's conference to be held in Fiji sometime in August or September; my friend Cristina, a graduate student in anthropology at Stanford University, tells me about her M.A. thesis on Native American organizing around and against the celebration of Columbus' Quincentennial. **10:00** A.M., pick up tickets for Pacific Rim Film Festival Sunday screening of Eddie Kamae's new film on slack-key guitar called, *The Hawaiian Way*. **10:30** A.M., grocery shopping. **11:30** A.M., lunch of yogurt, kiwi fruit, and vanilla cookies as I prepare for my 2:00 P.M. meeting with Joanne to figure the layout of this paper. **2:00** P.M., Joanne arrives; snack of tortilla chips and salsa, with coca-cola. **4:45** P.M., check mailbox: postcard from my sister holidaying in Brisbane, Australia. **5:00** P.M., ceremony to name Oakes College D-Block after Hawai'i's last sovereign monarch, Queen Lili'uokalani, and Bay-Area attorney and Asian Pacific Islander rights advocate, Dale Minami; dinner of barbecued chicken, rice, and noodle salad. **8:00** P.M., "Qwe·ti: Tales of the Makah Tribe," a performance by the Northwest Puppet Center at Porter College Dining Hall. **10:00** P.M., home again—sleep!

✳ ✳ ✳

An abbreviated history:

1804   A British vessel chances upon Banaba and charts it on Admiral T maps.

1900   A subject of the British Empire ascertains that Banaba is practically solid phosphates.

1901   The island is annexed and included under the colonial administration of the Gilbert Islands. Leases negotiated by the mining company with the islanders, provide mining rights to the Pacific Islands Company for 999 years and payment of 50 pounds sterling a year to the land owners.

1928   After islanders demonstrate increasing tenacity to land, British colonial government passes a mining ordinance to permit the companies compulsory acquisition of land. The government compensates the islanders by setting up trust funds for them.

1941   Japanese attack British colonial headquarters on Banaba; British flee and Japanese occupy the island, relocating most of the islanders to Tarawa in the Gilberts and Kosrae in the Carolines.

1945   British return.

1946   After convincing the scattered Banabans that their island was uninhabitable after the war, the British begin a project of resettling islanders.

1970s   Money from the Banaban trust funds is used to purchase Rabi island in Fiji. After two years, the islanders decide to stay on Rabi while maintaining their land rights on Banaba.

1970s   Mid-1970s. Mining winds down as island becomes little more than a jagged rock.

1977   Banabans sue the British Phosphate commissions for just compensations for the exploitation and destruction of their ancestral home. The matter is settled out of court and ten million pounds are added to the islanders trust fund.

1979   The Gilbert Islands become the independent Republic of Kiribati and Banabans make some demands for their own independence from Kiribati but nothing comes of these.

1990s   After more than a decade of mismanagement of funds by some of their own leaders, Banabans on Rabi are in financial and social crisis. The Fiji government appoints a three member commission to administer the island's affairs until things get better.

* * *

Vanishing Indian Speaks

It seems clear that the favorite object of anthropological study is not just *any* man but a specific kind of man: the Primitive, now elevated to the rank of the full yet needy man, the Native . . . The "conversation of man with man" is, therefore, mainly a conversation of "us" with "us" about "them," of the white man with the white man about the primitive-native man.[23]

What happens when "them" chooses to be located within the academy as a subject *of study, as a* speaker *without translation, on the* other *side of knowledge production?* "Them" arrives at the university, born of a history of territorial-identities already marked and occupied by the settler, anthropologist, film maker, and cowboy novelist.[24] The *first* place "them" are made to reside within when they arrive is quite simply that of the observed/informant, made to reaffirm and reform the authenticity of colonial forms of knowledge by being made into embodied testaments of its validity, made to speak to its History—*how much Indian did you say you were?*—and thus to an immobility within its systems—*you really don't look anything like an Indian.* In other words, the relative absence of "them" within the academy and the narratives of the "Vanishing Indian" combine and "them" are made to be *native informants* not of their cultural and political identities, which are both historically constituted and specifically changing, but of the "primitive-native man" frozen in the past that Anthropology and History have created in their greater schemes of Evolution.

Our not-generous suspicions of Anthropology as the first occasion of colonial forms of knowledge (of us) come with us when we enter institutions of "higher" education. We are here as still-suspicious intellectuals, interrupting the usual practices of knowledge production: *Observed/Informant   Anthropologist Text/Knowledge.* We refuse to be the passive recipients and practitioners of knowledges not ours in formation, submitting to the ideologies of "us." Rather, we insist on taking up an interruption of the "conversation of man with man," "a conversation of 'us' with 'us' about 'them,'" that ends up proving to be no conversation at all and instead calls attention to its very *constructedness* as knowledges belonging to U.S. colonialism, nationalism, modernism, evolutionism, *et cetera*:

> A conversation of "us" with "us" about "them" is a conversation in which "them" is silenced. "Them" always stands on the other side of the hill, naked and speechless, barely present in its absence. Subject of discussion, "them" is only admitted among "us," the discussing subjects, when accompanied or introduced by an "us," member, hence the dependency of "them" and its need to acquire good manners for the membership standing.[25]

* * *

Excerpts from the appendix of my report to the Fiji Association of Women Graduates on the International Federation of University Women's 1992 Conference at Stanford University:

- Throughout my attendance at the conference, white women (mostly American) would initiate conversations with me. Although my badge clearly stated that I was a delegate from Fiji, I had to correct them repeatedly when they asked me about *Fuji*.
- As I was browsing through the quilt exhibit, a woman from the American Association of University Women said "Bula" to me. I said "Bula" back with a tight smile. She told the woman next to her that she'd been to Fiji and the people there were very friendly. I was tempted to walk away then and there without another word, but I smiled saying, "Enjoy the rest of the exhibit," and walked away just as she opened her mouth to say something else to me. I hate being a "friendly, smiling native" on demand.

* * *

I get kinda scared here in Santa Cruz when I'm invited to speak "as a Pacific Islander" at events where I'm the only Pacific Islander. But you know what's scarier? The idea of going back to the islands and being asked to speak at events of all Pacific Islanders!

* * *

Conclusions Forming
The Natives InForming

Everybody wants to be an Indian. I don't want to be an Indian anymore.

JAMES LUNA
UCSC PERFORMANCE, 1993

The conversation envisioned herein works to transform the possibilities for native peoples within the academy. It allows us to speak to one another in our differences and thus (hopefully) towards a collaboration between them. We are then inter-locutors. Not romanticized storytellers of the Frontier attesting always and only to dead ancestors, but interlocutors in parity with claims and rights to writing and curating the terms of the discourse in which we travel (remember) and are trav-eled (remembered). We see possibilities *there* for (in)forming other narratives than the Vanishing Indian as other conversations are insistently reproduced and engaged that allow for our co-habitation within our individual and collective histories and identities without one being at the expense of the other. Conversations that form and sustain collaboration and not narratives that produce Subjects and Histories and Creation Stories to which we are always expected and anticipated to return as the speechless and naked "primitive-native man" on the other side of informa-tion/knowledge. Conversations that allow us to tell other stories than the one of our death. Conversations that allow us to dance, and pray, and sing, and transpose the histories in which we really live. The histories that are mixed within the blood.

* * *

Our protagonists, our heroines, Vanishing-Indian and Native-in-formation walk through the hollow halls of the academy. They pass some closed doors, some doors that are wide open, some doors that are ajar. They exchange know-ing glances as they pass rooms in which their ancestors' bones are numbered and catalogued. They exchange knowing glances as they pass rooms in which their contemporaries are the centerpieces on the smorgasbord at glamorous re-ceptions. "I was invited to that party," Native-in-formation whispers. "I know," nods Vanishing-Indian, "they've already numbered and catalogued me." At that moment, Native-in-formation feels a sense of loss. She turns to her compan-ion for reassurance, only to find that Vanishing-Indian has disappeared. In a panic, Native-in-formation runs down the hall. She runs past the glamorous re-ceptions. She runs past the rooms with her ancestors' bones. She runs past the doors that are ajar. She runs past the doors that are wide open. She runs past the closed doors. And then, Native-in-formation freezes. "What's happening?"

Table wax. Playdoh. Steam. Ice. Sun sets. Lava. Ozones. Land fills. The Spotted Owl. Portable nuclear weapons. Vanishing-Indian, Native-in-formation: the point is that *how* the name is pronounced makes all the difference between our vanishing and our formation. The name itself will not change to protect the innocent.

Native-in-formation relaxes. She realizes she is in the rotunda again. Then she remembers, as she looks at the statue—the one she saw when she first arrived. Yes, she remembers.

Native-in-formation turns and notices that Professors and Students of Information continue to hurry by. But with what she knows now, she can tell the difference between the ones who will hear and the ones who will listen. The ones who will look and the ones who will see. The ones who will touch and the ones who will feel. And there in the hollow halls of the academy, Native-in-formation smiles.

* * *

> Go away now
> We don't know you from anybody
> You must be some ghost in the wrong place wrong time
> Pack up your toys garbage lies
> We who are alive now
> have signed no treaties . . .
> Go so far away we won't remember you ever came here
> Take these words back with you.[26]

THIS IS NOT A TREATY! This is native *information*: autobiographical, fictional, anthropological, political, comical, statistical, governmental, theoretical, historical, ethnographic. Some of it you've solicited. Some of it we've given up. Some of it is meant to provoke. Some of it is meant to inform. And so here it is. And you will do with it what you want.

THIS IS NOT A TREATY! This is native *in formation*: as we have been informed by, as we are informing, as we are in-formed. It's about process, not stasis. It's not about romanticizing the dead of our history onto the sides of defaced mountains carved up for all time. It's about the way we move with time and with each other.

THIS IS NOT A TREATY! This is contestation, a conversation. This is not an entreaty for your signature. We're not looking for converts. We're not going to ride off into the sunset. We're not going to wrap things up for you or for us. And we're not going away.

THIS IS NOT A TREATY! Because we don't promise that the next time we meet you will find us here, still, waiting for what has become our inevitable removal to other places, waiting for our extinction.

Rather, we have taken up the work of interruption which is not necessarily a "native" thing to do but is necessary for our purposes at this time. And so we have intentionally constructed a place for us to speak from (to you, to each other) with the aim of denaturalizing the political subjects we have been created as by the Vanishing Indian. And hopefully, we have created the possibility for something else to say, on our terms, next time around: these words do not bind us, they free us. What do these words do for you?

Notes

1. Chrystos, *Not Vanishing* (Vancouver, BC: Press Gang, 1988), p. 71.

2. This was reported to me in a personal letter from the Principal Researcher at the Native American Language Preservation Project funded at the Anthropology Department at the University of Oklahoma (February 16, 1993), who had had personal correspondence with the Delaware Tribe's manager. I have subsequently written to the Delaware main office but as yet have not received confirmation or denial. It seems plausible but I'd be willing for it to be refuted.

3. This is not to suggest that the Delaware are void of traditional cultural practices or are not organized by a tribal government but that these activities are not centered or located within what would be *recognized* as "Indian" by the unbreakable links created by historical and anthropological knowledge between land, language, and religion.

4. Karen I. Blu in *The Lumbee Problem: The Making of an American Indian* as quoted by Louis Owens in *Other Destinies: Understanding the American Indian Novel* (Norman: University of Oklahoma Press, 1992), pp. 3–4.

5. Trinh T. Minh-ha. *Woman Native Other* (Bloomington: Indiana University Press, 1989), p. 67.

6. Geronimo and Pocahontas are, actually, two Indians I wouldn't mind seeing vanished for their use within the American Romance for dead Indians. Which is to say, haven't we tired of the way that Geronimo and Pocahontas are made to be representative of the quintessential Indian experience, and then reduced to colloquialisms—*Geronimo!"*— and used to further historical ignorance? Pocahontas has, just within the last year, returned in yet another novel of the tragic "Indian Princess" story that carries her name in the title. And I hear that Disney is working their next "Little Mermaid"/"Beauty" feature on her. Somewhere in between the slang and the animation, the real material conditions of indigenous histories are lost, or at least perpetually distorted.

7. Robillard, Albert B. *Social Change in the Pacific Islands* (London: Kegan, Paul, 1992), pp. 10–11.

8. U.S. Census Bureau 1990 Reports.

9. *Population Today*, February 1993; U.S. Census Bureau 1990 Reports.

10. According to *Population Today*, (February 1993).

11. *Digest of Educational Statistics*, 1992.

12. Nonresident alien doctor's degrees conferred: 23.4 (8,875). All student and graduate student figures unavailable.

13. Epeli Hau'ofa, *Kisses in the Nederends* (Auckland, Penguin, 1987), pp. 15–16

14. "We've got the Third World smack in the middle of America:" from *Thunderheart*, Directed by Michael Apted (TriStar Pictures, 1992).

15. Vine Deloria Jr., *Custer Died For Your Sins: An Indian Manifesto* (Norman: University of Oklahoma Press, 1988), pp. 78, 79, 80.

16. Unnamed Native American (of course) to missionary John Eliot in 1646 as quoted by Robert Berkhofer in *The White Man's Indian* (New York: Vintage Books, 1978), p. 4. The remainder of this paragraph is a paraphrase of pp. 4–5.

17. This is the same Captain Samual Argall who captured Pocahontas and brought her to Jamestown April 13, 1613, and who later took her to England in 1626. See J.A. Leo Lemay, *Did Pocahontas Save Captain John Smith?* (Athens: University of Georgia Press, 1992).

18. This paragraph is a summary of C.A. Weslager's in *The Delaware Indians: A History* (New Brunswick: Rutgers UP, 1972), pp. 31–32.

19. Territories were lands that the U.S. government set aside for Indian relocation. These lands were never given to native peoples for permanent settlement (despite treaty obligations), but were always eventually taken back in the name of "manifest destiny's" westward expansion.

20. See C.A. Weslager's, *The Delaware Indian Westward Migration* (Pennsylvania: Middle Atlantic Press, 1978).

21. *Delaware Indian News* (Bartlesville, Oklahoma. Vol XII, Issue II: April 1993), p. 1.

22. Trinh, *Woman Native Other*, p. 67.

23. Trinh, *Woman Native Other*, pp. 64–65.

24. I am indebted to Louis Owens' discussion of the relationship between American Indian territories and identities during a graduate seminar in which he was a guest lecturer and I was a participant (UCSC, Winter 1993). His argument, as I remember it, was that territories and identities "belonging to" American Indians have *always already* been desired for occupation and so constructed. For even when it could be said that the American Indian was living *there*, *there* has always belonged to the mythology of the Frontier in which lands lie in waiting for the settler's discovery and possession. Like the land, Owens posited that American Indian identities have been mapped out, discovered, and tended by everyone, and particularly the Euroamerican colonizer, but the American Indian.

25. Trinh, *Woman Native Other*, p. 67.

26. Chrystos, *Not Vanishing*, p. 71.

Photographic Memoirs of an Aboriginal Savant: Living on Occupied Land

8

HULLEAH J. TSINHNAHJINNIE

Photographic Memoirs
of an
Aboriginal Savant

(Living on Occupied Land)

"The vision of a 40 year old female aboriginal savant. Thought provoking pages photographically illustrated with unexpected post-assimilation grace. Journey to the center of an aboriginal mind without the fear of being confronted by the aboriginal herself."

The act of existing has been nothing short of wild west show. Designated an oddity because I am from this land called America. A oddity because I have the perfect tan. Odd because I love crossing the line, my T's, the border and my eyes. Life has definitely been a wild west show....

Born on occupied land where the American dream creates environmental nightmares. I awake each morning shaking my head with disbelief, just like my grandmother. It is a time, as poet Marci Rendon say's "When the white girls act more Indian than the Indians.." and If I may add "and when some Indians act more white than the whites" (of course you and I have no such friends but we have heard about them.). My existence has been influenced by the flotsam and jetsam of a navigational error, influenced by the ever present strength of Native thought, influenced by award winning advertisement firms. An existence that would make it easy to become a Native Louis Farrakan.

As the self described aboriginal savant, I have photographed and written about my observance of myself, family, community and those other people.

Forward (#1)
Hulleah J. Tsinhnahjinnie (Seminole/Muscogee/Diné).
Photographic Memoirs of an Aboriginal Savant.
Unique digital print on aged book stock, © 1994, 14 x 11 in.

...it should have been a warning to my mother when the first word I spoke was "Liberace" or perhaps she did have an idea,

maybe that's why she named me Hulleah, Hulleah was my maternal great grandmother, she swore, drank and carried a gun. I

have always thought my mother to be "progressive" in that she didn't give her children American first names.

1954

1954 (#2)
Hulleah J. Tsinhnahjinnie (Seminole/Muscogee/Diné).
Photographic Memoirs of an Aboriginal Savant.
Unique digital print on aged book stock, © 1994, 14 x 11 in.

GLORIA PINTO RUTH PITTMAN THERESA PRICE ESTHER REDHAT RUTH ROANHORSE MARY ROY

RAMONA TSINAJINNIE HULLEAH TSINHNAHJINNIE RONALD TSO BILLY TSOSIE DELLA TSOSIE EMMETT TSOSIE

ALFRED YAZZIE AURELIA YAZZIE BARBARA YAZZIE BERNICE YAZZIE DENNISON YAZZIE GLORIA YAZZIE

Non-native teachers preparing

native students

for the

outside world.

Outside the reservation.

Outside an aboriginal existence.

They meant well.

73

1973 (#3)
Hulleah J. Tsinhnahjinnie (Seminole/Muscogee/Diné).
Photographic Memoirs of an Aboriginal Savant.
Unique digital print on aged book stock, © 1994, 14 x 11 in.

PART TWO

Ever since I can remember Dad has told us the story about him and his buddies running away from Fort Apache Indian school, it was a 200 mile trek. The younger ones cried at night, to keep warm they covered themselves with sand. The older ones keeping watch acquired holes in thier clothing because they sat so close to the fire. They caught donkeys at Donkey springs and bribed a ranch hand with a wrist watch. Two weeks later they arrived home, at least the ones that didn't get caught. Dad slept one night at home and the next morning an Indian policeman arrived on horse back. Dad was taken to Chinle to the jail, there he saw the rest of his friends, they all had been caught. To prevent any methods of escape on the journey back to Fort Apache they were shackled and handcuffed. Back at school they were made to wear dresses awhile dragging logs around the school marching grounds. They were about 8 years old.

The March
of Culture

The March of Culture (#4)
Hulleah J. Tsinhnahjinnie (Seminole/Muscogee/Diné).
Photographic Memoirs of an Aboriginal Savant.
Unique digital print on aged book stock, © 1994, 14 x 11 in.

Gallup, New Mexico, The self-described Indian capital of the world. One of my Uncles died Gallup. Its a strange place where one can be wild and free, until you wake up. When I first began photographing I wanted to be a photojournalist. Gallup was a place to expose and exploit, I began taking photographs and then the pain came in waves. I couldn't do it.

A couple years ago I ran into a book by a white photographer about the border towns around the Navajo reservation, my first thought was "What if a native child sat down with this book, the damage to the spirit would be immense." I'm so glad that I didn't finish my documentation of Gallup, but I have thought of another project, documenting white voyeurism and alcoholism.

0

Gallup (#5)
Hulleah J. Tsinhnahjinnie (Seminole/Muscogee/Diné).
Photographic Memoirs of an Aboriginal Savant.
Unique digital print on aged book stock, © 1994, 14 x 11 in.

PEOPLE OF THE WANDERING FLOCKS

Ever since I can remember my family would take off to the Rez during the summer. The car would be packed for camping and we would head out from Pinnacle Peak to Rough Rock, where my dad was born.

Back then once on the reservation, paved roads were hard to come by and only the locals knew certain ruts were roads. we would drive north to Chinle on to Many Farms head west 15 miles and drive up to Margaret's hogan and not far would be grandmas hogan.

The dogs would be barking and Grandma would come out to see who had arrived and would yell back at the hogan telling Old Man to come out, she would hug everyone, talking in Navaho and crying because she was happy to see us.

These were the memories I kept replaying in my mind as the novice minister was delivering the eulogy for my grandmother. Grandma didn't go to church, Old Man had been a medicine man and I really didn't like the minister.

I had flown in from Oakland to Phoenix the night before and had driven up with my sister, the roads are all paved leading to Rough Rock and there aren't all that many hogans left.

Since the minister had no idea who my grandmother was, decided that the timing was right to shepherd new souls to the path of glory I figured I had better start thinking about grandma so I wouldn't abuse one of god's chosen.

Grandma was 105 and her life encompassed an incredible array of experiences, she was traditional in her living and traditional in her beliefs. Then I began to think about the outside influences, government policies, missionaries and I became overwhelmed, my grandmother who couldn't have been more than five feet tall had survived and had lived a long life despite everything in the world, from that thought I was strengthened.

From the memories of my grandmother I am made strong.
From the memories of my grandmother I am made strong.
From the memories of my grandmother I am made strong.
From the memories of my grandmother I am made strong.

Grandma (#6)
Hulleah J. Tsinhnahjinnie (Seminole/Muscogee/Diné).
Photographic Memoirs of an Aboriginal Savant.
Unique digital print on aged book stock, © 1994, 14 x 11 in.

Singing songs in your head
singing songs with motionless lips.
Don't let your eyes sing,
it'll give you away.

Voicing prayers in your head
inside you face East, West, North, South,
not one movement outside the body.
Don't let your eyes sing
'cause it'll give you away.

You dream in native tongue
no subtitles needed,
the morning comes and its "Good Morning"
in the official foreign tongue.
Awhile slammin' down a double expresso
with a jellied croissant,
you wonder about the young.

Late one night the stories are remembered
and your youngest one wants to write a novel,
eventually put it up on that big silver screen, why in
the hell does this make you scream?
Be careful of your dreams there's some white guy
ready to package and sell them.
White guy, shit,

Watch out for your economic-developed brothers
and sisters,
who have self-determined
that they can express your native experience
better than you.
Again you scream,
remembering this ain't no dream.

Our word isn't revolution.
Our word is sovereignty.
Sovereignty for all red nations.

Now, is the time to scream our dreams.
Now, is the time to pick up the weapon of thought
Now is the time.

October 22,1992
In the air heading to MSP

4

Heading to MSP (#7)
Hulleah J. Tsinhnahjinnie (Seminole/Muscogee/Diné).
Photographic Memoirs of an Aboriginal Savant.
Unique digital print on aged book stock, © 1994, 14 x 11 in.

Intertribal Lust

Vermilion Romance

Just Another

Two Spirited Indian love Call

101

Page 101 (#8)
Hulleah J. Tsinhnahjinnie (Seminole/Muscogee/Diné).
Photographic Memoirs of an Aboriginal Savant.
Unique digital print on aged book stock, © 1994, 14 x 11 in.

Irene Perez and I went to Tijuana, this is about the only border art we did, we ate, bought a plaster Virgin De Guadalupe, ate again, went to the mercado and bought a bottle of Centario.

Just so happens I was born on the northern side of the border, I remember reading somewhere, the Seminoles were requesting to be relocated to Mexico, rather than Oklahoma, but the United States government thought that would be a negative mark on nationalistic pride in that, they would be perceived as unable to handle the welfare of their Indians. So it was off to Oklahoma. Now the Oklahoma Seminoles have an Oklahoma accent, when we might just as well had a south of the border accent.

The Border to the south, tell me again how it differs from the Berlin wall.

237

Page 237 (#9)
Hulleah J. Tsinhnahjinnie (Seminole/Muscogee/Diné).
Photographic Memoirs of an Aboriginal Savant.
Unique digital print on aged book stock, © 1994, 14 x 11 in.

Native Children defuse this image (#10)
Hulleah J. Tsinhnahjinnie (Seminole/Muscogee/Diné).
Photographic Memoirs of an Aboriginal Savant.
Unique digital print on aged book stock, © 1994, 14 x 11 in.

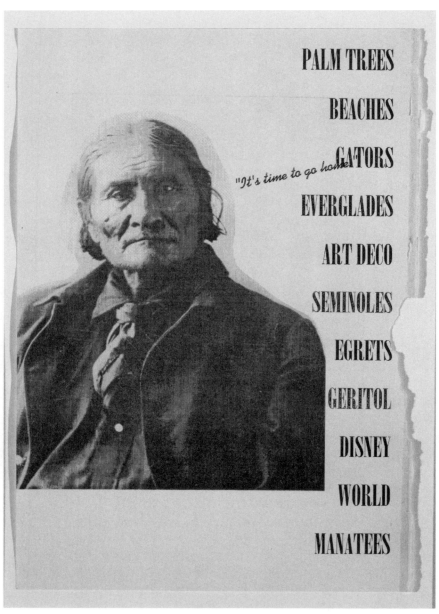

Geronimo (#11)
Hulleah J. Tsinhnahjinnie (Seminole/Muscogee/Diné).
Photographic Memoirs of an Aboriginal Savant.
Unique digital print on aged book stock, © 1994, 14 x 11 in.

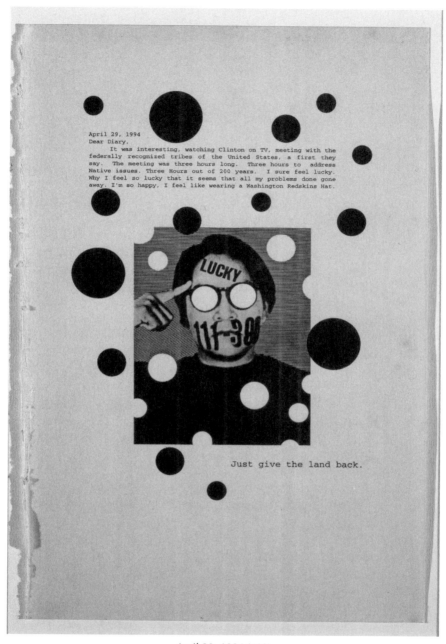

April 29, 1994 (#12)
Hulleah J. Tsinhnahjinnie (Seminole/Muscogee/Diné).
Photographic Memoirs of an Aboriginal Savant.
Unique digital print on aged book stock, © 1994, 14 x 11 in.

Don't leave the Rez Without It! (#13)
Hulleah J. Tsinhnahjinnie (Seminole/Muscogee/Diné).
Photographic Memoirs of an Aboriginal Savant.
Unique digital print on aged book stock, © 1994, 14 x 11 in.

Last night I had a dream that I had died and the first person I went to tell was my mother. She listened as if I was telling her about another adventure of mine. She was calm and understanding, and then she asked if some one had hurt me, I replied, "No one hurt me. It was an accident, an accident within my body." As I was talking, I knew I wasn't going to be able to hang around very long. I felt myself traveling on and found myself wondering if I should have attended church, just for insurance-- but something told me that there was no heaven or hell, at least not as the Christian churches preached. As I came to my destination, I asked the first person I met: "Where do the Indians live?"

While I was "dead," I came to an understanding about fulfilling dreams. I remembered close friends who had passed on, I could easily become upset, upset by the thought that loved ones had not attained certain dreams, dreams that I knew were important to them. Death stops every possibility of dreams. I became determined not to die with unfulfilled dreams. However, while I was "dead," I realized how insignificant the majority of my dreams in the past had been. What matters is finding one's people, finding one's family. As the thunder cracked and rolled from Bemidji to Lake Superior, my dreams strengthened, and when I woke up the next morning-- once I got over being alive-- I noticed a certain freedom, I felt freed of many expectations I had placed upon myself.

As the day unfolded, I related my dreams to the life of my grandmother and to other relatives long before me and wondered what their earthly dreams had been and how mine compared to theirs. My thoughts were of holding tight to family, to loved ones and to the essence of Native thought. I also thought about continuous dreams handed down from generation to generation, and the translations of dreams. I understood that dreams which travel from generation to generation do not involve the ownership of the current earthly possessions but rather the ownership of one's own well being and are a part in continuity of Native thought. Dreams can control. Dreams can heal. I have began the sorting of my forty years of dreaming.

July 20, 1994,
Bemidji, Minnesota

Page 40 (#14)
Hulleah J. Tsinhnahjinnie (Seminole/Muscogee/Diné).
Photographic Memoirs of an Aboriginal Savant.
Unique digital print on aged book stock, © 1994, 14 x 11 in.

Epilogue

I will never be American enough, because you have to be a foreigner to be a true American and no matter how hard my skin is scrubbed it will always be brown, no matter how hard my mind is bombarded with thoughts of Americanization, my mind will always return to the stories of Native survival. The books in my mind contain endless pages of Native intelligence, Native resistance, Native pride, countless pages I will carry for the rest of my Life.

Epilogue (#15)
Hulleah J. Tsinhnahjinnie (Seminole/Muscogee/Diné).
Photographic Memoirs of an Aboriginal Savant.
Unique digital print on aged book stock, © 1994, 14 x 11 in.

The Storyteller's Escape: Sovereignty and Worldview

9

REID GÓMEZ

W hen sovereignty becomes accepted as a single narrative moment in U.S. federal law or a categorical state of being instead of a process of bending and stretching, we, as Native American people, become limited in our response to, and our imaginings of, our current existence upon the landscape. Various singular and static narratives of sovereignty describe and establish an available and recognizable vocabulary for existence and interaction. If you engage in conversation with another vocabulary, your words, thoughts, and experiences are often viewed as unintelligible, fictive, or merely creative.

Within the authoritative vocabulary, a particular understanding of sovereignty is recorded. Gerald Vizenor, Anishinaabe writer, describes some of these records as the "new and diverse narratives of governance: the diplomatic narratives of treaties, executive documents, and court decisions that acknowledge the rights and distinctive sovereignty of native communities."[1] Vizenor locates colonial wars within the mouths of speakers and the ears of listeners. He intervenes in the "word wars" with a trixter discourse and a demand that "survivors" step over and around the parameters and meanings available in predetermined and predetermining vocabularies and story lines. Discourses that assume authority and demand allegiance, such as the origin story of the United States of America and U.S. federal policy toward Native Americans recorded in such "narratives of governance," enforce a single interpretation as the only (possible and legitimate) interpretation. Vizenor describes these discourses in his theory of terminal creeds, and Mikhail Bakhtin's notions of the authoritative discourse and of "pretenders"[2] also explore these ideas.

One understanding of sovereignty, within the "narratives of governance," is the ability to make your own laws and the ability to enforce them. The opinions given in *Johnson v. M'Intosh*, 21 U.S. (8 Wheat.) 543, 5 L. Ed. 681 (U.S. Sup. Ct. 1823),

Cherokee Nation v. Georgia, 30 U.S. (5 Pet.) 1, 8 L. Ed. 25 (U.S. Sup. Ct. 1831), and *Worcester v. Georgia*, 31 U.S. (6 Pet.) 515, 8 L. Ed. 483 (U.S. Sup. Ct. 1832) inform one reality with great consequence. In this reality, questions concerning the exercise of governmental (U.S. and tribal) powers and questions of jurisdiction are highlighted. Chief Justice Marshall wrote in reference and contribution to this consequence:

> Power, War, Conquest, give rights, which, after possession, are conceded by the world; and which can never be controverted by those on whom they descend.[3]

These narratives do not determine all realities, and though they are interesting and complex, they are limited. Those in power and completely convinced of this understanding and experience of power have subsequently sought the acquisition of more power (of this type). War and conquest "give rights" and require that all people's mobility be controlled and coerced, through the construction and defense of territorial borders as well as the creation and confinement of specific peoples on reservations or within institutional settings (prisons, mental hospitals, and asylums). This type and use of power requires a strategic manipulation of written evidence and narration, specifically tribal roll numbers; passports; and historical, governmental, and ethnographic narrative documents. Insidiously, this power feigns omnipotence and omniscience, and like the passive voice, it pretends it has no subject but exists in some state of primordial order, some a priori and nonresponsive moment, existing in an extended and unchanging declaration of what is real and possible. This declaration establishes an impoverished and demeaning narrative attempt to contain existence—resulting in the most pernicious use of power, that of ideological control.

I do not speak directly about the notion of sovereignty tied to the narrative practices employed in U.S. history and federal Indian law. Marshall's narrative reality claims a single source of power and locates it within itself, and within the act of conquest, as recorded in the documents and ideologies of the conquistadors. I speak of a different source of power, one that we retain and exercise in our ability to think, speak, and act as Native peoples on these our homelands. This requires us to understand sovereignty as motion and as a spiritual and intellectual recognition of the sources of power that we as Native peoples retain but do not always recognize (or are not recognized by others):

> Sovereignty is in the visions of transformation: the humor of motion as survivance over dominance; the communal movement to traditional food sources; dreams and memories as sources of shared consciousness; the stories of reincarnation, out of body travel; the myths and metaphors flying; communal nicknames and memories of migration; the spiritual and herbal powers to heal and locate lost

souls. These are evidence of natural reason and the personal power of creation; the native names and remembrance of motion and sovereignty.[4]

When we understand sovereignty as motion, an intellectual spiritual practice becomes available to the specific needs and peoples of the diverse communities currently understood as the group called American Indians or Native Americans. We live, always, with the risk of being trapped within the narrative frameworks that declare our complete subjugation and eventual and inevitable extinction. When we practice an intellectual spiritual sovereignty, we step outside those narratives and work from within our own worldviews and from our own origins and migrations.

escaping a story of our origins

When [accountability] is absent, as it invariably is in situations of colonialism, the whole treaty system becomes a weapon in the arsenal of the stronger power.[5]

As a Navajo, and as a being of language, I consider accountability not merely in terms of political or governmental accountability but in terms of the accountability we, all people, have in relationship to each other and to the cosmos at large. There is no refusing this accountability, and it necessitates an integrative approach to theorizing relations, not abstracting or erasing them. "There can be no formula for integrity, no substitute for each person's own project of selfhood, no escape from the ethical obligations of every situation at every moment."[6] There exists no moment when we as people—individual and community—are not required to show up and participate. No single person or group of people is exempt from the responsibility we have toward each other and the places we inhabit. Primary in this is to exist in relation to, not as separate from. Moreover, accountability extends to larger institutions and practices, such as the judicial and academic systems. Each is answerable. "There is no alibi for being."[7]

When sovereignty is conceived as a state of being, as it sometimes is in legal discourse, it is not viewed as a means of answering back. That view shifts centers away from geography and people's varied responses toward the application of power over territory and territorial subjects. In these arenas, courtrooms, and governmental (tribal and non-tribal) elections and proceedings, the need arises to determine group membership, ownership of territory, and the division of land without regard for it or its people. These systems abstract themselves, removing themselves from relationship with the land in attempts to control and restructure the land they now claim sovereign power over. In this narrative reality, people—like landscapes—become little more than subjects under systemic, governmental controls, able to do little more than assume a position within. We are allowed to speak, but only within a set of predetermined and predefined vocabularies. Legitimacy, proof, and authenticity, as concepts, become of prime importance, and conversation is usually circumscribed within the interrelated languages of law, history, and anthropology.

Consequently, the need becomes paramount to determine first rights and aboriginal title and to solve, with certainty, the question of origins. The problem of an American identity and the corresponding preoccupation with American Indian origins has consistently puzzled European colonials and fueled the spiritual commitment to the idea that this is in fact a nation of immigrants. We can observe the urgency to determine who was here first,[8] and who holds the oldest and most authentic claim to possession over both the territory and the past, in the stories of American history, in the lineage of American anthropology, and to a lesser degree in various models of Ethnic Studies.

In his essay "Anthropology and Responses to the Reburial Issue," Larry Zimmerman begins with a brief but interesting discussion of the way "American anthropology has intellectual roots inextricably linked to American Indians."[9] The most interesting aspect of this inextricable link is the question over American Indian origins. Confusion on the part of colonials about exactly who "Indians" were and where "they" came from shaped future scholarship, and that scholarship shaped public opinion and policy. To address the question of origins and the contemporary Indian presence, they attempted to pinpoint a time and means of arrival for American Indians to the continent. This knowledge seemed necessary to adequately explain the survivals and cultural "advancements" (pyramids and sophisticated arts) the colonials had encountered, especially in Meso and Central America.

Instead of listening and accepting tribal accounts of their own origins, American[10] intellectuals and theologians resorted to the collection and scientific study of human remains and archeological diggings in an attempt to establish and maintain control over the past. This control, in the form of historical and scientific explanation, determined an ostensibly proper and moral code of action toward the people perceived to stand in the way of further and continued occupation of the land. In the models and justifications for how to treat the contemporary Indian, the role of the Indian as Other and the importance of "the Indian" and "Indianness" as constitutive of American identity have been explored by numerous scholars.[11] One means of legitimating colonial occupation was to dehumanize "the Indian"; another was to claim that Indians were also immigrants, an idea still experiencing some popularity and authority in the form of the Bering Strait theory of eastern migration. These conceptualizations of Indian origins facilitate a variety of analytical attempts to establish legal right and precedent.

Zimmerman summarizes the various attempts to address the colonial question of Indian origins. These questions began surfacing and taking shape in the late eighteenth century. They continue today. Vine Deloria Jr.'s 1995 *Red Earth, White Lies: Native Americans and the Myth of Scientific Fact* speaks directly to this situation. The significance of Darwin's *Origin of the Species* itself reveals the tremendous effect the loss of origin stories has on a people. Early colonial confusion arose from existing and developing biblical conceptions and understandings and the corresponding beliefs of cultural evolution and social Darwinism. Debates between monogenists and polygenists soon followed, along with the explanations and creations of racial categories, demonstrating (to these scholars) the rising need to preserve cultural specimens, practices, and histories once understood (and to some extent still understood) to be headed toward extinction, especially given enlightenment concepts of savagery and civilization. He notes, "It is from this intellectual medium that American anthropology was born; with little question, though its motives were scientific, it was a tool of colonialism."[12]

The question of Indian origins was and is largely a non-Native concern in that Native peoples have clear articulations and memories of origins and subsequent migrations. It is to these stories that we must turn, whatever our disciplinary or community memberships. Deloria Jr. clearly argues for precise attention to and respect for tribal histories and elders, which would allow a movement outside of the narratives of Christianity and evolution that seek to trap each and every one of us. He notes that most scientific narratives are capable of only a single understanding and explanation of reality and creation, whereas tribal peoples have stories accounting for the varied experiences and memories of creation and migration within their ancestral homelands.

Instead of listening to those "American Indians [who] were here 'at the beginning' and have preserved the memory of traumatic continental and planetary catastrophes"[13] in tribal stories, American scholars have developed an almost pathological obsession with control over the past. This need and hunger are evident in natural history museums and in the ethnographic approach to Native American literature in general. Furthermore, the past has been afforded legal protection in the passage of the Antiquities Act of 1906 and is celebrated (and coupled with property value and ownership) in the PBS series *Antiques Road Show*. Expert archeologists and anthropologists are still called upon in court to give testimony, mainly in relation to establishing legal power over access to, and interpretative meaning and value of, ancestral lands and cultural objects.

Though "we [Tewa people and most tribes in general] do not share the assumptions underlying what museums do: collection preservation, documentation and exhibition,"[14] our literature and our histories are frequently framed in this light, and many scholars and approaches share those same underlying assumptions.

Deloria's tight and humorous critique of books containing great Indian oratory is still pertinent today as contemporary authors are expected to perform some aspect of Indian culture, relay some ancient spiritual insight or secret, or at the very least look Indian, if not come dressed like one.[15] He argues that Americans continually refuse to let go of their conception of "the Indian" and refuse all interaction, intellectually or experientially, with living Native Americans and contemporary Native American agendas.

Many texts continue to share an ethnographic framing of Indian content or subject matter and anthropological notions of pre-literate oral cultures. Readers, scholarly or not, approach Indian literature looking for old-time Indian myths and legends, while contemporary writers writing about contemporary realities are often seen as being inauthentic, unrepresentative, or somehow less Indian.[16] The idea of the Indian (as a racial Other, with a single anthropological, religious, or scientific origin story) in powerful ways serves as a limiting factor to narrative and analysis. Often people do not listen to stories in contemporary work but judge their verisimilitude to America's Indian of history, law, and science. This theoretical approach, if taken with other texts such as Gloria Naylor's *Linden Hills*, with its reality so far removed from the physical plantation, and as a reworking of Dante's *Inferno*, would render them largely incomprehensible.

The narratives of U.S. Indian relations constructed in federal law have explicitly shaped relations between tribes and between tribes and the new colonials. Within these, quasi-sovereignty,[17] as detailed by Chief Justice Marshall, can be seen merely as an exhibit, in the psychology and spirit of the world's fairs, "of the Native American's place in American culture."[18] Issues of representativeness, authenticity, and preservation of ancient tribal secrets (religious or cultural in slant) go hand in hand with the desire to stay and contain Native American mobility in colonial narratives and language. These issues go beyond the courthouse and law archives and shape the memory and imagination of the American public in general.[19] Frederick Hoxie notes that during the late 1800s, with continued westward expansion, "the race would become more important [to the narratives of American identity and American history] for what it represented than for what it might become."[20]

Hoxie discusses the representations and displays constructed at the early Smithsonian Institution and at various "world's fairs," linking the role of Indian simulations in the narration of the past. The forty years of projections began in 1876, touring the cities of New Orleans (1884), Atlanta (1895), Nashville (1897), Omaha (1899), Buffalo (1901), Philadelphia, Chicago, St. Louis (1904), San Francisco (1915), and San Diego (1915), and were to be "the 'university of the masses.'"[21] At these schools, the importance and understanding of the Indian's position in American history and as a piece of the American landscape was established.

The exhibits revealed shifts in the presentation and perception of the Indian by the American public and had little to do with Native people living at the time. They coincided with an increased demand for and exotification of Indian mythology and artistic expression, insofar as they continued to foster and exist in line with existing static representations and narratives of the eventual and impending extinction. The Indian was and is continually being absorbed as a part of an American past and tradition. In her recent work, *Why I Can't Read Wallace Stegner and Other Essays: A Tribal Voice*, Elizabeth Cook-Lynn notes that Louise Erdrich and Michael Dorris have been received and absorbed as American authors coming from an American tradition.[22] Of central insight here is the control and manipulation of "the Indian's" appearance on the land, post-dating it at a single migratory moment in human history. Tribal stories (epistemologies of origin and migration) are ignored or reworked to fit into pre-Colombian or pre-Cortezian history or as ethnic experiences within an all-consuming American history.

This narrative framing, and the Indian identity created as a result, has consequences for the understanding of sovereignty where Native Americans become domesticated within an ethnic model of identification and articulation of the "national and natural history" of America. Ethnic Studies scholarship focusing on immigration (histories of) and increasing inclusion and participation within an American politic or identity necessitates the dismissal or replacement of Native American thought and story. Instead of beginning with origin stories that detail site-specific births and migrations, many Ethnic Studies models describe, deconstruct, and define community memberships and territorial boundaries. One example is the "reclamation" of Aztlan, whether the territorial or spiritual homeland of the Chicano people; another example is the current burgeoning field of mixed-race scholarship, with its re-inscription of racialized bodies and ideologies. These practices are clearly tied to the state and concern regulating behavior and defining boundaries (even if those boundaries are then theorized across, in a sort of border crossing).

Within scholarship, the regulation of behavior often takes place in the regulation of methodology. Questions concerning how and where to access information, in addition to the manner of description, shape and limit what is found, as well as what is found lacking. This process, where language and discovery are predetermined, exists in clear contrast to methodology that not only encourages but also requires imagination and creativity. Boundaries of reality, authenticity, accuracy, and validity are regulated in ideas of genre, as products are categorized into areas that inform and in many cases determine analysis. There is no space or opportunity here for vision—either for artists or those participating in artistic moments. Instead, scholars carefully write for an audience that passively reads and at times consumes information for later reiteration and recitation.

In this way, things—ideas and people—stay put or are at least pulled toward stasis. We see this in the rigid disciplinarity of David, the historian in Anna Lee Walters's novel *Ghost Singer*, and in the limitations of language exercised in some scholarly practices. Most notably, with those that understand themselves as existing categorically outside of the creative arts, for to engage in language and story making is at its very center an act of creative expression.

> The sovereignty of motion is mythic, material, and visionary, not mere territoriality, in the sense of colonialism and nationalism. Native transmotion is an original natural unison in the stories of emergence and migration that relate humans to an environment and to the spiritual and political significance of animals and other creations.[23]

In context, mobility is an act of resistance. Imagination and creativity, practiced in an understanding of sovereignty as motion, enact an ideological living and resist physical and spiritual containment. Recognizing sovereignty as actively moving with and across all aspects of experience opens a moment where we can all step through and word out some order and meaning to that particular and site-specific migration.

approaching the changing world

The presence of natives on this continent is an obvious narrative on sovereignty.[24]

Through ideological life we can resist physical and spiritual containment. Birthed in thought and speech, story and language, we sustain and invigorate ourselves through creative application (a continual mental or physical effort imbued with diligent and close attention) and the continual exercise of thought and speech, story and language. Existence itself is a profound articulation. Tradition, the adaptability of the people to continue without losing a sense of who they are, understands motion as the very quality of living. Motion of body, fluidity and changeability of all matter, nothing enters or exits from a great and empty nothingness but exists in transformation, from this to that. This process is described in the stories and in the simultaneous act of making and engaging in them. Understanding sovereignty as motion allows for important process-oriented theorizing, calling forward the need to experience language and land instead of "understanding" them.

For Vine Deloria Jr., time-centered religions, such as Christianity, rely on a progression of unmoving moments. Living in a time-centered reality shifts the way we engage or disengage with life, with our surroundings. In *God Is Red*, he writes, "the reality of religion . . . becomes its ability to explain the universe, not experience it. Creeds and beliefs replace apprehension of whatever relationship may exist with higher powers."[25] The shift toward explanation shapes what we read and think, in addition to how we read and live. Of great intellectual importance here is the non-separability of experience from being, not the false couplet of theory and experience where the two exist in opposition, with one in subordination or perceived more authentic, depending on your paradigmatic approach. Language as a representative system, and not a transformative practice, attempts to represent the world instead of invent and create it. This fragmenting leads directly to the dissociation of experience from worldview and theory. It is a reductive process in which things are reduced and reduced until there is nothing, not even the memory of existence.

In the introduction to *Tribal Secrets: Recovering American Indian Intellectual Traditions*, Robert Allen Warrior comments on his use of the word *sovereignty*: "I recognize that these words are problematic in spite of continuing to carry a certain political, emotional, and critical force. This is perhaps most true of sovereignty, a term from European theological and political discourse that finally does little to describe the visions and goals of American Indian communities that seek to retain a discrete identity. To simply abandon such terms, though, risks abandoning their abiding force and utility."[26] I write with that same awareness in the attempt to highlight neglected meanings and opportunities in language, to facilitate the fluidity of analysis and continuity of storytelling necessary for continued survival (growth and adaptation). Understanding sovereignty's role in respect to "the visions and goals of American Indian communities that seek to retain a discrete identity" requires an active engagement with those discrete identities and corresponding homelands. Our method of engaging with the world informs the manner in which we theorize that world and understand its scope and our place within that scope.

Though Warrior's own work could appear to focus on treaty-based nationalism, in light of the close investigation of Deloria Jr.'s work, his employment of reading styles and selection of reading materials reveal a wonderful application of the type of (intellectual) sovereignty that informs and is characterized by a more inclusive notion of sovereignty. He contends that neither John Joseph Mathews nor Deloria Jr. fits into any genre or academic discipline. The idea of sovereignty as motion precludes these types of containment, as does Mathews's and Deloria Jr.'s views of land and community and Warrior's own commitment to "reading across American Indian writings," in a practice he terms intellectual sovereignty, in order to facilitate "fresh ways of reading Native material."[27] This is further complemented and initiated by the particular use of language that informs and initiates process, not product.

In this spirit, I look toward Native American writers as creators of a collection of written literary explorations, evocations of language, and storytelling theories. This collection, and the ideas expressed therein, informs the reading of all texts (across disciplinary and community lines) as well as sovereign artistic expression, easing an engaged expression of the storytelling moment composed of land and language. The threads of story and land run through everything. All work must, therefore, be at its core interdisciplinary and multifaceted because it must institute a means of experiencing each thread. The failings of much contemporary thought have originated with the attempt to sever the very ties between peoples, earth, and language or in the failure to recognize the placement and limited power of individuals within an entire cosmic system. Warrior notes in his investigation of Deloria Jr. that "one of the problems of the modern condition is its loss of the impulse to seek direct, unmediated religious experience."[28] An intellectually sovereign practice rests on the impulse to seek a religious experience of land and language. There is no separation of theory from practice: each makes up the other.

Language is more than but inclusive of individual tribal languages. Native peoples, regardless of location and relocation, need language retention and acquisition programs, as well as the application toward English of the values we hold to and within our own languages. We must then use each fully, requiring and allowing English and writing to stretch, bend, and move to our experiences and expressions of those experiences. Given the changing landscape, we also need a re-emergence of multilinguality and polyphony across and within languages, genres, and artistic mediums. Writing can be done within, not against, an oral tradition.[29] Warrior warns against reducing expression and experience by cutting ourselves off from other theoretical expressions. Holding onto an idea that certain languages, mediums, or fields of study are white while others are Indian can only limit and diminish our lives. Avoiding English or the written word falls directly into the "trap of Western religion, which seeks to freeze history in an unchanging and authoritative past,"[30] ultimately resigning us to the death of the word, and to the death of our stories, if only because we then believe our stories are less than they are. Our decisions to do, think, or say certain things are informed by our singular worldviews, not by the idea that certain fields are categorically outside of our identity. If our worldviews do not foster a means for engaging and surviving a changing world, then how have we survived so many worlds already?

"Land and community are necessary starting points for the process of coming to a deep perception of the conflicts and challenges that face American Indian people and communities."[31] It is necessary that we employ a way of expressing ourselves that does not flatten either notion. Though both have changed dramatically, given their utmost importance we need processes in which we, as a manner of approach, can call forth the experience of those varied and specific expressions—a listening, a showing up, a going toward where the storyteller is taking you. Deloria Jr. follows the logic as far as it goes; in reading him, you too must follow. What is revealed in that journey is a fuller appreciation and awareness of those assumptions along with their limitations. In seeing how far the various logics go, we stand to also see how far they don't.

Warrior's own "literary critical strategy . . . has been to read across the texts."[32] I have followed this example and continued to read across the land and inside the language. This all requires a fluidity of usage and analysis, along with a certain and necessary motion. "The return to tradition . . . cannot in Deloria's analysis be an unchanging and unchangeable set of activities, but must be part of the life of a community as it struggles to exercise its sovereignty"[33] and its mobility. A story is not a creation of texts or textlike moments; it is an entire event eclipsing a time-centered reality, eclipsing the positioning of the storyteller, the listeners, and the people in the story. It requires a knowledge of the world of the story, as well as that each listener know his or her own world. Stories occur in intergenerational meetings and celebrations related to seasonal cycles. They instigate, establish, and develop growing relationships among tellers, listeners, and their particular surroundings. A story is not a book you buy through the Internet from Amazon.com, never having even seen, let alone touched, the seller or the author. You can approach a book like a story, but you cannot approach a story like a book without killing it and the world inside it.

Considerable scholarship moves forward by proving and establishing discontinuities, in time, among peoples and their intellectual experiences and practices. Such attempts at establishing discontinuity cannot contain our existence. Our mere presence is an act of sovereignty. Contemporary intellectuals who center colonial regimes of knowledge and their corresponding structures deny the presence and power of the land, the gods of each land, and the people living upon the land—as well as the relationships between these presences and powers that describe and create a fully integrated way of life. What needs centering or practicing is a process, not an unchanging or evolving collection of human insights or analytical advancements. Like Johnny Navajo, we must test information, not assemble a reading list of conceptual truths. An orienting toward process as a way of life informs how we approach the changing world. It does not try to stop it from changing.

"Unlike many other religious traditions, tribal religions . . . have not been authoritatively set 'once and for always.' Truth is in the ever changing experiences of the community. . . . 'religious forms must, in order to be meaningful, relate to a dramatically changed community in a dramatically changed environment.'"[34] One way to open up notions of community and land is through the words we use to describe them (e.g., Vizenor's urban reservation resists the idea that America retains spiritual or ideological possession of the land merely because it currently occupies it). Occupation, through ideological control, and the desire for territorial control shape one reality. Through language and story we exercise the power to exist in other realities. Similarly, Walters's discussion of Anita in *Ghost Singer* allows for a more complex understanding of Navajo community, specifically, and Native American communities in general.[35] With a varied and voluminous narrative approach, as demonstrated by Pura Fé's song "Going Home,"[36] we are able to relate to the dramatically changing community and the dramatically changing landscape. Language and story as spaces, means, and approaches to moving through make up the very fiber of continuing existence, as such. This is sovereignty.

The use of language will change you, but it requires you to engage it and practice a place-centered experience of your immediate reality. "Deloria's abiding criticism of modern Christianity is its concern for interpreting experience rather than having an experience."[37] He also maintains in *God Is Red* that for experience to occur, it has to occur somewhere. Emphasizing his "place-centered" philosophical and metaphysical approach to grounding experience of particular peoples in particular geographies, Deloria Jr. "suggests that to become ourselves requires that we 'begin to probe deeper into [our] own past and view [our] remembered history as a primordial covenant.' Through such a process, . . . Natives would 'discern, out of the chaos of their shattered lives . . . a new interpretation of their religious traditions with a universal application.' This universal application would not result in principles or doctrines, however, but in examples to others of the necessity of authenticating human experience with the particular places humans inhabit."[38] This challenge points to the continuity of existing theoretical approaches to, not necessarily models of, the world as experienced at specific geographical locations.

Warrior contends that the seed of importance lies in analysis, "opening ourselves . . . to a wide range of perspectives." He emphasizes this in relation to cross-cultural/cross-theoretical engagement, and it simultaneously holds true for cross-disciplinary engagement. Warrior's own work engages with pan-African intellectuals as well as pan-Indian intellectuals. Analysis and engagement across tribes, in the U.S., is comparative work and should be acknowledged as such. There is little reason to believe that the Osage or the Lakota bear much in common aside from their "context" as tribal people who, like the "others around the world, . . . face similar situations."[39] Likewise, investigating the theorized experience of language and story across peoples offers tremendous opportunity, in relation to openness of perspectives and the possibility and transformation of circumstance, specifically of those lands and peoples currently under colonial rule.

Language is an interdisciplinary event; it is an all-encompassing creative happening. "We respect tradition . . . by confronting the chaos of contemporary life and asking where we have been and where we are going."[40] We listen and remember. There is nothing outside of language, neither memory nor experience. It doesn't represent reality, either by standing in for it or allowing one to step back from it:

> I don't remember a world without language. From the time of my earliest childhood, there was language. Always language, and imagination, speculation, utters of sound. Words, beginnings of words. What would I be without language? My existence has been determined by language, not only the spoken but the unspoken, the language of speech and the language of motion. I can't remember a world without memory. Memory, immediate and far away in the past, something in the sinew, blood, ageless cell. Although I don't recall the exact moment I spoke or tried to speak, I know the feeling of something tugging at the core of the mind, something unutterable uttered into existence.[41]

If we devalue language, we demean ourselves with a diminished experience; we withdraw and effectively cut ourselves off from the power available to us, alienating ourselves from our very means of survival, community, and land. "If our struggle is anything, it is the struggle for sovereignty, and if sovereignty is anything, it is a way of life. That way of life is not a matter of defining a political ideology or having a detached discussion about the unifying structures and essences of American Indian traditions. It is a decision . . . to be . . . and to find out what that means in the process."[42]

the storytellers escape

The narrative of "the Indian" does not allow for Native American worldviews or the sovereignty of thought or language. It enforces an entrapment and stagnation, in narrative realities (of race and ethnicity) and in representative images and objectifications (of red men and squaws). In escaping, we can create and continue to tell stories of our shared experiences, shaped by the naming and corresponding treatment of us as Indians. The Indian origin story initiates the idea that we are dead, dying, or somehow less than our ancestors and "a burden on the grandchildren of those 'real Indians' who are 'gone.' It is a weight on the spirit and it is time it be lifted."[43] Precisely because this Indian is an earlier immigrant, assuming a place in an "American" ancestral lineage, it has served as a way for colonials to ground themselves in a constructed past (not the experience) of this continent and thereby speak with greater authority and insight. Both Cook-Lynn and Vizenor write in response to, and critique of, this cultural appropriation and "wanna be" sentiment in popular and academic cultures.

Importantly, each individual person and tribal community exercises a site-specific experience and expression alongside this burden. I speak of this now:

> One day a story will arrive in your town. There will always be disagreement over direction—whether the story came from the southwest or the southeast. The story may arrive with a stranger, a traveler thrown out of his home country months ago. Or the story may be brought by an old friend, perhaps the parrot trader. But after you hear the story, you and the others prepare by the new moon to rise up against the slave masters.[44]

These words reflect the basic understanding that story has the power to effect great change on the very face of the earth. The early colonials have applied their narrative realities to great personal advantage. As experience must take place somewhere, the stories must also arrive somewhere and be experienced there. There is no thread cutting, no severing the links between story, place, and people. Deloria Jr. points this out in *God Is Red* when he questions the "missionary" aspect of religion:

> Space has limitations that are primarily geographical. . . . The danger that appears to be lurking in spatial conceptions of religion is the effect of missionary activity on a religion. Can it leave the land of its nativity and embark on a program of world or continental conquest without losing its religious essence in favor of purely political or economic considerations?[45]

As we move, we carry with us our specific cohesive worldviews and the stories of our movement as characterized and informed by those cohesive worldviews. The work, the story, the writing must be experienced, and as people move they must participate in a religious experience of that movement, through continuous engagement with the land and contiguous moments of connection. People cannot transplant themselves and superimpose their existence on the landscape. Neither can they transplant or superimpose their ideologies regardless of landscape. They must engage in a type of bidirectional reaction and interpenetration. This relationship is characterized by their specific aspect, as well as the aspect of their moving and the lands they are moving within.

Silko emphasizes the storyteller as the keeper of stories, but she also (most specifically in *Almanac of the Dead* and *Yellow Woman and the Beauty of the Spirit*) explicitly emphasizes the land as the keeper of stories as well. Importantly, storytelling is not the act of an individual; it is the act of a situated community, all working within each other's presence and influence—the mesa, the grandmother, and the littlest one there, in the cradleboard learning. In *Storyteller*, she begins,

> As with any generation
> the oral tradition depends upon each person

> listening and remembering a portion
> and it is together—
> all of us remembering what we have heard together—
> that creates the whole story
> the long story of the people.[46]

She joins the pieces in order (not of hierarchy or explanation but of meaning). They are not fragments. Claiming the fragmentary nature of "this" narrative assumes the "wholeness" or untenability of the "wholeness" of another narrative. Instead, this is a universe made up of parts: parts that are not fragmented but merely and beautifully overlap, conjoin, relate in some dimension, and connect to some place or person in particular. There is no finished story, because like the people, it too is always in motion. It is a breathing and changing thing. Like the landscape, it will exist and continue on long after this writing and your reading—in motion, with no final word and no retractions.

> The storyteller keeps the stories
> all the escape stories
>   she says "with these stories of ours
>   we can escape almost anything
>   with these stories we will survive."
> The old teller has been on every journey
> and she knows all the escape stories
>   even stories told before she was born.
> She keeps the stories for those who return
>   but more important
>   for the dear ones who do not come back
>   so that we may remember them
>   and cry for them with the stories.
>   "In this way
>   we hold them
>   and keep them with us forever
>   and in this way
>   we continue."
>   This story is remembered
>   as her best story
>   it is the storyteller's own escape.[47]

The story of her own escape keeps her alive. Returns her to the village. With it she establishes the very thing she has always established: connections between the people, their memory of her, and their relationship to her, all there inside the story and their compulsion to tell it. She could live there, in the story. But there is no one there to tell it, to look onto her, so she thinks it herself. Each element is necessary—her thinking, the child she imagines looking back, and in doing so, telling a story of continuance.

There are many enemies; she tells a story, waiting for them. She will get them because she will tell the story of her death before they arrive there to kill her. The end of storytelling, the enemy that never arrives, because the storyteller sat there thinking, telling this all through. She has "always had a way with stories / even on the last day."[48] She could not die. There would be no one there to tell this; she would take it with her, and with that removal there would be no way of relating.

There was a day she sat down in a place, on "the north side of Dough Mountain." It is a very important linking, her imagining the child there to tell. The ancestors and the little ones are tied there with this story to a place where a survival was thought up and remembered. This child that looks back to tell the story is especially significant in light of the continual attempts to sever the experiences of children from their tribal realities, as well as attempts to sever relations altogether. Forbidding speech and creative intellectual thought is a method of destroying tribal languages. Attacks on expression limit the influence our worldviews "are allowed" to have on the English we speak. Many Native Americans converse in a tribally influenced English (whether that influence be in content or in creative alterations of accepted grammar and pronunciation), only to be corrected by proper laws of usage and English idiom. Colonial severings such as these continue occurring, sometimes in formal laws undercutting, delegitimizing, and disempowering tribal realities and at other times in the form of desensitization to the word and to the telling of stories. The danger herein is not the belief that stories have no power but that *our* stories have no power and are somehow less real and less reality shaping. This alters the relationship (and in some cases the access) the youth have to tribal and multiple languages and stories. The diminished relationship becomes accepted as an unchanging and originless fact. Living languages become recorded in linguistic systems or conceived of as tribal mythologies subordinated to an entirely foreign and facile understanding of language power and transformation. These youth become the elders that teach the youth who become the elders.

Community is made from the interconnection of people through these shared experiences, beginning most importantly with origin stories and the ascending migrations through worlds. "The old teller has been on every journey."[49] The stories are alive; we participate in them, along with the ancestors—the spirit beings—and with our enveloping land base. The storyteller has participated in the movement of the people, their travels and their escapes, all experienced within the context and the creation of the stories. With survival, she does not continue in the way literary merit affords many Western authors the illusion of immortality, but it is the people who continue, and she is connected.

This is precisely where the importance of intellectual sovereignty and Vizenor's conception of the motion of sovereignty stand upright with great importance and tie in with Cook-Lynn's highlight of the centrality of worldview, to American Indian intellectual practice. These practices and approaches resist a severing and disconnecting from the power and process that peoples and languages have had since time immemorial. They help us realize, in experience and expression, that the "power of those traditions is not in their formal superiority but in their adaptability to new challenges."[50] We need this to continue addressing the journey of colonialism, which though brief in terms of tribal memory has had dramatic effect on both the peoples and their homelands. These effects have been experienced and storied in the survival of each distinct people and each specific landscape, as well as in the survivals of those displaced, removed from their homelands and their communities and re-educated, however multiple the tracings. For African Americans, Afro-Latinos, indigenous Latinos, and some Native Americans such as Anita from *Ghost Singer*, the telling of getaway stories, by survivors and by the generations, is vital and relates to the strengthening of the land and the tribes in general.

One response to calls for colonial discontinuities is sovereignty as a language process of motion. The expression of a worldview forms continued survivals of peoples, through traditional imaginations and memories, as they connect to each other and their geographical surroundings. A story is an experience-based means of addressing so-called urban land and the experiences and ancestries of removed peoples. As new clans are introduced or new challenges met, relatives are not always made through shared origin but shared migration:

> all of us remembering what we have heard together—
> that creates the whole story
> the long story . . .
>
> I remember only a small part.
> But this is what I remember.[51]

in 1864

> *The old folks said the stories themselves had the power to protect us and even to heal us because the stories are alive; the stories are our ancestors.*[52]

Destroying our memories of and our relationships to the stories splits ties between the generations. It is an attempt to remove us from our proper lineage and place us as objects outside of histories and conceptual understandings. The enemies, in the word wars and to the storytellers, "are liars, of course, and they want the people to lose heart; so the destroyers always tell the people that the old stories are ended. The old stories don't matter anymore."[53] Our first defense must always be existing in relationship, to the land and to language, telling stories with reverence and celebration. Keeping aware of the enemies' desire to appropriate, carelessly catalog, and ossify the language and the people, then acting responsibly in light of that awareness. The same drive to collect and preserve within museum structures also arises in various literary traditions that still and rank the written word, judging its authority, authenticity, and genre category. The stories are not packets of information that belong to everyone. They are living powers that offer protection as well as destruction. In our storytelling and story sharing we must account for the realities we create. This is part of the core of imaginative play and survival in Vizenor's naming of the word wars and his warning against believing and consuming ideologies not tasted and tested and taken for what they can and cannot be. We approach words with care, knowing where they came from and where they take you if you mindlessly ride them out, in speech, thought, and action.

A carefulness in language, based at its center on an intelligent respect for that power, is not a silencing or deadening of speech. It is not characterized by a stoic paucity of words. It is something quite opposite:

> We are all part of the old stories; whether we know the stories or not, the old stories know about us. From time immemorial the old stories encompass all events. . . . The sprits of the ancestors cry out for justice.[54]

With care we are able to tap into the extraordinary vastness of the "earth power coming," a generational force rising upward and descending downward. At the storytelling event, listeners are invited to call out things they've heard otherwise, offer their own versions, each holding and telling details and differences that together make up the people in their varied experience. Necessary in this is a developed reverence for the act of listening as an integral part of the moment, as well as a complex understanding and experience of listening. Connections are made and further enhanced in the relationships created and strengthened through the shared event of story making. Storytelling involves a touch and exchange between teller and listener, a sharing of power and experience across the generations and across particular geographic realities. Teller, listener, and story interpenetrate each other and exist forever in and outside of that reality; they compel action, and this action takes you to deeper levels of knowing.

In her essay "The American Indian Woman in the Ivory Tower," Elizabeth Cook-Lynn maintains that Indian participation is essential to a well-thought-out and responsible Indian Studies program. Native Americans need full participation in their own field of study, and for this to happen, she articulates the need and description of a paradigmatic restructuring:

> Indian Studies is a development which is dependent upon two parameters. . . . The first is the religious, philosophical consideration of tribal life (culture), in which *worldview* is a major subject of inquiry; and the second is the legal and historical relationship of Indian Nations to the United States of America and other nations of the world (history), the essential principle of *sovereignty* being a primary focus of examination and definition. Because these parameters have been established over a very long period of time and because they are tribally specific, they do not operate as barriers to intellectual freedom; rather they operate as defensive, regulatory, and transformative guidelines that take into account rather than dismiss the experiences and values of our ancestors.[55]

This model of Indian Studies revolves around the dual cores of worldview and sovereignty. Not all peoples are recognized tribes, and not all tribes have the recognizable, or documented, "legal and historical relationship of Indian Nations to the United States of America" detailed in Cook-Lynn's directive. Thinking of sovereignty as a spiritual intellectual process of mobility is a way of extending our understanding of this model. Cook-Lynn's own emphasis on worldview is another. The basic tenet of most tribal worldviews is to contribute toward and ensure the continued survival of that particular tribal community and their expression, which for Warrior is the real meaning behind sovereignty itself. Both words, *worldview* and *sovereignty*, seem to name, with a different history and nuance, a way of life.

Cook-Lynn's work and emphasis on a Plains Indian treaty paradigm emphasize the importance of both worldview and sovereignty and the subtle distinctions between each as we address discrete and particular tribal worldviews as well as their experiences of, and responses to, geographically situated articulations of sovereignty.[56] Her model for Indian Studies establishes a clear directive for American Indian scholars. First and foremost, stop theorizing Native Americans as a single racialized and unified body. Determine with precision and clarity the means of addressing and experiencing the world, as described by the tribe, and then engage in scholarship that responds to, but more important contributes to, the continuing life of that tribe. Precision comes in the attention given to language and detail of people and landscape, not in the settling on any single definitive narrative.

In "The American Indian Woman in the Ivory Tower," Cook-Lynn offers this model, which for some scholars may have little explicitly to do with gender or its sister, feminism. Her approach to gender is grounded in her model of Indian Studies in addition to an understanding of what anthropologists term as egalitarian societies, and she begins her introduction with that very observation. In this approach, sexual differences do not equal inadequacies or inharmonious distributions of power; they are informed realities unique to the worldviews of the tribes in particular. The Crow Creek Sioux are not the Diné, and the scholarship will necessarily reflect that. The bottom line always is the survival of the tribe as a community of vision and integrity (meaning a cohesive wholeness)—a survival accomplished through the individual contribution of unique personal attributes, talents, and expertise. Within this process decisions are made, primarily by those individuals who are both responsible and willing to carry them out. The tribe acts not with one mind but through the numerous contributions of each aspect of the minds surrounding.

We, the Diné, acknowledge anything that weakens the people, or introduces ill health and imbalance, as something obstructing survival. Imbalance and ill health must be addressed through a specific means of medicine: political, spiritual, social. In 1864, such an event came among the people, with the sole purpose of limiting and destroying the expression of living that is uniquely Navajo. The response to this event was a continued existing as such, along with modifications of food, dress, and beliefs around the geographical efficacy and boundary of ceremonial life. Together, they form the basis of Navajo worldview: resourceful responses that ensure health and survival of the way.

Luci Tapahonso, a Navajo then living in Lawrence, Kansas, writes:

> For many people in my situation, residing away from my homeland, writing is the means for returning, rejuvenation, and for restoring our spirits to the state of "hohzo," or beauty, which is the basis of Navajo philosophy. It is a small part of the "real thing," and it is utilitarian, but as Navajo culture changes, we adapt accordingly.[57]

It has happened this way forever. In her story/poem "In 1864," Tapahonso writes of a journey in which a younger daughter sleeps and the wheels turn along the highway as they move toward Hwééldi. The narrator remembers the story of a man working the power lines of western New Mexico. "The land was like he had imagined from the old stories,"[58] and "He heard the voices wavering and rising in the darkness. . . . No one else heard the thin wailing."[59] Their influence everywhere, the same story changing us as we ride into it. Reminding us, in the car, at the edge of the page, that we are here "because of what happened to [our] great-grandmother long ago."[60]

Under Kit Carson, the Bilagáana marched 8,354 Navajo from Navajo country out to Fort Sumner. Many died, pregnant women were shot, elders were left behind to starve and suffer alone in the snow, the people suffered on the walk, and at Hwééldi they faced starvation, smallpox, illness, and depression. Like the man working the lines in Tapahonso's poem, those Diné in the newly partitioned joint use area (JUA), and Navajos far outside and deep within the sacred mountains, we remember this and believe always in one thing. We told each other,

"We will be strong as long as we are together."
I think that was what kept us alive. We believed in ourselves
and the old stories that the holy people had given us.
"This is why," she would say to us. "This is why we are here.
Because our grandparents prayed and grieved for us."[61]

The role of traditional Navajo ceremonial life in ensuring the return of the people cannot be overemphasized. This is some of what we know, and do:

Because of her [Blanca Peak], we think and create.
Because of her, we make songs.
Because of her, the designs appear as we weave.
Because of her, we tell stories and laugh.
We believe in old values and new ideas.[62]

It is said by some that "the Long Walk" and the resulting Treaty of 1868 constituted the political unification and identity of the people into the Navajo Nation. Not all Navajo walked the path toward Hwééldi; some fled and hid high and deep in the canyons. Their hiding is not separate from the walk or the return, each participation now and always connected in a response, as a people, to remain alive on the land as we know it.

Likewise, scholarship is obligated to contribute toward the restoration of harmony among communities. The special understanding each tribe or people has and creates is bounded by their spiritual relationship to the places they occupy and is enacted in the tribe's ceremonial life and practice:

Ceremony, in literary terms, can be said to be that body of creative expression which accounts for the continued survival and development of a people, a nation. In this instance, it relies upon ancient symbols which are utilized spontaneously in a communal effort to speak with the givers of prayers, to recall the knowledge about life and death that has its origins in mythology and imagination.[63]

Scholarship, like the conversations and negotiations within the tribe as well as among tribes, needs to occur in these worldviews, firmly grounded in ancient experiences and passed down through the tribe's oral and written history. This tribal history, or worldview, takes all things into consideration.

Everything is changing. Everything is remaining the same. The stories do not change but have innumerable versions and allow unlimited possibility in the changing world, countless possibility for making more stories and restoring hozho. You change in your relationship to, in your level of participation in, and your understanding of each story made and being made around you. They may be the same stories you have heard every winter since you were one, two, three, four, or five, but you are thirty now, and everything is different and moving. They inform your understanding of that movement, give you a way of participating in your own changes and in your own changing landscape, especially "for those of us living away." For as everything is changing and the stories are alive, moving all around us, the land remains the same.

Notes

1. Gerald Vizenor, *Fugitive Poses: Native American Indian Scenes of Absence and Presence, The Abraham Lincoln Lecture Series* (Lincoln: University of Nebraska Press, 1998), p. 181. Very important work can be done with these narratives, but often they are viewed as the only understanding of sovereignty. Vizenor's importance as an indigenous scholar lies in his consistent demand that all Native peoples engage in constant intellectual and spiritual participation with all aspects of life and not contain language or experience within a single discipline or within a particular understanding or preformed response. For Vizenor, it is not so much the exact response that is important, but the method of arriving at that response. For an example of the work to be done, and the work that is possible, within the recognized notions of sovereignty, see the work by Elizabeth Cook-Lynn, Vine Deloria Jr., and the members of the American Indian Movement.

2. Bakhtin's "pretenders" refuse interaction and creative understanding in the world. Like Vizenor's terminal creed believers, they simply go along, not so much accepting a place provided in a pre-existing narrative frame, but acting as if they stand completely outside of narrative framings altogether. A pretender is "someone who tries to live in no particular place at all, or from a purely generalized abstract place. . . . Each of their acts is merely a sort of 'rough draft for a possible accomplishment, a document without a signature, obligating no one and obligated to nothing.'" Caryl Emerson and Gary Saul Morson, *Mikhail Bakhtin: Creation of a Prosaics* (Stanford: Stanford University Press, 1990), pp. 180–81.

3. *Worcester v. Georgia* 31 U.S. (6 Pet.) 515, 8 L. Ed. 483 (U.S. Sup. Ct. 1832).

4. Vizenor, *Fugitive Poses*, p. 185.

5. Dorothy Jones in Vizenor, *Fugitive Poses*, p. 181.

6. Emerson and Morson, *Mikhail Bakhtin*, p. 31.

7. Emerson and Morson, *Mikhail Bakhtin*, p. 31.

8. For an additional explanation and exploration of some of the legal arguments in relation to the doctrine of discovery, see Vine Deloria Jr., *Behind the Trail of Broken Treaties: An Indian Declaration of Independence* (Austin: University of Texas Press, 1974), chapter 5.

9. Thomas Biolsi and Larry J. Zimmerman, eds., *Indians and Anthropologists: Vine Deloria, Jr., and the Critique of Anthropology* (Tucson: University of Arizona Press, 1997), p. 94.

10. The process of making Others and the ability to be and become "American" has a long and interesting trailing of story. By "American" I mean to identify those claiming unquestioning membership in, and allegiance to, this identity, as it was and continues to be in the process of formation, as well as the values and ideology described and upheld

within the process of contesting exactly what it is to be "an American." My choice of language here does not reflect a category of people or a necessary race, class, or gender designation, though those policing the boundaries of membership often used such categories in their policing. I mean here the assumed subject and those who took their place within that assumption as American subjects, not objects.

11. Most famous among these are Robert F. Berkhofer Jr.'s *The White Man's Indian: Images of the American Indian from Columbus to the Present* (New York: Random House, 1978) and Roy Harvey Pearce's *Savagism and Civilization: A Study of the Indian and the American Mind* (Berkeley: University of California Press, 1953). In the spirit of intellectual sovereignty, I encourage people to read Philip J. Deloria's recent work, *Playing Indian* (New Haven: Yale University Press, 1998).

12. Biolsi and Zimmerman, *Indians and Anthropologists*, p. 96.

13. Vine Deloria Jr., *Red Earth, White Lies: Native Americans and the Myth of Scientific Fact* (New York: Scribner, 1995), p. 251.

14. Biolsi and Zimmerman, *Indians and Anthropologists*, p. 82.

15. I am referring specifically to chapter 3 in *God Is Red*.

16. This is common in the readings, or avoidance of readings, given gay American Indian texts or science fiction, such as Chrystos's wide body of poetry, including one book of erotica, and A. A. Carr's novel *Eye Killers*. See also, Robert Allen Warrior's critique of essentialisms and the imposition of unifying frames around a Native American literature in *Tribal Secrets*.

17. In the opinion Chief Justice Marshall delivered, in relation to *Worcester v. Georgia*, he defined Indian nations as having a "quasi-sovereignty" as "domestic dependent nations." He admitted that the "very fact of repeated treaties with [Indians recognized their entitlement to self-government] . . . and that a weaker power does not surrender its independence—its right to self-government, by associating with a stronger power, and taking its protections." But the Cherokee, and by extension all Indian nations, were in his opinion significantly weaker and therefore not nations in their own right but nations needing protection. The three Marshall opinions lay the framework for talking about a legal sovereignty as related to self-government and established the basis for the trust relationship between tribes and the U.S. They also provided unique language that Native activists can use, and that has been used against us, as our status is officially less than quasi, and our sovereignty is considered somehow weaker with the modification. This paternal relationship continues to characterize most scholarship on policy toward Indians.

18. Frederick E. Hoxie, *A Final Promise: The Campaign to Assimilate the Indians, 1880–1920* (New York: Cambridge University Press, 1992), p. 86.

19. For a more thorough exploration of this, see Philip Deloria's *Playing Indian*.

20. Hoxie, *Final Promise*, p. 85.

21. Hoxie, *Final Promise*, p. 86.

22. Without engaging in a lengthy or detailed exploration or explication of Erdrich's and Dorris's work, it is important to note them as problematic figures in Native American literature, not so much for what they write but for how it is positioned and received. In his introduction to *Tribal Secrets*, Warrior points out three key observations of Native

American critical work: (1) "the discourse continues to evidence an avoidance of internal criticism," (2) work is usually accorded "unmitigated praise or unbridled criticism [which] stands in the way of sincere disagreement and engagement," and (3) "both American Indian and Native Americanist discourses continue to be preoccupied with parochial questions of identity and authenticity." These tendencies are reflected in the reception given to Erdrich and Dorris, by Indians and non-Indians alike. At one time it was easy to categorize them as model breeds, happily married, extolling American nuclear family values while being deeply critical and punitive of Native American women (in particular). This, of course, has changed given Dorris's recent death and its surrounding circumstances, but the previous categorization avoids an intelligent and informed examination of their political and spiritual views and the real intertribal differences evidenced in Cook-Lynn's important critique of *The Broken Cord*, as well as their popularity in American culture and corresponding positioning as "spokespersons" for Indians and Indian culture. It is precisely their political position(s) that have made them palatable, but it only serves to weaken Native American discourse to dismiss the differences as resulting from their perceived Indianness or non-Indianness.

23. Vizenor, *Fugitive Poses*, p. 183.

24. Vizenor, *Fugitive Poses*, p. 181.

25. Vine Deloria Jr., *God Is Red* (New York: Grosset and Dunlap, 1973), p. 79.

26. Robert Allen Warrior, *Tribal Secrets: Recovering American Indian Intellectual Traditions* (Minneapolis: University of Minnesota Press, 1995), p. xxi.

27. Warrior, *Tribal Secrets*, p. xxi.

28. Warrior, *Tribal Secrets*, p. 72.

29. Kimberly M. Blaeser's wonderful work *Gerald Vizenor: Writing in the Oral Tradition* (Norman: University of Oklahoma Press, 1996) argues this in specific reference to Vizenor's large body of literature.

30. Warrior, *Tribal Secrets*, p. 84.

31. Warrior, *Tribal Secrets*, p. 85.

32. Warrior, *Tribal Secrets*, p. 86.

33. Warrior, *Tribal Secrets*, p. 93.

34. Warrior, *Tribal Secrets*, p. 84.

35. Anna Lee Walters, *Ghost Singer* (Albuquerque: University of New Mexico Press, 1988).

36. Pura Fé, "Going Home," on *Follow Your Heart's Desire* (Music Maker Relief Foundation, 2004).

37. Warrior, *Tribal Secrets*, p. 104.

38. Warrior, *Tribal Secrets*, p. 111.

39. Warrior, *Tribal Secrets*, p. 113.

40. Warrior, *Tribal Secrets*, p. 112.

41. Brian Swann and Arnold Krupat, eds., *I Tell You Now: Autobiographical Essays by Native American Writers* (Lincoln: University of Nebraska Press, 1987), p. 187.

42. Warrior, *Tribal Secrets*, p. 123.

43. Anna Lee Walters, *Talking Indian: Reflections on Survival and Writing* (Ithaca: Firebrand Books, 1992), p. 222.

44. Leslie Marmon Silko, *Almanac of the Dead* (New York: Simon & Schuster, 1991), p. 578.

45. Deloria Jr., *God Is Red*, p. 83.

46. Leslie Marmon Silko, *Storyteller* (New York: Arcade Publishing/Little, Brown, 1981), pp. 6–7.

47. Silko, *Storyteller*, p. 247.

48. Silko, *Storyteller*, p. 253.

49. Silko, *Storyteller*, p. 253.

50. Warrior, *Tribal Secrets*, p. 94.

51. Silko, *Storyteller*, p. 7.

52. Leslie Marmon Silko, *Yellow Woman and a Beauty of the Spirit: Essays on Native American Life Today* (New York: Simon & Schuster, 1996), p. 152.

53. Silko, *Yellow Woman*, p. 153.

54. Silko, *Yellow Woman*, p. 154.

55. Elizabeth Cook-Lynn, *Why I Can't Read Wallace Stegner and Other Essays: A Tribal Voice* (Madison: University of Wisconsin Press, 1996), p. 108.

56. It is important to note here that her understanding of sovereignty is shaped by the particular experiences of her tribe/nation and will have very different meaning and application for urban Indians as well as non-Plains treaty Indians. The centrality and unwavering adherence to this perspective reflects the unique and specific worldview and experience of her people. Utilizing her directive as an approach to scholarship allows each worldview and tribal experience to then name for itself what is of utmost importance and meaning.

57. Luci Tapahonso, *Sáanii Dahataal: The Women Are Singing*, Sun Tracks: An American Indian Literary Ser. 23 (Tucson: University of Arizona Press, 1993), p. xii.

58. Tapahonso, *Sáanii*, p. 7.

59. Tapahonso, *Sáanii*, p. 8.

60. Tapahonso, *Sáanii*, p. 8.

61. Tapahonso, *Sáanii*, p. 10.

62. Luci Tapahonso, *Blue Horses Rush In: Poems and Stories*, Sun Tracks: An American Indian Literary Ser. 34 (Tucson: University of Arizona Press, 1997), p. 39.

63. Swann and Krupat, *Native American Writers*, p. 60.

Relocations Upon Relocations: Home, Language and Native American Women's Writings

10

INÉS HERNÁNDEZ-AVILA

> Give me back my language and build a house
> Inside it.
> A house of madness.
> A house for the dead who are not dead.
> And the spiral of the sky above it.
> And the sun
> and the moon
> And the stars to guide us called promise.
> Joy Harjo[1]

> How I love this tragic valley of South Texas . . . this borderland between the Nueces and the Rio Grande. This land has survived possession and ill-use by five countries: Spain, Mexico, the Republic of Texas, the U.S., the Confederacy, and the U.S. again. It has survived Anglo-Mexican blood feuds, lynchings, burnings, rapes, pillages . . . . This land was Mexican once / was Indian always / and is. / And will be again.
> Gloria Anzaldua[2]

This essay is about homes, positions, and (re)locations, in relation to language and in relation to Native American women writing today. The essay is also, in a sense, an interrogation of the terms "feminism" and "feminist politics," as they might apply to Native American women writers. Drawing from the essay by Biddy Martin and Chandra Talpande Mohanty, "Feminist Politics: What's Home Got to Do with It?" I would say that Native American women writers are also "interested in the configuration of home, identity, and community; more specifically, in the power and appeal of 'home' as a concept and a desire."[3] As I position myself in relation to Martin and Mohanty, however, I find that my notions of "home" in the patterning of identity and community in some ways resemble what these feminists are articulating, in some ways not. While "home" occurs as a metaphor in feminist writings, it is, after all, a metaphor in the work of many, if not most, Native American women writers as well. At the same time, I do not find many Native American women writers particularly interested in locating, in their writings, an "all-encompassing" or even "discrete" home within feminism, or at least feminist scholarship per se.

I appreciate Martin and Mohanty's admission that "women of color cannot easily assume 'home' within feminist communities as they have been constituted."[4] They suggest that "feminist communities" have assumed (or presumed) a body (or membership) that excludes the acknowledgement of the participation of "women of color" (a problematic term); therefore women of color do not feel at "home" with these "feminist communities as they have been constituted," since they often appear to be associated primarily with white women. This perspective opens up the discourse around feminism to reveal the possibility that other "feminisms" might have found a home and assumed a body (or membership) among, for example, Native American women.

In her essay, "The Politics of Location as Transnational Feminist Critical Practice," as she critiques the universalizing, naturalizing, and totalizing tendencies of Western feminism, Caren Kaplan acknowledges how the "concern with location and space, with rooms of one's own, with expanding 'home' from the domestic to the public sphere, has been one of the hallmarks of Western feminist practice."[5] Herein lies a major difference, or as Mohanty would say, a difference as history, between "Western feminist practice" and what might be called a Native American "feminism." For many activist native women of this hemisphere, the concern with "home" involves a concern with "home*land*." Even when native women activists no longer reside on their ancestral landbases, and many still do, they continue to defend the tribal sovereignty of their own communities as well as communities of other indigenous peoples.[6] Sovereignty encompasses the cultural, spiritual, economic, and political aspects of the life of the communities and of the individuals who make up the communities. Issues of sovereignty are intimately interwoven with issues pertaining to the land(base) of each people.[7] For native people, any notion of "home" within the domestic sphere was largely and intentionally disrupted by the colonialist process. Considering how we were seen literally as the enemy by colonial and then (in the United States) federal forces, native people were and have been forced historically to address the issue of "home" in the "public sphere." Any "renegotiation" between Native American women and "other" feminists must recognize this point.

I agree with Martin and Mohanty when they convey the need and "the responsibility [feminists have] for remapping boundaries and renegotiating connections."[8] This remapping and renegotiating is a necessary process within communities as well as between communities. One of the specific ways that boundaries need to be remapped, or better still transformed, in the study of Native American literature is in the si(gh)ting of "Indianness" and "Americanness" with respect to this hemisphere rather than simply with respect to the United States and Canada. Connections should also be renegotiated regarding issues of identity and mixed-bloodness that is of other combinations besides native and white. I began this essay with a passage from Chicana/Tejana writer Gloria Anzaldua, as well as the one from Creek mixed-blood poet, Joy Harjo. Harjo's poem "We Must Call A Meeting" illuminates the power of the creative (writing) process itself, the inscription of our lives and our communities' lives, the relocating of our languages in the homes of our words, and our homes in the words of our languages. Anzaldua's passage from her chapter "La conciencia de la mestiza/Towards a New Consciousness," focuses upon the repeated colonial subjugation of her land base and of the original inhabitants of that land, and on her vision of a returning sovereignty, for both the people and the land. She, too, proclaims the power of naming, in her willful insistence on this land being Indian again. In her language she also creates a "house for the dead who are not dead," just as Harjo does; these "dead" are, after all, the spirits of our ancestors, "not dead," finding form in our voices and informing our words.

My own vision, as well as the vision of the Native American Studies Department in which I teach, is inclusive of Chicanas/Chicanos in definitions of "Indianness,"[9] which in itself disrupts the definition of "Indian" that is commonly associated with the study of Native American literature, as well as with most Native American Studies programs in general. This particular position is apparently as unpalatable, in the realm of academia, to many Indian scholars as it is to many Chicana and Chicano scholars, due to the internalized racism and historically regulated animosities that have obstructed the si(gh)ting of both communities with respect to each other.[10] It is possible that the foothold we (those of us in Native American Studies at the University of California at Davis) have managed in the rocky terrain of identity politics is one of our contributions to the ideas of "home" within Native Americanness. It might be unsettling to some (scholars in particular) to consider and include Chicanas/Chicanos within the United States and "Indians" from south of the U.S. border in the conceptualization of Native American Studies. At Davis, it is and has been a distinguishing principle of our program from the inception of Native American Studies over thirty years ago. Since January of 1994, the unfolding events in Chiapas, Mexico, have been dramatically highlighting the necessity of our hemispheric perspective, which grounds our experiences as indigenous peoples of the Americas. Almost eight years after the beginning of the armed uprising of the EZLN

(Ejército Zapatista de Liberación Nacional), it is clear that the army of Maya Indians who declared war on the Mexican state have been writing new chapters of contemporary indigenous history, with implications for us all.

This project of remapping boundaries and renegotiating connections, according to Martin and Mohanty, is "partial in at least two senses of the word: politically partial, and without claim to wholeness or finality."[11] In her essay, "Response to 'Black Women's Texts,'" Barbara Christian emphasizes, "In the last few years issues of how we read as well as what we read have become critical ones as literary critics acknowledge the politics that has always been at the center of our enterprise."[12] I would say the same regarding writing: Issues of how we write as well as what we write have become critical ones as writers, literary critics and scholars in other disciplines acknowledge the politics that has always been at the center of our enterprise. In this context, I also appreciate Kaplan's admission that "[t]oo often Western feminists have ignored the politics of reception in the interpretation of texts from the so-called 'peripheries' . . . ."[13] Admitting the political partiality as well as the dynamic process of any project is crucial to the addressing and informing of our strategies as conscious human beings. Christian creates a discursive space for us to consider both the rewards and the obstacles that accompany these admissions.

As she calls upon her reading of *Jane Eyre* to reflect upon her own location in relation to the characters of Jane and the Caribbean woman Bertha, Christian demonstrates how a reader's "sense of who she is, as subject, [can be] disrupted."[14] She notes how Bertha's

> history, carefully coded by Charlotte Bronte, was the underside of British colonialism, a colonialism which was the source of Rochester's wealth and made it possible for him to even hire Jane as a governess.[15]

While she identifies with Bertha, Christian admits that she also identifies with Jane's "strategies of survival, enmeshed as she was in a patriarchal [and classist] context."[16] Iroquois artist George Longfish speaks of going beyond survival and moving on to the creative act, the creative response, which reveals complexity rather than predictability, multilayers rather than merely stereotype. In his art, he imprints his process of working through that space between himself and the canvas, which is the critical/creative space of location and relocation. Christian's essay also represents this strategy of impression and expression.

Going beyond survival has to do with subversion and creative agency. When I and other Native American women are central as subjects—as sovereign subjects—we often unsettle, disrupt, and sometimes threaten other people's, particularly many white people's, white scholars', white women feminists' sense of self as subjects. That may not have been my or our primary motivation, but it is necessarily inherent in Native women's claiming our right to speak for ourselves. Our own personal and collective struggles notwithstanding, Native American women are writing our own scripts and playing roles we ourselves have created; we are negotiating our own terms, even "Reinventing the Enemy's Language" (as Joy Harjo and Gloria Bird have indicated in their important anthology). Trinh T. Minh-ha says in her essay, "Not You/Like You: Post-Colonial Women and the Interlocking Questions of Identity and Difference, " . . . [I]n the unfolding of power inequalities, changes frequently require that the rules be reappropriated so that the master be beaten at his own game."[17] As Native women determine our own rules, and therefore, as it were, change the game, we reveal and reinscribe our own historical cultural identities.

These historical cultural identities are contextualized within the personal and collective historical processes which we have undergone and the cultural pedagogies which have sustained us and our families and communities, not without suffering or grievous loss, but with courage, beauty and dignity as well. The experience of invasion, genocide, dispossession, colonization, relocation, and ethnocide, is marked at different historical moments by singular imperial, then governmental policies. These systemic policies which sought, and seek, to destroy, or at least subvert, native sovereignty and render us dependent wards of the state, continue today throughout this hemisphere. My use of the term "relocation" deliberately recalls the historical fact of relocation of native peoples (including my own, Joseph's band of the Nez Perce), the policies which created the urban Native populations we have today, and the policies which forced Native children to be sent away from their homes to boarding schools. One of the tactics of indoctrination at the boarding schools was, of course, the silencing and denial of Native voices and Native languages. In the United States, because we were forced to adopt English only, many of us could, and can, only locate ourselves, position ourselves in the English language. Now it is the English language, and for some of us, Spanish as well, that we make use of in si(gh)ting our and our people's sovereignty, not only in academia, but also in local and international political and cultural arenas.

Kaplan, in "Deterritorializations: The Rewriting of Home and Exile in Western Feminist Discourse," says, "First world feminist criticism is struggling to avoid repeating the same imperializing moves that we claim to protest. We must leave home, as it were, since our homes are often sites of racism, sexism, and other damaging social practices."[18] While the homes of Native people are just as likely as anyone else's to be these destructive kinds of sites, and at the level of the individual, Native people might indeed "leave home" due to any number of factors which make them feel unwelcome, it is also an historical fact that Native communities were (and are) the object of colonialist, imperialist "moves." For most Native people, "leaving home" at the level of the collective has meant relocation, through war or "peacetime" governmental policies. We were given no choice but to "leave home," and to move unwillingly to *other* homes which were "often the sites of racism, sexism, and *other* damaging social practices." In pursuing Gilles Deleuze and Felix Guattari's notions of "deterritorialization," Kaplan says,

> I would have to pay attention to whether or not it is possible for me to choose deterritorialization or whether deterritorialization has chosen me . . . If deterritorialization has chosen me—that is, if I have been cast out of home or language without forethought or permission, then my point of view will be more complicated.[19]

I appreciate Kaplan's acknowledgement of this potential of "complication," and I believe that it applies to Native people.

Concurring with Deleuze and Guattari, Kaplan notes that often, and for many groups of people, "leaving home" has also meant leaving voice, leaving language. She repeats a crucial question asked by them, "How many people live today in a language that is not their own?"[20] For Native Americans, "leaving language" is too benign a term for the attempted and sometimes successful eradication of our languages. This campaign of eradication had and has the purpose of destroying our sovereignty by destroying our connections to our landbases, given that the home(land)s or landbases inform the cultures, belief-systems, and the languages. However, Native people have managed to sustain, through memory and the constant presence of the land, their connections to their home(land)s in this hemisphere. This realized connection has made it possible for many Native people to reclaim and recall their languages (native and otherwise) as their own, as an act of si(gh)ting sovereignty. Kaplan says, "Exploring all the differences, keeping identities distinct, is the only way we can keep power differentials from masquerading as universals."[21] In this sense, location as a contextualizing factor must be claimed as a necessary element in the struggle for self-reflexivity. So, yes, the situation of Native people, and Native women, is complicated, and not all reflections are the same.

One of the issues that Native American women cannot help but draw attention to is the fact that racial identities are also white, and as Henry Giroux notes in *Border Crossings: Cultural Workers and the Politics of Education*, white ethnicity is constructed in its attempts to position others.[22] Martin and Mohanty, in their discussion of Minnie Bruce Pratt's narrative, "Identity: Skin Blood Heart," also attest to Pratt's exploration of "the exclusions and repressions which support the seeming homogeneity, stability, and self-evidence of 'white identity,' which is derived from and dependent on the marginalization of differences within as well as 'without.'"[23] In the section, "Afro-American Feminist Writers and the Discourse of Possibility," Giroux says,

> Once dominant culture is racialized within the discourse of ethnicity and existing power relations, it becomes possible to write history from the perspective of those engaged in the struggle against cultural genocide. Voices now begin to emerge

from different locations and are no longer authorized to speak only through a Eurocentric perspective that defines them in its own interests.[24]

The poems and poets mentioned here cite their own authority as they interrogate "whiteness," including its attempts to dominate native people in language and through language, thereby taking us away from home, relocating us, as it were, in a foreign, violating and inhospitable place (of language) also called home. This questioning represents self-revelation as well and demonstrates concretely through language that this relocation home has been opened up, as a site of both contestation and reconciliation. The family has been invited in to live in the words, and the dead who are not dead have come to express themselves in silence and in voice, now moving freely, back and forth, between the new languages and the old.

In their interrogation of whiteness, Native American women writers inscribe their locations in such a way that the multiplicity of audiences addressed remains clear. In my own poem, "He Says He Just Can't Get Enough" / for all the Indi'n men with their white women groupies," the message is dedicated ostensibly to Indian men (and white women), but the scene that takes place within the poem is intended first for Indian women:

> Say *hey*
> It's that taking-his-stuff
> out-the-door-leaving-it
> out-in-the-yard-for-him
> to-*go*-time
>
> I mean
> it's when
> no story
>   line
>   "con"
>   sweet words
>   self-delusion
>   mutual confusion
>   or so-called
>   satisfaction-in-spite
>   of-it-all
> will work
> no more
>
> ain'it
> sister

you know what
I mean

Those stretches
of the imagine
          nation
are worse than stretches
of the body
or the budget
or any athlete's
or aerobics dancer's
I know

He wants it all
his way
Indi'n women
to keep his
"traditional" stance
when it looks good
. . . after *all* . . .

White women
when Indi'n women
make things too hard
don't hang around
him enough
nor gasp at his
every word
nor let him come
in the middle of the night
or any hour
thoughtless
of all but satisfaction
for himself

He wanders around
in-and-out-of-the-forest
out of touch
with his own self
much less the *trees*

picks fruit
that's already
on the ground
it's easier to eat
no work involved
except
the occasional
stooping.

Even though I usually qualify the dedication of this poem whenever I include it in a poetry reading by acknowledging that not all white women are groupies, I have seen white women become incredibly offended with the content. At Humboldt State University, in February of 1993, I was a keynote speaker for a native women's conference; later in the evening, I also participated in the poetry readings. One white woman came up to me to say that this one poem invalidated everything else that I had said earlier in the day. Interestingly enough, my main address concerned issues of representation (including the ethics of representation) of Native American women, as well as issues of commodification and exploitation of Native American spirituality.

When I read the poem, I explained that many white women have contributed with genuine solidarity to Native American causes. Other types of white women (and men) are fairly notorious for the ways in which they pursue (and make themselves available to) Native people, in gestures that betray their own exoticizing (and objectifying) of Native people. The poem, from a Native woman's perspective, is foremost an internal critique of Native men who also, in turn, objectify this kind of white woman. Yet, for this woman (and possibly other white women who did not voice their protests to me), their "whiteness" would not allow them to see the issues the poem raises. Kaplan suggests that part of the process of first world feminist critics "becoming minor" is the need for them to "learn about what [they] have been taught to avoid, fear, or ignore."[25] The clear discomfort (and occasional outrage) of some white women regarding the poem and others like it perhaps belies their shock at the possibility of their behavior being interpreted and critiqued from another's perspective.

In Barbara Christian's discussion of Alice Walker's character Meridien, she says that Walker "exposes white women's real position in their own society, a byproduct that often results when black women write from their point of view."[26] Christian comments on Meridien's meditation:

Meridien's analysis is initiated by her realization that white women might be desired by black men, not because they were women but because they were *white women*.[27]

The poem "He Says He Just Can't Get Enough" traces a similar line of thinking. The poem has received an enthusiastic reception among Native women whenever I have read it. Why does this poem resonate so roundly with them?—because in the language of the poem we come home to ourselves in familiarity. The relocation, the humorous si(gh)ting, is of our own doing, and therefore a creative act worthy of laughter, including laughter at our selves.

Another such si(gh)ting was created by Native artist Judith Lowry, who is Mountain Maidu. She has a 94 1/2 by 69 inch painting titled "Medicine Man" which she says

> represents the direction that some of our Native people are following. I appropriated an 1811 Jean Auguste-Dominique Ingres painting of Jupiter because of its depiction of the power of male dominance. I replaced Jupiter and Thetis with a young Indian man and a white, "new-age" woman.[28]

Using an acrylic medium, and intense, vibrant color, Lowry places the "Medicine Man" on a throne, one of his arms resting on clouds, the other holding up a staff from which hangs a dream catcher complete with feathers and bird claw. He is a "typical" Indian warrior in appearance, shirtless, in jeans, longhaired, handsome, his sleepy eyes gazing out into the distance beyond the viewer. He is wearing thongs and, tellingly, a beaded belt buckle that depicts none other than "the end of the trail" motif. The "brave" may as well ride off into the sunset with his head hanging, given that he has succumbed to the role prescribed to him by a society that would only "honor" him as a vision of the past.

At the lower left-hand corner of the painting a blond, long-haired woman kneels before this Indian man. She is wearing Birkenstock sandals, beaded earrings, a long dress and a vest; her attire suggests that she is a "New Ager" or a "liberal," possibly a "progressive." With her right hand she places what looks like an offering of a U.S. flag across his knees—the nation will be his if only he will continue to provide a romantic image for her with his looks and with his voice. With her left hand cupped she reaches up to his mouth as if to catch whatever precious words he would deign to give her, all the while gazing adoringly at his face. Both of these individuals are wearing the "requisite" bracelets and rings to accessorize the outfits that ostensibly manifest their respective roles of "medicine man" and devotee. The painting reflects a tension in the situation. How long can either figure remain in the position he or she has apparently chosen? Lowry says,

> These personifications reveal aspects about illusion and hypocrisy that occur in both Native and non-Native societies. We as Native people need to critique ourselves. We need to stay honest if our cultures and communities are going to continue to grow and be healthy.[29]

Her painting is strikingly humorous, yet provocative, particularly in its internal critique.

Chrystos' poem "Dear Indian Abby" also engenders humor from a Native American woman's perspective. The persona of the poem says in her letter to "Indian Abby,"

> What should I do
> about those ones who try to crawl down my throat
> bulging eyes are going to Understand
> me or Else
> Get some of my spirit   get some of my magic
> OOOOOHHHHHHOOO they want it
> Want to explain how I could have a better grasp
> of Native issues if I read this book or that by some
> white person   Want me to listen to them with traps
> dangling from their back pockets
> Gonna get some   gonna get some of me now
> from *Sincerely Puzzled*[30]

Martin and Mohanty's discussion of "the ways in which appropriation or stealth, in the colonial gesture, reproduces itself in the political positions of white feminists"[31] informs my reading of this poem, although I would say these gestures are common enough among many non-Indian people, not only white feminists. In this instance, I do read "those ones" in the poem as a certain type of white women, a certain type of white feminists, the kind who, perhaps like Lowry's figure, are prompted by some sectors of the women's (spirituality) movement, the progressive movement, or the New Age movement (although New Agers and progressives could just as easily be men) to take what they want from native spiritual traditions and leave the rest.[32]

What Sincerely Puzzled experiences is "those ones'" entitlement of intrusion, a replicating invasion that seeks to steal cultural vitality under the assumption (and with the voracity) of privilege. As Theresa Harlan has stated, "[Native American women] are objectified as mystical beings with a genetic disposition to touch everyone's lives and leave them in a state of harmony and balance. If we are not at peace, we are at war."[33] To respond to this insistent objectification requires a humor that gives back the objectified image served up in exaggerated (and reappropriated) language, sending "those ones" back home to their own words. "Indian Abby's" reply to Puzzled is,

> . . . Best thing to do is tell them you've heard
> there's a great Indian wise woman named Whale Rabbit

over anyplace around 3,001 miles away
& you're real sure
she's waiting patiently for them to show up
& they'd better hurry cause her fee goes up in 2 weeks
& your fee for giving them the directions is only $350
Don't forget to smile
as you wave goodbye
Yours Truly, Indian Abby[34]

In this poem, Chrystos creates a home and a discursive space for Puzzled and Indian Abby, just as she negotiates that space for other Native women. As a narrative of bitter testimony and creative amusement, "Dear Indian Abby" inscribes one of the more public spheres of Native women's lives. In contrast, Beth Brant's prologue to her collection, *Food & Spirits*, draws from the intimate secret spaces of raw wounds and willful healing. She calls upon the diary form to create a somewhat hushed yet powerful buffer zone of protection for the confidences which have been shared with her. At the same time, she insists on the voice that will break the silence by the "Telling"—"Dear Diary" / "What do I do with this *Dear Diary*? / A writer can read. She can hear. She can write. / What does she do with the need of someone to tell?"[35] Brant's reflections in the prologue and throughout *Food & Spirits* reveal an internal critique, within herself, within the Indian community. Trinh T. Minh-ha has stated:

> Differences do not only exist between outsider and insider—two entities. They are also at work within the outsider herself, or the insider, herself—a single entity. She who knows she cannot speak of them without speaking of herself, of history without involving her story, also knows that she cannot make a gesture without activating the to and fro movement of life.[36]

Brant takes on this telling, and with the telling the issues of misogyny, rape, violence, child abuse, homophobia, within the Indian community, and between the Indian community and the larger community. She also, with loving skill, weaves for us the healing power of voice.

In Toni Morrison's essay, "The Site of Memory," Morrison addresses the need of "[ripping] the veil drawn over 'proceedings too terrible to relate.'"[37] Brant rips the veils, locating herself, arming herself with the weapons, with the words for si(gh)ting voice. "If love could be made visible, would it be in the enemy's language? It is the only weapon I hold [Brant says]: this pen, this knife, this tool, this / language."[38] Morrison reminds those of us "who belong" to any marginalized category . . . [that] historically we were seldom invited to participate in the discourse even when we were its topic."[39] For native people, these exclusive conversations took place (and take place) in our own home, on our own land, where even questions of identity and community are regulated largely by federal policy. Through language, Native people, Native women, have been disgraced and violated in our own home(land) and robbed of our sovereignty. In our own home(land), we recover our grace and our sovereignty through language and through struggle, even if that language is the enemy's made ours.

Rigoberta Menchú, the 1992 Nobel Peace Prize winner from Guatemala, years ago demanded her own participation in the global discourse of struggle. Her (mediated) autobiography, *I, Rigoberta Menchú,* indeed rips the veil drawn over proceedings too terrible to relate, just as her voice at the international level continues to subvert notions of "democracy" that are perpetuated by militaristic regimes. Menchú is fortunate in that she speaks her native language, as well as Spanish, and she is beginning to speak publicly in English, too. In her poem, "Ella" ["She"], printed in Spanish, Menchú honors the dignity and beauty of her Mayan sisters in struggle. She grounds this representative woman in the history and lived experience of their everyday lives, saying,

> Es mi madre torturada, es mi hermana, es mi nieta,
> es aquella que rectificó después de un señalamiento
> colectivo
> Es la compañera que apenas culminó una larga
> caminata por rumbos, charraleras, veredas,
> subiendo y bajando cerros sembrando mucho maiz
> Es la mujer que guardó sus gritos y cantos de júbilo
> para mañana.[40]
> [She is my tortured mother, she is my sister, my
>   granddaughter
> She is the one who thought things over after a signal
> from the collective
> She is the comrade who just finished the arduous
> walk along roads, through fields, on paths
> going up and down hills, sowing much corn
> She is the woman who saved her cries and songs of joy
> for tomorrow.]

Once Menchú contextualizes her si(gh)ting of "Ella's" voice, she establishes "Ella's" relocations which take her away from home, yet also bring her back home.

In many ways, Ella never leaves home, because home is in her language, in her voice, as Menchú tells us,

> Es ella, la que cruzó fronteras y no le dió
> tiempo de despedir el novio desaparecido,

la que gritó la verdad por el mundo,
dijo un discurso frente a militares asesinos
y no se le terminó la voz.
Es la que venció su miedo, aceptó ser acompañada
por la soledad de lejanas tierras, cruzando
fronteras esperando un avión de allá pa cá, da acá pa llá.[41]
[It is she, the one who crossed borders, which did not
give her time to say farewell to her disappeared sweetheart,
She is the one who yelled out the truth throughout the world,
made a speech before military assassins
and did not lose her voice.
She is the one who conquered her fear, and accepted
being accompanied by the solitude of faraway lands,
crossing borders waiting for a plane from there to here,
from here to there.]

The path of consciousness and struggle is solitary for Ella, but she is not alone as she crosses and recrosses borders, insisting, too, on the voice that will break the silence. In her traveling, she does not forget her landbase; she does not forget her own or her people's histories. In fact, she takes strength from the land and from the history, using them to forge her weapons and her tools, as do all the other native women writers mentioned here. Theresa Harlan has said, "When we criticize and challenge hegemonic thinking and attitudes we are then characterized as being angry. We are often asked, 'Why do you take history so personal?'"[42] These personal and collective histories, including our cultural responses to experience, ground our theoretical perspectives and our reinscriptions of ourselves.

What are the pedagogical implications of the study of these reinscriptions by Native American women writers? bell hooks says, "In my classrooms, we work to dispel the notion that our experience is not a 'real world' experience."[43] I feel the same about my own classes. I ask my students (Native and non-Native) and myself, "How might the works of Native American women, as mediated sites of recollection and witness, recreate possibilities of discovery and transformation for the readers as well as for the writers themselves? How might Native American women's literature contribute to students (including me) coming home to language, to voice, and to them(our)selves?" In the classroom, as students and myself consider the "feigned homogeneity of the West,"[44] we also distinguish the feigned homogeneity of Native Americans. The attention to difference as history and complexity releases students to critique their own possibly essential understandings of themselves as well as the world in which they live; it releases them to consider their own "homes" and "communities." In some cases their considerations might lead them to realize what Martin and Mohanty state,

"Being home" refers to the place where one lives within familiar, safe, protected boundaries; "not being home" is a matter of realizing that home was an illusion of coherence and safety based on the exclusion of specific histories of oppression and resistance, the repression of differences even within oneself.[45]

The texts, including the text of the classroom itself, mediate at many levels because of the locations and relocations of the readers.

Native American students do not fit into neat categories of readerships any more than any other readers. Native American students might realize their own people's histories of oppression and resistance, yet they might not be so aware of the histories of oppression and resistance of other peoples, or the repression of differences within themselves, or any combination thereof. The same is true for any readers. In the best of circumstances, they (and we) will see, as Christian says, the "sameness/difference in texts . . . as a creative possibility rather than a threat."[46] Many students come home to language itself and to their own place in relation to it. In "We Must Call A Meeting," Harjo speaks of an "arrow, painted / with lightening / to seek the way to the name of the enemy."[47] As students become these arrows, they (re)create their own language, and in language relocate and re-member their homes and realize community. In si(gh)ting their own voices, Native American women writers create for Native American students and readers the possibilities for si(gh)ting their own voices and their own and their people's sovereignty.

Notes

This essay is an expanded version of a presentation originally given at the University of California, Riverside, conference "Reading Into Diversity: Native American Studies in a Multicultural Curriculum," held on March 3–4, 1994. I would like to thank Theresa Harlan and Dorette Quintana English for our conversations as I was completing this essay.

1. Joy Harjo, "We Must Call A Meeting," *In Mad Love and War* (Middletown: Wesleyan UP, 1990), pp. 9–10.

2. Gloria Anzaldua, *Borderlands/La Frontera: The New Mestiza* (San Francisco: spinsters/aunt lute, 1987), pp. 90–91.

3. Biddy Martin and Chandra Talpande Mohanty, "Feminist Politics: What's Home Got to Do with It?" *Feminist Studies/Critical Studies*, ed. Teresa de Lauretis (Bloomington: Indiana UP, 1986), p. 191. The authors also call attention to the "challenging presence [of home as a metaphor] in the rhetoric of the New Right" (Ibid.).

4. Martin and Mohanty, p. 192.

5. Caren Kaplan, "The Politics of Location as Transnational Feminist Critical Practice," *Scattered Hegemonies: Postmodernity and Transnational Feminist Practices*, ed. Inderpal Grewal and Caren Kaplan (Minneapolis: University of Minnesota Press, 1994), p. 137.

6. I am using the term "activist" in a broad sense to include community organizers, educators, writers, artists, media people, environmentalists, health professionals, etc., who consciously advocate for the betterment of Native communities.

7. Issues regarding ancestral lands, sacred places, fishing and water rights, etc., all pertaining to landbases, are best articulated in concrete terms by Native activists rather than in the romantic or generic "earthbound" manner that some environmentalists and many New Agers use.

8. Martin and Mohanty, p. 193.

9. I will use "Indian," "Native American" and "Native" interchangeably in this essay; the terms are generic and problematic, "Native American" and "Native" being possibly the more exact, at least in English, "Indian" being a complete misnomer. Many native people in the United States, however, have made "Indian" their own and use it as a term in English to refer to indigenous people whose ancestral landbase is now known as the United States.

10. This expanded definition of "Indian" is also unsettling to many of the non-Indian scholars who, like their Native and Chicano/Chicana counterparts, would rather not have to shift their paradigms and rethink their "territories."

11. Martin and Mohanty, p. 193.

12. Barbara Christian, "Response to 'Black Women's Texts,'" *NWSA Journal,* Vol. I, No. I (1988), p. 34.

13. Kaplan, "Politics of Location," pp. 138–139.

14. Christian, p. 35.

15. Ibid., p. 32.

16. Ibid.

17. Trinh T. Minh-ha, "Not You/Like You: Post-Colonial Women and the Interlocking Questions of Identity and Difference," *Making Face/Making Soul/Haciendo Caras: Creative and Critical Perspectives by Women of Color,* ed. Gloria Anzaldua (San Francisco: aunt lute foundation, 1990), p. 373.

18. Caren Kaplan, "Deterritorializations: The Rewriting of Home and Exile in Western Feminist Discourse," *The Nature and Context of Minority Discourse,* ed., Abdul R. Jan-Homaned and David Lloyd (New York: Oxford UP, 1990), p. 364.

19. Ibid., p. 363.

20. Ibid., p. 360.

21. Ibid., p. 364.

22. Henry Giroux, *Border Crossings: Cultural Workers and the Politics of Education* (New York: Routledge, 1992), p. 127. Chapter 5, "Redefining the Boundaries of Race and Ethnicity: Beyond the Politics of Pluralism," is useful regarding this discussion.

23. Martin and Mohanty, p. 173.

24. Giroux, op. cit.

25. Kaplan, "Deterritorializations," p. 364. I am assuming that the term "first world feminist" refers to white women. On another note, I am not in agreement with the terms "major" and "minor," but my dissension is the subject of another essay. I realize these terms are not Kaplan's; she herself asks, "Who is the 'us' that is circulating in [Gilles Deleuze and Felix Guattari's] essay 'What is a Minor Literature?'" (Kaplan, "Deterritorializations," p. 362). Suffice to say that much in the same way Martin and Mohanty voice their concern "that critiques of what is increasingly identified as 'white' or 'Western' fem-

inism unwittingly leave the terms of West/East, white/nonwhite polarities intact" (Martin and Mohanty, p. 193). I want to voice my same concern about the seemingly intact polarity of "major/minor," or more specifically, the use of those particular terms to create even a "revolutionary" distinction, as Deleuze and Guattari suggest.

26. Christian, p. 34.

27. Ibid., p. 33.

28. Judith Lowry, "Artist's Statement," prepared for the catalogue to the Fall 1994 Heard Museum exhibition *Watchful Eyes*, curated by Theresa Harlan.

29. Ibid.

30. Chrystos, "Dear Indian Abby," *Dream On* (Vancouver: Press Gang Publishers, 1991), p. 21.

31. Martin and Mohanty, p. 207.

32. I have written of this phenomenon in an essay titled "Mediations of the Spirit: Native American Women and the Ethics of Representation."

33. Theresa Harlan, "As In Her Vision: Image Making by Native Women Artists," ms., p. 9.

34. Chrystos, op. cit.

35. Beth Brant, *Food & Spirits* (New York: Firebrand, 1991), p. 12.

36. Minh-ha, p. 375.

37. Toni Morrison, "The Site of Memory," *Out There: Marginalization and Contemporary Cultures*, eds., Russell Ferguson et. al. (New York: New Museum of Contemporary Art, and Cambridge: MIT Press, 1990), p. 302. I also agree with Minh-ha, however, when she points out, "If the act of unveiling has a liberating potential, so does the act of veiling. It all depends on the context in which such an act is carried out, or more precisely, on how and where women see dominance" (Minh-ha, op. cit., p. 372).

38. Brant, p. 17.

39. Morrison, op. cit.

40. Rigoberta Menchú, *1492–1992: la interminable conquista*, ed. Heinz Dieterich Steffan (Mexico, D. F.: Joaquín Moritz/Editorial Planeta, 1990), p. 292. The translations to these two sections of Menchú's poem are mine.

41. Ibid.

42. Harlan, p. 9.

43. bell hooks, *Talking Back: thinking feminist, thinking black* (Boston: South End Press, 1989), p. 51.

44. Martin and Mohanty, p. 193.

45. Ibid., p. 196.

46. Christian, p. 36.

47. Harjo, p. 9.

The Trick Is Going Home: Secular Spiritualism in Native American Women's Literature

CAROLYN DUNN

Literature is one facet of a culture. The significance of a literature can be best understood in terms of the culture from which it springs and the purpose of the literature is clear only when the reader understands and accepts the assumptions on which the literature is based. A person who was raised in a given culture has no problem seeing the relevance, the level of complexity, or the symbolic significance of that culture's literature. We are all from early childhood familiar with the assumptions that underlie our own culture and its literature and art. Intelligent analysis becomes a matter of identifying smaller assumptions peculiar to the locale, idiom, and psyche of the writer.

—PAULA GUNN ALLEN, *THE SACRED HOOP*

American Indian history and culture remain a footnote in history to many resident aliens of this country who are of European non–American Indian descent. *Resident aliens*, a term favored by the majority regarding persons who have immigrated here from elsewhere, is a phrase that should be used self-reflexively by the powers that be in this country—but sadly it is not—since the descendants of the original resident aliens have seized power here from its original inhabitants and continue to misappropriate history, culture, and political power from the continent's aboriginal inhabitants. In literary and scholarly circles, this misappropriation continues. Literary critics, with few notable exceptions, have virtually ignored the importance and value of American Indian literature in contemporary canonical American works. For that matter, in the larger scope of things, American Indian history and culture remain a footnote in history to many Americans. How can we be identified as sovereign nations or distinct peoples with our own history, our own art, our own music, and our own spiritual practices if the larger society still believes we ceased to exist after Wounded Knee over one hundred years ago? Commentator and columnist Andy Rooney so eloquently stated in his newspaper column six years ago that (I'm paraphrasing here) there is no great Indian literature, no great art, unless you consider a few totem poles worthy of artistic note. Our fight to gain acceptance, Pulitzer Prizes and National Book Awards notwithstanding, within the field of canonical literature seems trivial compared with the struggles Indian people face daily: the right to practice traditional religions, the right to wear hair long due to religious practices, access to traditional homelands integral in our spiritual and social practices, access to quality health care and prevention programs, poverty, alcoholism, suicide, and day-to-day matters that some members of society take for granted.

Stories traditionally were handed down in Native life to be used as teaching tools among tribal societies. Creation myths and rituals were taught through vast oral traditions that kept culture alive and vibrant, generation to generation. Perhaps in looking to some of these stories we, as Native peoples, can form our own aesthetic, our own canon that informs and signifies that which is truly unique about our cultures. Perhaps, in forming our own literary criticism, our own anthropological studies, our own religious institutes, we can heal the vast schisms that seek to threaten our families, our communities, our tribes, our nations. Perhaps works such as this anthology are the first steps to define ourselves on our own terms, and those of us struggling in academia can create a methodology for contextualizing our aesthetic.

In *The Sacred Hoop*, Laguna Pueblo scholar Paula Gunn Allen notes that American Indian literature is classified in generic culture- and language-specific terms by most Anglo- and Euro-American critics.[1] Applying a Western template to literature based firmly in non-Western traditions steals the work's meanings, recasts it, and in a word, colonizes it. While Western American literature is entirely secular, modern American Indian literature, particularly that of American Indian women, is firmly based in Native spiritualism.

After much thought and discussion on alternative forms of criticism, especially within my own work in regard to American Indian literature, I feel it is necessary to address spiritualism and myth in American Indian literature, especially the presence of archetypal tribal spirits in American Indian women's writing. Chickasaw writer and poet Linda Hogan describes the presence of such spirits in her work:

> As my interest in literature increased, I realized I had also been given a background in oral literature from my father's family. I use this. It has strengthened my imagination. I find that my ideas and even my work arrangement derive from that oral source. It is sometimes as though I hear those voices when I am in the process of writing.[2]

It is important to note that in the Indian world, there is no division between the sacred world of spirits, deities, myth, ritual, and cosmology and the secular world of political structure, economics, family life, and personal life. Our religion, our culture, and our traditions are seamlessly woven together and cannot be separated. Our religions are part of our social lives, and our social lives are connected to our spirituality. In this regard, ethnobotanist Dr. Wade Davis, author of *The Serpent and the Rainbow* and *Passage of Darkness*, speaking at a pharmaceutical conference in Germany, notes:[3]

> For the people of these societies, there is no rigid separation of the sacred and the secular. Every act of the healer becomes the prayer of the entire community, every ritual a form of collective preventative medicine.

The fluidity of boundaries Davis comments on is echoed in the words of Gregory O'Rourke, a young man from Northern California deeply rooted in his Yurok spiritual traditions. I asked Greg about the state of mind of both participants and spectators in the healing Brush Dance traditions of the Northern California coastal Indian communities:

> The spectators are quiet between songs out of respect for the singers and dancers, as well as for the healing ceremony itself. When the dancers and singers are directing our thoughts toward the health and well-being of the baby the dance is for, then the community prays along with us, until all the prayers become one and are focused directly upon the child.[4]

Davis points out that there are aspects of politics and familial structure in tribal societies that are directly related to the sacred world through ritual prayer and storytelling, shamanistic healing, and re-creations of certain tribal myths pertinent not only to the individual but to the entire society as well. Gunn Allen calls this process, or worldview, "tribal aesthetics"—a view echoed by Greg O'Rourke in regard to the Yurok Brush Dance. According to Gunn Allen,

> The aesthetic imperative requires that new experiences be woven into existing traditions in order for personal experience to be transmuted into communal experience.[5]

John (Fire) Lame Deer, in his narrative recorded by Richard Erdoes, explains further the idea of the sacred and the secular, void of divisions:

> These things are sacred. Looking at that pot full of good soup, I am thinking how, in this simple manner, Wakan Tanka takes care of me. We Sioux spend a lot of time thinking about everyday things, which in our mind are mixed up with the spiritual. We see in the world around us many symbols that teach us the meaning of life. . . . We Indians live in a world where the spiritual and the commonplace are one.[6]

Tribal aesthetics renders in structural and transcendent form the commonly held reality by a group of people: a community is a group that shares a common reality.

To the tribal societies and community members, spirits simply exist, and there is no way to articulate the presence of these spirits using scientific reasoning or theory. These spirits not only exist, they are also seen as kin—relatives to all. Inanimate objects such as a rock, a tree, or a cloud are all seen as relatives. The chemical or scientific composition of these objects is not important, but the relationship of these objects to the natural living world is. It is difficult, then, for literary critics, especially those of Indian blood, to explore the possibilities of an Indian literary criticism that excludes the presence of these spirits, a presence acknowledged and alive in the work of writers today. While Native myths and legends have been trivialized, seen as "pagan" or "childlike"[7] or as part of the new mysticism currently sweeping the New Age movement, or given one-dimensional characteristics as portrayed in the film and book *Dances with Wolves*, they are as viable and vital to our literary production as to our lives. The modern world has been divided between the sacred and the secular, and into this division fall the myths and legends and rituals of Native peoples all over the world. Our myths, in the world of Western empiricism and logical positivism, are viewed as falsehoods, trivialities, quaint curiosities. The Western world seeks to destroy its own myths and those of indigenous cultures because the Western tendency to secularize requires the separation of the "ordinary" from the "extraordinary," the sacred from the description of reality, the intellect from the emotion. We, as tribal peoples viewing the world from an aesthetically different viewpoint, have been unable to see our myths and traditions as truth in the scientific world of Western literary criticism.

In his book *Elements of Creation Myth*, author R. J. Stewart discusses the Western tendency to negate spiritualism with science:

> This urge to reduce the power of a mystery by labeling it, by filing it into a little box assembled from a dogmatic or pre-contrived system, is one of the most dangerous and inherently weakening or disabling aspects of Western culture.[8]

While Euro-Americans have decidedly divided both their own and others' worlds into the sacred and the secular, they have also categorized Indians; in turn, Western literary critics have categorized Indian literature.

Kenneth Lincoln, in *Indi'n Humor*, draws attention to this mode of classification:

> The American Indian, to recapitulate, seems mythically our fresh origin in the new world: a romantic paradox that images ancient, beginnings mythopoetically new, Adam and the fallen angel superimposed on Caliban.[9]

So we have been doubly reclassified, reconceptualized. It is time to strip off these alien classifications and develop a critical approach that can illuminate our literature, both oral and written, in which the presence of spirits is acknowledged, welcomed, and accepted within the parameters of everyday life. I suggest an approach I call "secular spiritualism": a discussion on how the beings of the spirit world inhabit the writer's consciousness and manifest themselves in the writer's work.

American Indian writers are at the crossroads, the juncture of these two worlds; and at that crossroads, lines become blurred and no longer distinct. The spirit world pervades the physical world; in that rock, tree, or cloud there exists a presence, definable not by science but as a physical, literal being who exists within the framework of a tribal society. The writer, or storyteller, then becomes the mystic who can see into both worlds and report on the activities in the boundaries, record them, shape them, and point to a meaning, a significance that transcends the petty mundanities of secular preoccupations. The tribal community understands that spirit is part of the community, understands that spirit is part of the world, in both its spiritual and physical dimensions. Things may not appear extraordinary, but people and things are healed when the spirit world is approached correctly—that is, in a very ordinary, commonplace manner. Sacred and secular are seen as intertwined, woven, and laced together with great care and purpose, great respect for life and death, and an understanding that goes beyond mysticism as seen by modern Western society: spirits simply exist.

There is indeed an acknowledged spiritual presence in American Indian poetry and prose. The concept of tribal consciousness[10] becomes important while studying spiritualism and myth in American Indian literature, and the concept of tribal aesthetics, as defined by Gunn Allen in *Spider Woman's Granddaughters*, shows the reader and critic alike the collective vision of Indian peoples.

The Western Euro-American critic first must be aware of the tribal concept of aesthetics when discussing American Indian literature. What motivates the Indian writer is not the sense of self and individuality but working for goals that are common within the community. It is a shared consciousness, working for the whole of the community rather than the whole of the self. Analytical work has been done on the trickster figure in American Indian mythology. This is where Carl Gustav Jung's ideas of tribal consciousness combined with Gunn Allen's concept of tribal aesthetics becomes important in the research of this article. In his essay "The Trickster," from *Four Archetypes*, Jung discusses tribal consciousness:

> It is a personification of traits of a character which are sometimes worse and sometimes better than those the ego personality possesses. A collective personification like the Trickster is a product of an aggregate of individuals as something known to him, which would not be the case if it were just an individual outgrowth.[11]

Jung's work, like Gunn Allen's, focuses on tribal beliefs, which she sees as of value to the community as a whole rather than to the individual as an isolate entity. Gunn

Allen writes in her introduction to *Spider Woman's Granddaughters*, "The aesthetic imperative requires that new experiences be woven into existing traditions in order for personal experience to be transmuted into communal experience, that is, so we can understand how today's events harmonize within the communal experience. . . . We use aesthetics to make our lives whole, to explain ourselves to each other, to see where we fit into the scheme of things (*Spider Woman's Granddaughters*, 7).

Following our own aesthetic becomes vital when looking to our own traditional cultures for illumination and contextualization of our own canon. Our world shifts between the sacred and the secular effortlessly yet without ease; in this duality of life, we become the trickster figure within our own context.

Trickster Aspects in American Indian Literature

Henry Louis Gates's contribution to the study of the trickster figure and the mythological return to that trickster in *The Signifying Monkey* is impressive and useful for understanding tribal aesthetics and aspects of the trickster figure in American Indian mythology and sacred stories, although Esu Elegbara/Legba is a tribal figure.[12] Building on Gates's critical example and using his culture-specific method, we can look at the pan-Indian tribal trickster figure Coyote, here Coyotesse[13] when speaking of American Indian women, as a way to an American Indian literary criticism. We can discuss Coyotesse as trickster, as spirit, as re-integration of tribal concepts, and using Jung's trickster essays, as a precedent in the study of the collective (tribal) spirit presence in American Indian women's literature.

While Gates uses Esu/Legba as the central trickster figure or spirit at the crossroads in the African American cultural psyche, Coyote can be the archetypal—in Jungian terms—trickster in American Indian consciousness.

In *Indi'n Humor*, Kenneth Lincoln gives extensive biographical information on just who Coyote/Coyotesse is:

> Coyote is a tricky personage—half creator, half fool; he (or she in some versions) is renowned for greediness and salaciousness. . . . S/he is a marginal figure who scavenges the leftovers and here s/he somehow assembles the edges toward the tribal center. Indeed at times the Trickster serves as the Comic Hero or the Culture Bearer, bringing fire or foodstuffs or survival skills. . . . S/he's all too human . . . animal at his [sic] best, godlike in dreams."[14]

If we are to discuss the trickster-like qualities of the Indian author, then it should begin here, at the juncture where Lincoln stands.

Lincoln writes that Coyote Old Man is also Coyote Old Woman: "She has been slighted, if not slurred, in the mythmaking of America, and now she snaps back as a bushy tailed, non-conformist trickster Indian feminist" (165). Yet we must note that feminism is not an ethnic woman's concept but an Anglo middle-class woman's struggle. Indian women's power comes from and through home and hearth, our place in the natural world—its ritual center; its continuance of existence, rebirth, and survival—not in reaction to any presumed powerlessness. In returning to the storytelling traditions, we affirm our ancient place with our words and provide in them our continued existence, simply by telling the traditional stories. We therefore become tricksters at the crossroads—and in so doing evoke the presence of the spirits alive around us. We become Coyotesse, and, as Leslie Silko says, simply by telling the stories, we resist. "In contradistinction," Lincoln says on page 170 of *Indi'n Humor*, "to Anglo feminists, she was never without gender power, essential tribal work, self definition, an equal vote (though this varied from tribe to tribe), or generally the physical and cultural respect of the other sex."

In her story "Yellow Woman," Silko embodies many characteristics of the author as trickster, or Coyotesse: the use of tribal consciousness, with the application of the modern Yellow Woman story to the traditional tribal concepts and values (Yellow Woman/Evil Katsina stories), and the act of retelling the story in the face of Anglo- or Euro-American onslaught. In the invoking of the spirit Evil Katsina as the tall Navajo Silva and giving the narrator's identity as "Yellow Woman," Silko demonstrates how an Indian literary work is grounded firmly within a spiritual tradition. In this modern story, Silko's Yellow Woman asks Silva if he is indeed Evil Katsina:

> "But I only said that you were him and that I was Yellow Woman—but I'm not really her—I have my own name and I come from the pueblo on the other side of the mesa. Your name is Silva and you are a stranger I met by the river yesterday afternoon."
>
> He laughed softly. "What happened yesterday has nothing to do with what you will do today, Yellow Woman."
>
> "I know—that's what I'm saying—the old stories about the ka'tsina (kachina) spirit and Yellow Woman can't mean us."[15]

Silko invokes the presence of the traditional Yellow Woman spirit several times in her story. In looking at the traditional Yellow Woman stories, especially Gunn Allen's translation/adaptation of "Whirlwind Man Steals Yellow Woman" (*SWG*, 187), we can see how Silko ties a modern love story to Laguna consciousness. As in the old stories, Silva spirits the narrator away. Whenever any woman within the community disappears, Silko suggests that the woman was spirited away by the mountain spirit, like Silko's Yellow Woman and Gunn Allen's Irriaku:

> Brought her up when some woman was missing for a while. Said she ran off with a Navajo, or maybe a mountain spirit, like Kochinennako.[16]

The presence of the "Navajo" Silva in Silko's story evokes Evil Katsina/Sun/Whirlwind Man. Silva himself knows the Yellow Woman stories, and it is implied by Silko in her story (not just inferred but believed and accepted—of course that implies the sacred and the ordinary are perceived as a seamless whole[17]) that Silva really is Evil Katsina, the mountain spirit:

> "I'm leaving."
> He smiled now, eyes still closed. "You are coming with me, remember?" He sat back up now, with his bare dark chest and belly in the sun.
> "Where?"
> "To my place."[18]

In Silva's nonresponse to Yellow Woman's question, Yellow Woman truly knows she has stepped into the story. Has she become the traditional Irriaku of the old stories, she wonders? She is confused because "she is from out of time past and I live now and I've been to school and there are highways and pick up trucks that Yellow Woman never saw" (191).

It is Yellow Woman's connection within a tribal framework or consciousness that motivates her in the contemporary version of the story. The part of her that lives in the modern world, that went to school and travels the highways in pickup trucks refuses to believe their story is also hers:

> "You must be a Navajo."
> Silva shook his head gently. "Little Yellow Woman, you never give up, do you? I have told you who I am. The Navajo people know me too."

And later,

> "You don't understand, do you, little Yellow Woman? You will do what I want."[19]

But Yellow Woman knows the stories, the connection between Irriaku and the spirit of the mountains. Yellow Woman has heard the stories all her life and so wonders if she is the story. She knows the one person who would understand her predicament is her grandpa, who long since has passed:

> "But if Grandpa weren't dead he'd tell them what happened—he would laugh and say, 'stolen by a ka'tsina, a mountain spirit. She'll come home—they usually do.'"[20]

And Yellow Woman does go back, after she acknowledges the spirit power in Silva: "I looked at Silva and for an instant there was something ancient and very dark—something I could feel in my stomach—in his eyes" (196).

Silko's narrator wonders, early on in the story, if the Yellow Woman of the traditional stories had another name she was known by to her children and family and husband (191). By the time the white rancher arrives, Yellow Woman accepts her own belief in the story she is part of:

"And I told myself, because I believe it, he will come back sometime and be waiting by the river," . . . and "I decided to tell them some Navajo had kidnapped me, but I was sorry old Grandpa wasn't alive to hear my story, because it was the Yellow Woman stories he liked to tell best." (197)

Silko as Coyotesse

Of course, Silko's story has elements that will have Western feminists up in arms, most notably the captivity elements and the decidedly cultural female act of Yellow Woman's cooking after her "abduction." But such objectives are most likely to be confused by non-Indian academics. Some women of color feel excluded by the modern Western feminist renaissance. While modern middle-class academic feminists try to regather and remember the power they once had, we women of color never forgot our power. Kenneth Lincoln talks extensively of the female role in some Indian nations in the "Feminist Indi'ns" chapter from *Indi'n Humor*. Citing Mary (Brave Bird) Crow Dog in her autobiography *Lakota Woman*, Lincoln notes that

> a volunteer white nurse berates Indian women on 'feminist' grounds but Mary answers the war at hand must be fought, then the warrior's machismo can be deconditioned—for the moment every effort counts under fire, and the pecking order is irrelevant. 'We told her that her kind of women's lib was a white, middle class thing and at this critical stage we had other priorities. Once our men had gotten their balls back, we might start arguing with them about who would do the dishes.' The old gender loyalties bond her with the tribe as a whole, beyond new social definitions, and she is renamed *Ohitika Win* or Brave Woman after the siege.[21]

To the Indian woman, Silko's story and the traditional Cochiti and Laguna Pueblo stories are not what could be considered as traditional Western captivity narratives but rather as the sacred stories detailing the relation of the tribe to the lands and the sacred gifts of corn to the people—the Yellow Women or Irriaku. What may be seen as antifeminist in regard to the content of Silko's story by some in the white world is irrelevant to its tribally derived meaning. When discussing a tribal story, we must look at the context of tribal aesthetics rather than the dominant worldview and aesthetics.

In Lincoln's terms, Silko, as trickster, is the scavenger who turns the leftovers of a culture of storytelling, long abused by many years of Anglo- and Euro-American domination, into a meal that returns to the tribal center. In so doing, her gender role is clear. Coyotesse, that "bushy tailed, non-conformist Indian feminist," wears many hats and is called many names—Gunn Allen, Silko, Harjo, Hogan, Erdrich, Walters, TallMountain—but she still remains the storyteller and pieces the tribe together again, given her power and vision of the stories collected at the center of the tribal world.

"Home for the Coyotesse involves placing herself in collaboration with her origins," Lincoln writes.[22] Silko's "Yellow Woman" places Silko, as Coyotesse, at home. She is in "collaboration with her origins"—the retelling of an Irriaku story is itself an affirmation of the storytelling tribal traditions of the Laguna Pueblo people. Silko's Coyotesse quest takes us back to the traditional Pueblo land, to the connection of Yellow Woman (the Irriaku)—yellow ears of corn to the Laguna people. The Irriaku are a gift to the people; and once the Irriaku have been stolen by Evil Katsina, the people lose their connection to Iyetiku, their connection to the divine. The people and the land are no longer one because once the corn is gone, there can be no longer a sacred connection between people, land, and goddess.

To make a further connection to the archetypal Coyotesse and the writer or storyteller, we must further examine aspects of the Coyotesse, or trickster character. In the male form, Coyote, the trickster is many things to many tribes. To the Pueblo, Coyote tales are spun to teach the Pueblo children correct forms of behavior; thus Coyote is oriented toward a negative aspect of Pueblo reality and is the antithesis of the ideal Pueblo character. "He mediates between the way of the tribe and the way of the unrestricted ego."[23] Jarold Ramsey, in *Reading the Fire*, further explores Coyote's identity:

> Enter the Trickster as mediator. His outrageous sexual antics, his thorough selfishness, his general irresponsibility, his polymorphous dedication to the perverse in the stories that must have allowed the "good citizens" of the tribe to affirm the system of prohibitions and punishments . . . at the same time they could vicariously delight and find release in his irresponsible individualism.[24]

Gender roles become blurred when speaking of Coyote/Coyotesse, especially in the Laguna society where gender roles are not those of the Western majority. Confusion enters in because of conflicts within Anglo and Laguna ways of life. Within gynocratic tribes, asserts Paula Gunn Allen,[25] males are nurturing, pacifist, and transitory; females are self-definitive, assertive, decisive, and continuous. Thus, gender roles are reversed in Pueblo society—so perhaps what Lincoln gives as "Coyote" traits are "Coyotesse" traits. The trickster is not only distinctly female in Laguna Pueblo culture, but she's male as well, blurring the definitive crossroads of gender. Thus, both Gunn Allen and Silko can not only cross over between the worlds of the divine and the mundane but also as tribal women, as Coyotesse, continue to blur the lines, Anglically speaking. The feminism in these stories is tribal: telling the story is female because it centers upon tribal tradition—the gynocratic Pueblo tradition. The Yellow Woman in Silko's story has no choice but to return to her family, just as the Yellow Woman of the traditional stories must return to her people. She is a gift of that tribe, bringing sacred knowledge from the wilderness back to the people, strengthening the connection between Iyetiku and her people. Silko also has no choice but to return to the tribal traditions because she is a storyteller, and as that storyteller, she is inexorably tied to the storytelling traditions of her people. The acts of Coyotesse, the storyteller in a Laguna Pueblo context, then, are distinctly female: self-definitive, assertive, decisive, continuous.

According to the late Ernest G. Wolfe Jr., in his paper "Coyote: A Contrary Character," one of Coyote's aspects is representative of the sinister and destructive side of Pueblo life. "He roams alone in the dark; the time for an evil person begins at sundown. Called an ass barker by the Hopi, his howling near a village portends evil events to come. . . . his self-deceptive and credulous nature usually leads to destruction."[26] However, the sinister and destructive side of life may be considered the knowledge the landscape has to offer. As Coyote/Coyotesse walks that fine line between the spirit world and the secular world, the land embodies several spirit beings, Evil Katsina being one of them, who have knowledge to offer the people as well. In the traditional stories, Yellow Woman is abducted by Evil Katsina and is taken outside of the community to the wilderness beyond. There, she is given gifts of knowledge that she brings back to the people, thus cementing the relationship once again between land, people, and deity. According to Patricia Clark Smith in her essay "Earthly Relations, Carnal Knowledge" in the anthology *The Desert Is No Lady*,

> Southwestern Indian cultures do not approach wilderness as something to be either raped or domesticated. . . . in both traditional and contemporary literature wilderness often appears not as a mere landscape-backdrop but as a spirit being with a clearly sexual aura.[27]

In the Silko retelling of the Yellow Woman stories, Silva represents the land, embodied in the river that flows past on the mountain and in the translation of his name (*silva* means "river;" and even the Latin derivative *sylvan*, meaning woods). To the Pueblos, Navajos embody aspects of the wilderness, freedom, the sense of wandering and wilderness. The Navajos are perceived as "beautiful and free."[28] Silva is the wilderness: beautiful, nonpredictable, the perfect metaphor of the spirit in the real world. The modern Yellow Woman takes some aspect of knowledge back to the people upon her return: the aspect that the spirits do exist and the stories of the people and the land continue; the stories never end.

"The human protagonists," Smith goes on to state, "usually engage willingly in literal sexual intercourse with the spirits. . . . this act brings the land's power, spirit, and fecundity in touch with their own and so ultimately yields benefit for their own people."[29] Sexuality is a celebration of life and the continuous act of life, and in the world where there is no division between the sacred and the secular, spirits, land, people, and Iyetiku are one. Procreation brings life; and the tribal traditions and rituals are passed on through generations. Thus sexuality becomes survival, interwoven within the fabric of all things at the tribal center. Silko, as the storyteller, as Coyotesse, embodies the spirit who translates the power of the land to the people. It is Coyotesse who must venture into the darkness to bring back the knowledge to the tribe. These are shaky crossroads Coyotesse walks, as the spirit world is treacherous, but the knowledge gained and brought back will benefit the tribe, and survival in the face of devastation becomes the knowledge received in these modern times. "The coming together of a person and spirit may lead to magical children," Smith tells us, "the discovery of rich sources of food or water, or the gift of a specific ceremony."[30] Silko, again as Coyotesse, is telling the story and in so doing gives birth to the text as a magical child, metaphorically speaking; the story gives credence to ceremony and ritual (stories are part of the larger ritual); stories are sources of spiritual sustenance; and the child is Coyotesse's story, given from an encounter with the spirit world. The storyteller is Coyotesse, creatrix and mother, who through ritual and ceremony with the land gives birth to an ongoing dialogue between Iyetiku, the tribe, and the spirit world.

What then is the trick Coyotesse possesses? What is her function in society, and as the storyteller, what must she do to maintain her tribal role? Lincoln points out that Coyote is infinitely regenerative—a possessor of wisdom and ironic wit.[31] Coyote is the Yurok man who lives high on a hill in a big white house that resembles *the* White House; Coyotesse is the Laguna Pueblo woman storyteller in academia who receives recognition and accolades for her critical theoretical approach to modern literature—modern American Indian literature—in a university system that refuses to recognize the very aspect of tribal aesthetic literature the storyteller embodies. Yet she continues to do what she does best: telling stories. As the storyteller must go into the wilderness and bring back a story, she reforms it, gives it life, and regenerates the spiritual life of the people. She takes a story from the traditions, the spiritual center, and reforms it to suit a modern context and a modern tribe. Coyotesse negotiates the borders between the spirit world and the mundane world, forms a story, and must bring it back to the tribe in a nonmalevolent manner. She must face the wilderness and not only return a whole tribe to its traditions but also trick the nontribal world into her world as well. She must trick the Western world, in its division of sacred and secular, into believing that the character of Silva, the tall Navajo, is a wilderness spirit and that the modern Yellow Woman really has stepped into the story that was left behind long ago.

Whereas Coyote, to paraphrase Lincoln once again, is "infinitely regenerative—a possessor of wisdom and ironic wit," Coyotesse becomes that and much more: the weaver of stories and of life that illuminates tribal life, urban life, and signifies those aspects of our lives by telling the stories she brings back from the wilderness to the tribal center. It is Coyotesse's humor ("ironic wit") that allows her to be a signifier. By reworking the language and calling it her own, she has stolen from the language what the language had stolen from her: her tribal identity. It is Coyotesse's own multiplicitous nature that ties this all together. Coyotesse is a feminist whether she accepts that label or not: by writing about women's experiences she takes on the cause. Her reworking of language makes her the trickster. She steals back the fire, the fire being language, and makes it her—the tribe's—own. Because she walks tenuously between the spirit world and the ordinary world, she transcends both sacred and secular, becoming *both* sacred and secular.

Sacred spiritualism is the idea that Coyotesse has a "trick" up her sleeve. Her tricks are twofold. As Coyotesse, the storyteller (author as trickster), she negotiates borders and brings back stories from the wilderness to the tribes and provides sustenance and survival. In providing that sustenance and survival, Coyotesse performs a gender role that is clearly defined. That sustenance is cultural survival. That language is irony. That Coyotesse's regenerative power is her trick. That Coyotesse takes the language of colonization and makes it her own. That survival is humor. That survival is home. That survival is Coyotesse embodied in the soul of the storyteller.

Notes

1. Paula Gunn Allen, *The Sacred Hoop: Recovering the Feminine in American Indian Traditions*, 2nd ed. (Boston: Beacon Press, 1992), p. 54.

2. Interview with Linda Hogan, 1985, conducted and transcribed by Laura Coltelli, *Winged Words: American Indian Writers Speak* (Lincoln: University of Nebraska Press, 1990), p. 71.

3. *Shaman's Drum*, Spring 1991.

4. Personal interview with Gregory O'Rourke, July 3, 1991. The Brush Dance is a healing ceremony given for an ill child, be it physical or emotional illness, in which the prayers of the dancers, singers, and medicine woman combine with the prayers of the spectators and community members to heal illness. This ceremonial ritual is practiced by the Yurok, Hupa, Karok, Tolowa, and Klamath Indians of Northern California.

5. Paula Gunn Allen, ed., *Spider Woman's Granddaughters* (Boston: Beacon Press, 1989), p. 7.

6. Richard Erdoes, *Lame Deer, Seeker of Visions* (New York: Simon & Schuster, 1972), p. 86.

7. Gunn Allen, *Sacred Hoop*, p. 127.

8. R. J. Stewart, *Elements of Creation Myth* (Longmead, UK: Element Books, 1989).

9. Kenneth Lincoln, *Indi'n Humor* (Oxford, UK: Oxford University Press, 1993), p. 113.

10. Carl Gustav Jung, *Four Archetypes: Mother, Rebirth, Spirit, Trickster (from Archetypes and the Collective Unconscious)* (Bollingen Series, Princeton, NJ: Princeton University Press, 1986).

11. Jung, *Four Archetypes*, pp. 4–5.

12. Henry Louis Gates, *The Signifying Monkey* (Oxford, UK: Oxford University Press, 1988).

13. The term *Coyotesse* is applied as a feminine derivative of *coyote*. Ken Lincoln gives an Italian reading to the origin of the actual word *coyotesse*; in my opinion the word is French

in origin, the meaning remains the same as a feminization of the word *coyote*. However, Gunn Allen asserts that *coyotesse* is a feminine derivative of the original Aztec *coyotl*.

14. Kenneth Lincoln, *Indi'n Humor* (Oxford, UK: Oxford University Press, 1993), pp. 176–78.

15. Leslie Marmon Silko, "Yellow Woman," in *Spider Woman's Granddaughters*, ed. Paula Gunn Allen (Boston: Beacon Press, 1989), p. 190.

16. Paula Gunn Allen, "Whirlwind Man Steals Yellow Woman," in *Spider Woman's Granddaughters*, ed. Paula Gunn Allen (Boston: Beacon Press, 1989), p. 187.

17. Gunn Allen, *Spider Woman's Granddaughters*, introduction.

18. Gunn Allen, *Spider Woman's Granddaughters*, p. 190.

19. Gunn Allen, *Spider Woman's Granddaughters*, p. 191.

20. Gunn Allen, *Spider Woman's Granddaughters*, p. 193.

21. Lincoln, *Indi'n Humor*, p. 166; Mary Brave Bird Crow Dog with Richard Erdoes, *Lakota Woman* (New York: Grove Press, 1990), p. 137–38.

22. Lincoln, *Indi'n Humor*.

23. Ernest G. Wolfe Jr., "Coyote: A Contrary Character" (Unpublished paper, Department of Anthropology, UCLA, 1990), p. 11.

24. Jarold Ramsey, *Reading the Fire* (Lincoln: University of Nebraska Press, 1983), p. 32.

25. Gunn Allen, *Sacred Hoop*, pp. 2, 82

26. Wolfe citing Ekkehart, "Coyote," p. 8.

27. Patricia Clark Smith, "Earthly Relations, Carnal Knowledge," in *The Desert Is No Lady*, ed. Vera Norwood and Janice Monk (New Haven: Yale University Press, 1987), p. 178.

28. Interview with Paula Gunn Allen, Seal Beach, California, 22 October 1991. Gunn Allen related that as children Lagunas are taught the mystery and allure of the Navajo. She remembers the first time she ever saw a Navajo in her father's store in Cubero, New Mexico, and saying, "I want him to take me with him. Oh, please, can I go into the wilds with you?" She went on to say, "Identifying Silva as a Navajo was a perfect metaphor within Leslie's story."

29. Smith, "Earthly Relations," p. 178

30. Smith, "Earthly Relations," p. 178

31. Lincoln, *Indi'n Humor*, p. 114.

Dildos, Hummingbirds and Driving Her Crazy: Searching for American Indian Women's Love Poetry and Erotics

DEBORAH A. MIRANDA

In University course descriptions one finds classes about American Indian Literature in varying degrees, depending on the institution, faculty, and location. To find a course on American Indian women's writing is truly difficult, and to find one on Native women's poetry even more extraordinary (unless, as I have, you teach it yourself). Still, you would think that given the interdisciplinary trend that academia is currently experiencing, one would run across Native women writers in other departments. Certainly when I enrolled in a course at the University of Washington—*Women's Love Poetry and Erotics*—I had reason to hope that some Native women writers would be included in the course readings and/or discussions. After all, this was Seattle, a ferry ride away from one of the most prolific, infamous and famous writers of erotica, Chrystos![1]

Unfortunately, the syllabus did not include any women of color at all; my instructor had never heard of Chrystos or Joy Harjo, another excellent writer of sensuous love poetry. My professor did suggest that I bring in some samples of Native women's love poetry and erotics, and I accepted eagerly. "Real, ripe, ripping erotica" was my instructor's criteria. Well, I had volumes of the stuff at home. Alas, I was then told, the difficulty was not that this material did not exist, but that critical treatments of these women's work were non-existent. This was a serious problem, yes; but why did it mean that we, as a class, could not discuss Chrystos or Harjo? Why, without "proper documentation," did these two poets drop off the love poetry map?

Three subsequent years of searching revealed the extent of this invisibility. Well-written texts by smart women academics carry no articles, essays or critical treatments of Native women's love poetry or erotics. Take my primary piece of evidence, *Stealing the Language: The Emergence of Women's Poetry* in America by Alicia Ostriker. This book contains absolutely no reference to any American Indian woman writer.[2] Published in 1986 by Beacon Press, Ostriker's otherwise adequate and sometimes even insightful text includes critical work about white, Black, Chicana and Asian American women writers, as well as the works of the lesbian community; there is a brief examination of early poetics (categorized as '1650–1960'), as well as sections on nature writing, anger, revisionist mythology, and women's erotics. But even in the "nature" section—where lost Indian writers are usually relegated—there are no references to any nature-loving Indians. More recent analyses of American women's poetry exist, but they are no better; I use this one in part because of the influential nature of its publication, and because it has become a template of exclusion which subsequent analyses have perpetuated.[3]

Curious, and not yet completely conscious of such a systematic exclusion, I looked at my personal collection of Native women's poetry, checking publication dates. Perhaps, I thought, this text was published prior to the great American Indian 'Renaissance' (the name given to a group of American Indian authors who became active in the late 1960's and grew in importance during the 1970's).[4] However, books that had been published in or prior to 1985, the year before Ostriker's text came out, include *Mohawk Trail* by Beth Brant (1985), *Burning the Fields* by Anita Endrezze (1983), *That's What She Said: Contemporary Fiction and Poetry by Native American Women*, ed. by Rayna Green (1983), *She Had Some Horses* by Joy Harjo (1983), *What Moon Drove Me to This* by Harjo (1979), *Seeing Through the Sun* by Linda Hogan (1985), *The Halfbreed Chronicles* by Wendy Rose (1985), *Hopi Roadrunner Dancing* by Rose (1974), *Lost Copper* by Rose (1980), *Storyteller* by Leslie Marmon Silko (1981), *Star Quilt* by Roberta Hill Whiteman (1984).[5] Native women also had substantial presence in the following American Indian anthologies (in no particular order): *The Remembered Earth: An Anthology of Contemporary Native American Literature* ed. by Geary Hobson (1978), *Voices of the Rainbow: Contemporary Poetry by American Indians* (1974) ed. by Kenneth Rosen, *Carriers of the Dream Wheel: Contemporary Native American Poetry* ed. by Duane Niatum (1975), *Coming to Power; Eleven Contemporary American Indian Poets* ed. by Dick Lourie (1974), *The First Skin Around Me: Contemporary American Tribal Poetry* ed. by James L. White (1976), *Songs From this Earth on Turtle's Back: Contemporary American Indian Poetry* ed. by Joseph Bruchac (1983).[6]

It cannot be said, then, that Ostriker had no materials from which to draw examples of American Indian poetry; in fact, many of these writings were readily available due to the "green Indian" or "Pocahontas" effects of the 70's and 80's; i.e., the phenomenon by which Americans see Indians as the first ecologists, or romanticized Indian Princesses. Significantly, a remarkable collection edited by Marge Piercy, *Early Ripening: American Women's Poetry Now* (1987) bucked the exclusionary trend by publishing thirteen poems by five Native American women, including less anthologized pieces by Beth Brant and Roberta Hill Whiteman.[7] The amount of energy that a serious scholar of American poetry would have to invest in *missing* these Native women authors and their publications must be tremendous. In my use of Ostriker's text as an example of how American Indian women's poetry has been ignored or invisibilized in American poetry discourse, then, I am not creating a straw critic but examining a truly representative piece of American literary criticism that has contributed to a great silencing. Marilyn Frye uses a brilliant metaphor to make this same point. She writes,

> Consider a birdcage. If you look very closely at just one wire in the cage, you cannot see the other wires . . . you could not see why a bird would have trouble going past the wires to get anywhere . . . it is only when you step back, stop looking at the wires one by one, microscopically, and take a macroscopic view of the whole cage, that you can see why the bird does not go anywhere . . . [then] it is perfectly obvious that the bird is surrounded by a network of systematically related barriers, no one of which would be the least hindrance to its flight, but which, by their relations to each other, are as confining as the solid walls of a dungeon.[8]

Being excluded or ignored in one or two collections of critical discourse about women's poetry functions like one or two slender bars of steel; in and of themselves the exclusions do not construct a constraining cage around Native women's poetry. But the systematic, consistent, tacitly approved practice of exclusion in the field of literary criticism works to weld those individual bars into the shape of a barrier that severely restricts what we can learn about Native women's poetry. While this loss is immeasurable for Native writers seeking audience, feedback, professional acknowledgment and respect, I believe the larger women's community suffers an even greater loss in talent, opportunity for connection, and a rich body of work that is virtually unknown.

It's important to note that Native women have been marginalized within our own writing communities, as well. Publishers of Native literature are like most other publishers: they choose to publish men, a proven and profitable pattern. N. Scott Momaday, Simon Ortiz, Duane Niatum, James Welch and other male American Indians gleaned what few token publication opportunities there were for many, many years. These same men—with the recent and notable addition of Sherman Alexie—still claim the lion's share of publications, particularly by larger presses such as Norton, while Native women poets continue to be published mostly by small and/or feminist presses. Gloria Bird and Joy Harjo talk about this in their anthology *Reinventing the Enemy's Language*, where the two poets also discuss the countless difficulties encountered in their ten-year effort to compile and publish an all-woman Native anthology.[9] Aside from perks like mass marketing, actual royalties, and prestige-enhanced employment, large presses often insure that a writer's works remain in press longer, are more readily available, and can be reprinted in the future. Small presses frequently close up shop, remainder an author's books, or—as is the situation currently faced by Chrystos with Press Gang—simply stop publishing, make regaining copyrights very difficult, and essentially leave a writer suddenly out of print with no recourse.[10] Anita Endrezze was "luckier"—when Making Waves (her British publisher) folded, the press allowed her to purchase all remaining copies of her book.[11] The career of any author published by small presses is precarious, and with the notable (and more recent) exceptions of Joy Harjo, Leslie Marmon Silko and novelist Susan Powers, most Indian women are published in small presses.

But there are other additional reasons why Native women's love poetry and erotics are so invisible. Stereotypes about Native women, for example, may take up all the available disk space in the American public's head, leaving no room for writers who are not either Squaw Sluts, Pocahontas, or Indian Princesses. Like minority women everywhere, Native women carry varying levels of marginalization within our identities: woman, native, poor, lesbian, disabled, reservation/urban, and so on. However, for Indian women there is the added effect of internalized colonization and of what I call Intergenerational Post-Traumatic Stress Syndrome (Eduardo Duran, a psychologist specializing in Native mental health, calls it more generically, "Post-colonial Trauma"[12]). Five hundred years of colonization and its many painful wounds result in many Native women living at basic survival-level emotional lives: we accept invisibilization as a kind of Novocaine rather than endure the constant grinding of historical traumas that directly targeted Native women's bodies and ability to express themselves (in language and literacy).

Frequently, colonizing Europeans kidnapped Native women purely for the purposes of death by rape. The rape of Native women was also considered an act of sacred duty during the Spanish colonization of Mexico and much of the American West and Southwest; the resulting mixedblood children could then be baptized as new citizens of a Nueva España.[13] Widespread European rape of Native women from First Contact onward often resulted in fatal epidemics of sexually transmitted diseases, as well as children whose mixed ancestry contributed to cultural and linguistic diminishment.[14] Later, Native girls, especially, were kidnapped or coerced into the government's Indian Boarding Schools, where they were kept forcibly for 5–10 years, and sometimes sexually abused ("If we get the girls, we get the race," was a typical rationale). As an especially hard blow, separation from parents and extended family resulted in Boarding School adult survivors who had no idea how to parent.[15] During the 1950's, 60's, and 70's, Native women on reservations and in urban Native communities were targeted for massive sterilization campaigns, resulting in generations of Indian women unable to conceive. All of this was legal. The current high levels of Fetal Alcohol Syndrome in the children of Indian women are only the latest stress that damages Indian women's creative energies at the core.

Insidious, too, is the multi-cultural shift which emphasizes including work by American Indians into pedagogical curriculums. How can publication possibly be damaging? These high school and college texts use the same Indian authors, even the same pieces, over and over. Not only are the authors and the work tokenized, but they also ultimately harm representations of American Indians through that repetitious and non-contextualized use. Often, such poems fall into one of three categories for convenient discussion: a) a generalized grief; b) "nature writing" in which the Indian "connection to the land" is highlighted; and c) "ceremony" or description of a ritual event. Thus, stereotypes about Indians are perpetuated in the education of children and young scholars, who, rather than being enlightened about Indian lives, struggles or history, are typically left unaware that a much more complex genre of American Indian literature exists, or that Indians engage in passionate, intensely intimate affairs of the heart and body which have been, somewhere, expressed in poetic, published form.[16]

In my search for the invisible American Indian erotic self, I have discovered that there are no collections of American Indian erotica in existence (although she has been collecting Native erotica writings for almost ten years, Kateri Akiwenzie-Damm, a Anishnawbekwe poet, has not been able to sell the idea to any publisher, large or small).[17] I did, however, easily uncover many anthologies and collections of erotica with various themes and audiences including Latina, Latino, African American, Korean, Asian American, Jewish, erotic sci-fi, erotic queer sci-fi, futuristic prostitution, magickal sex, surfer-sex, foot-fetishes, blow jobs, vampire sex, lesbian vampire sex, Roald Dahl fantasies, horror-sex, cybersex, Elizabethan sex, kitchen sex, gothic gay encounters, and so on. However, not one of these collections exists solely as an anthology of American Indian erotica.[18]

Many collections contain creative critical essays and articles that reflect on the erotic as it intersects with race, class, gender, culture, AIDS and/or age. The collections compiled by racial minorities, especially, take time to bear witness that they are the first, or one of the few, erotica anthologies by people outside the dominant culture, and attempt to answer that question, *why?* For my purposes here, I use examples only from anthologies by people of color, in hopes of uncovering influences that may help explicate invisibilization of Native erotics. The editors of *Erotique Noire/Black Erotica*, for example, conclude early on that,

> Black erotica has not been considered an art form and has not been the subject of serious study for a variety of reasons, some historical, some cultural. One of the legacies of slavery was the "genteel tradition," which shaped Black life and letters. Many nineteenth-century and early-twentieth century Afro-American writers and artists felt compelled to prove the moral worth and intellectual integrity of Blacks by avoiding literary representation of physical desire and sexual pleasure . . .[19]

This fear of appearing primitive or reinscribing stereotypical minority sexuality makes clear that possession of black bodies did not cease with the Emancipation Proclamation, but became a concept deeply embedded in American culture. For American Indians, the constant barrage of literary representations depicting native men as "buckskin rippers" and native women as either Squaw Sluts or Indian Princesses left very little room for any kind of acceptable expressions of personal sexuality in the few literary venues open to us. These inhibitions are echoed by other writers of color, as when Ntozake Shange writes,

> We are lost in the confusion of myths and fears of race and sex. To be a 'good' people, to be 'respectable' and 'worthy citizens,' we've had to combat absurd phantasmagoric stereotypes about our sexuality, our lusts, our lives, to the extent that we disavow our own sensuality to each other . . . so how do we speak of our desires for each other to each other in a language where our relationships to our bodies and desires lack dignity as well as nuance?[20]

Internalized racism and sexism often cause people of difference to demand perfection from themselves, to do twice the work for half the credit. As Shange notes, to be "worthy citizens" means denying or erasing a sexuality that has already been completely misrepresented by the dominant culture. Self-hatred or self-fear is often combined with a kind of erotic starvation brought about by histories specific to a community's experience, such as the frequent separation of African American families by slaveowners, or in the case of American Indians, the strict separation of boys and girls during long stints at Indian Boarding School (such distances not only changed Native courtship and coming-of-age experiences, but also inscribed a European, Christianized dogma regarding the "dirtiness" of Native bodies and sexuality in general). Russell Leong, in his forward to *On a Bed of Rice: An Asian American Erotic Feast*, points out that for decades only male Asians were allowed to immigrate to the United States, leading to a cultural, familial schism of silence about anything surrounding love or sex, including how to endure or ameliorate desire when one's wife was in another country, and interracial sex (which was grounds for arrest and/or execution in most states). Leong also writes,

> simply put, throughout this history of Western subjugations and colonization Asians were seen by whites as both threatening and desirable—the men as dangerous and threatening, and the women as sexually available and desirable. Racial and sexual depictions converged, forming a distorted lens which we— Asians and Asian Americans—were viewed by non-Asians.[21]

That distorted lens, Leong concludes, delayed or inhibited Asian American writers' explorations of sexuality and erotic life in their works until very recently.

Ray Gonzalez, editor of *Under the Pomegranate Tree*, the first major collection of Latino erotica, comments on the effects of Catholicism making eroticism taboo for many writers; he also acknowledges that most Latino (and Latina) writers are brought up "in patriarchal societies, [with] the suppression of women's art."[22] However, more significantly, Gonzalez mentions the one fact that all anthologies of minority erotica cite in common as the major obstacle to writing the erotic: the basic need to ensure bodily survival vs. the "non-essential" needs for erotic fulfillment. He writes,

> In the U.S., the political struggles of Mexican American, Puerto Rican, and Cuban writers focused on social issues such as racism, poverty, and problems in the cities . . . in order to establish a vibrant Chicano culture, the personal had to be given up so that social and political concerns could lead the way . . .[23]

Gonzalez' words are reminiscent of Leong, who writes, "The sheer energy we expended on survival and the building of our communities did not always find its way into sexuality or experiments with erotic pleasure."[24]

Each of these reasons for belated erotic acknowledgment—the need to counteract dominant cultural stereotypes about minority passion, traumatic changes in how sexuality can be expressed within one's own cultural group, and lifetimes spent living on the precarious edge of disappearing, can be applied to the lives of Indian peoples and native writing. Although getting the all-woman anthology *Reinventing the Enemy's Language* published in 1997 was a triumph for American Indian women writers, it is still jarring to realize that even here no section titled "Love Poems" exists, and that love poetry in general is absent from the collection (using the term "love poetry" very loosely, of course; I acknowledge the theory that all poetry is love poetry, but here I am referring to poems which celebrate intimate and/or erotic relationships between lovers and life-partners). Reluctantly, we could conclude that the erotic is a luxury, something which must be earned *after*, not during, a more primal struggle for physical survival; and which, in many cases, can never be earned at all. But I am reminded of Audre Lorde's essay, "Poetry Is Not a Luxury," in which Lorde exhorts women of color to live, and write, the poetry of their experiences; to not let poverty or oppression silence the poet within. Lorde writes, "if what we need to dream, to move our spirits most deeply and directly toward and through promise, is discounted as a luxury, then we give up the core—the fountain—of our power, our womanness; we give up the future of our worlds."[25] Surely, Lorde is suggesting that poetry and the erotic are not mutually exclusive but, in fact, equal parts of the same struggle toward gaining one's full life-force.

Yet there is a significant difference between the creation of poetry, and the embracing of the erotic, and it may be that a crucial level of physical safety must be reached before erotica can be publicly shared by an oppressed population. Created by people of color or sexual minorities, poetry can be dangerous; living the erotic (as do women of color who break stereotypes such as gender roles, sexual orientation expectations, or silence) *within your poetry* can get you killed, or severely threaten your ability to earn a living. Perhaps this is due to the power of publication, which sets out an author's lifestyle or life-choices in print, creating a public forum that identifies the author by name as well as becoming testimony to that author's acts, beliefs or experiences. The publication of erotic writing, for example, often draws fire from conservative or religious fundamentalist groups. It is a small step from letters and demonstrations of protest to the hate crimes that people of color or difference routinely face—however, for a writer in the same position, the very accessibility and publicity that allows success can make him or her more vulnerable to physical violence. Other minority communities have worked through this, while simultaneously the dominant culture (currently) seems to have "given way" enough to allow for publications which celebrate eroticism in many non-mainstream ways. *Why not Indians?* Are there specifics to American Indian writers' circumstances that prevent us from feeling "safe," or that prevent U.S. culture from feeling safe enough to stop repressing the erotic in Indian literature?

"I Like a Woman Who Packs"

At this point, I want to consider the forces specifically emerging from within the poetry and poets themselves, forces that may threaten the dominant cultural mythology. I have chosen two poems by Menominee poet Chrystos that seem to me fertile ground for this discussion. "I Like a Woman Who Packs," and "Na'-Natska" are both clearly erotica; perhaps not as clearly, they are a Native lesbian's erotica and as such, challenge the very foundations of United Statesian ideology. Let's look at "I Like a Woman Who Packs."

> I Like a Woman Who Packs
> not because she wants to be a man because she knows
> I want a butch
> who can loop my wrist with leather, whisper *Stay right here*
> *I have something I need to do to you* . . .[26]

The title flaunts the specter of a dildo—unattached to any man, making male participation not only unnecessary but also unchosen—in close conjunction with "woman." Betty Louise Bell, a Cherokee writer and professor, writes, "I am your worst nightmare: an Indian with a pen."[27] Chrystos takes this even further: she is an Indian woman with a dildo. Not only does she write her truth, but she also helps create erotic pleasures in ways that confound the agendas of both heterosexism and colonization. If the pen is mightier than the sword, Chrystos seems to say, the dildo is mightier still in that it does not destroy one's enemy, but completely ignores him.

The first line of this poem is absolute rejection of the conservative rational for lesbianism: ". . . not because she wants to be a man"—and to have that right up front, so to speak, laughs in the face of patriarchal pride and the foundation of homophobia. After all, penis envy is supposed to be part of every woman's psyche, right? But here, we get the distinct impression that the speaker of this poem doesn't want a man with a penis, and doesn't want to be a woman with a penis: the speaker wants a woman with a dildo. The speaker continues, "I want a butch/who can loop my wrist with leather, whisper *Stay right here/I have something I need to do to you*"; these lines not only pass over male options, but complicate the supposedly fixed notion of *woman*. With the word "butch," the poem makes the first of many assertions that don't challenge, as much as simply bypass, codes of behavior constructed by the dominant culture. Playing with the enemy's language further, Chrystos piles reversal on reversal, as the butch lover "loops my wrist with leather," or symbolically binds someone who will not be bound to societal assumptions, and then says not "*Stay right here, I have something I need to do*," and walks away, but "*Stay right here, I have something I need to do to you*" and, we presume, comes closer. Perpetually making unpredictable, sudden turns in her language trail keeps the reader guessing and in a constant state of re-balancing within the already ambiguous liminality of the poem's eroticism.

A little further along, the speaker continues, "I like a woman who'll make me beg her for it/Ride me till I forget my name, the date/the president, prime minister & every head of state." Here again, the seemingly simple replacement of "woman" for man, "her" for him, and the phrase "ride me" all dislocate heterosexual privilege and comfort zones; further, "ride me till I forget . . . the date, the president, prime minister & every head of state" indicates a butch woman whose power is such that she can distract her lover from the kind of knowledge typically asked of mentally ill people, or old folks in rest homes, when checking to see if they are still in touch with reality ("Ms. Miranda, what year is this?"). In other words, this butch woman literally drives her lover crazy, into an unbalanced state of being, and rather than crazy being *bad*, it is exceedingly *good*. I imagine Chrystos laughing as she penned this poem, giving the lover powers to erase even distinguished male political figures. Chrystos simultaneously creates the rhythmic image of "ride me" through strategic alliteration, rhyme and increased pace of syllabic combinations; she's not just throwing this poem together, but carefully crafting multi-levels of sensory information and resistance.

Although there may be some element of flaunting lesbian pleasure in the Great White Father's face, the work of the erotic in this poem is not to punish but to simply ignore patriarchal presence by allowing the erotic to acknowledge itself. By doing this, the lover makes herself visible, and patriarchal culture suddenly invisible; and in that instant, as she creates herself, each lover grasps what Audre Lorde calls the power of the erotic, what I suggest here to be more specifically *the power to create, to become visible.* For American Indian women, this power comes about by being the creatrix of her own visibility, to assert presence in physical, historical and political form.[28]

Turning to "Na'Natska," we find a wonderfully carnal and surprisingly complex poem. As I briefly mentioned earlier, Indian writing has often been stereotyped as "nature poetry," leaving Indian poets to wrestle with this problematic imagery. We know that if we use natural landscape as metaphor, we are being predictable; but on the other hand, these are not "just" natural images to us. Often, the natural world contains much religious, culturally specific importance that is impossible to ignore but difficult to negotiate. Chrystos comes up with an intriguing solution to this dilemma. In "Na'Natska" she writes,

> Teasing your eyes flicker like tongues on my lips
> little roses your nipples become red mountains
> My tongue climbs into you
> shaking our legs sweat sliding
> Your fingers in me are ruby-throated
> humming birds Your eyes iridescent wings . . .
> You laugh a gurgle of nectar
> We go shining in the rainy road your palm kneading
> my thigh mine yours
> I murmur *Am I affecting your driving too much?*
> Tossing your head smiling you answer
> *I want you to . . .*[29]

Here, we enjoy a deliciously graphic moment between the speaker and her lover, complete with the metaphorical inclusion of ruby-throated hummingbirds feeding on images of opening roses that blossom into mountains, the whole natural-Indian-sex thing (you know it must be about Indians, because the title is some strange native word you can't understand—an old Indian trick), when suddenly, bam! line 12 arrives: "I murmur *Am I affecting your driving too much?*" The juxtaposition of Primordial Indian and car sex is stunningly effective. This rhetorical move tweaks notions about who is civilized, who is modern (as opposed to "traditional" or "vanishing"), and how deeply imbedded our expectations are about American Indians. There is an Indian woman in this love poem, but she's not that Barbie Doll from Disney, and she's not riding a pony or a canoe, but feeling up her girlfriend in a car. There's no way you can miss seeing that girl, thanks to the ways

Chrystos has framed her so perfectly in a car driving through the center of an Edenic love poem.

This poem does not allow readers to cling to preconceptions about "Indian love songs." We see an Indian woman who is lustful, happy, who exists in the real world of automobiles and daily life ("I paint/while you study falling asleep after 26 pages of greek"), yet still sees the iridescent wings of humming birds in the eyes of her lover (or, in a classic Chrystos turn, becomes the humming bird that laps the nectar of her lover/rose). The women in this poem love, make love, paint, study, laugh: they create. But are there consequences for a representation such as this, consequences that determine who must *not* see this picture?

Repatriating the Erotic

If Native women, who bear the scars from five hundred years of erotic murder in this country, suddenly become visible, there is hell to pay. The crimes against Native women—crimes against the humanity of indigenous peoples of the Americas, crimes committed in the name of colonization—become visible alongside these women, while the U.S. Constitution and the Bill of Rights, as well as every treaty ever written, and every protest against genocide in "other countries," suddenly become testimony which strangles American mythology and identity. In other words, we cannot be allowed to *see* indigenous women in all their erotic glory without also *seeing* and acknowledging all that has been done to make those women, their bodies and cultures, extinct; and we cannot see that criminal effort of genocide without also acknowledging that 'our America,' our own democratic and superior nation, has committed crimes on a par with the gender—or ethnic-cleansing campaigns in other countries against which United States politicians ceaselessly rail. The mythic foundation of the United States is not a bedrock of democracy and freedom, but a shameful nightmare of unstable and treacherous sandstone, crumbling with each true vision of a Native woman's erotic existence.

In thinking about the erotic as the creative or generative force, it seems to me that American Indian women's love poetry and erotics do two things. First, they threaten to reveal heinous crimes and equally horrific cover-ups, revelations that attack the most vulnerable point in American identity: the jarring intersection of a democratic "Nation" and genocide. Secondly, American Indian women's erotics make more 'real', less stereotypical, artificially constructed American Indian women visible; this writing allows us to fully experience our creative strengths—something no one now alive on this continent has yet truly seen. As Joy Harjo, Muskogee Creek, says, "To be 'in the erotic' . . . is to be alive . . . the dominant culture can't deal with a society of alive people."[30] *People* is the key word here: Indian as *human* is still unthinkable for most Americans. For Indian women to express the erotic is almost as frightening to America as if the skeletal witnesses in anthropology departments and national museums had suddenly risen from their numbered boxes and begun to testify: the mythology of a nation built on "discovery," "democracy," and "manifest destiny" begins to fall apart, and the old foundation, bereft of bones, cannot hold it up.

I once asked Chrystos what she thought about the poor publication record and lack of critical analyses of American Indian women's erotics and love poetry. She thought for a moment, then replied, "American Indian writing is invisible; American Indian women's writing is more invisible; American Indian women's poetry, still more invisible. And Native women's love poetry and erotics are so invisible, so far back in the closet, that they're practically in somebody else's apartment."[31] This, I think, is the most astute analysis of the situation to date. It is not that American Indian women have chosen to keep erotic writing closeted; as Kateri Akiwenzie-Damm's unpublished anthology attests, the willingness to go public is there. But our "closet" has, indeed, been appropriated into somebody else's apartment, and the inhabitants of that rental (or maybe they're just squatters!) cannot afford to crack the door just yet.

Audre Lorde writes about the erotic as a form of communication between human beings. "The sharing of joy," she explains, "whether physical, emotional, psychic, or intellectual, forms a bridge between the sharers which can be the basis for understanding much of what is not shared between them, and lessens the threat of their difference."[32] Anything with that much power is sharp on both sides! American Indian women's erotics do, in fact, threaten the status quo of larger American concepts of history, mythology and nation precisely *because* this erotics is not merely a reinvention of the enemy's language, but *a reinvention that accesses the most powerful kinds of communications human beings can experience.* Thus, love poetry and erotics go far beyond the original intent of literacy for American Indians, the U.S. Government's Indian Boarding School 'education' which tied Indians to labor-intensive vocations weighed down by issues of race and class. Love poetry and erotics are a kind of "elite" literacy that express truly consequential discourse about power, souls, well-being, and the transformational aspects of relationships based not only on injustice and trauma, but also on celebration of pleasure and our humanity. European and Western academics have called this kind of knowledge "philosophy" or "metaphysics"; higher-level cognitive and spiritual practices, indeed. Could it be that more than five hundred years after First Contact, Indians are still thought incapable of bearing these most human of characteristics: desire, imagination, and a facility with language to articulate intangible possibility?

Few substantial avenues of expression currently exist for American Indian women, still fewer for representations of an Indian women's erotics. The repression of such writing accomplishes nothing less than the shutting down of our best writers based on fears of the transformational potential of their work. To revise an old activist aphorism, we might say that if we want justice, we must work for the erotic—and that is no easy task. But poets like Chrystos imagine the erotic for her readers as a lover kneading your thigh while you attempt to drive the straight and narrow highway. When the erotic asks demurely, "Am I affecting your driving too much?" know that affecting your driving is exactly her intent!

Be brave. Smile back at her and say, "I want you to."

Notes

Thank you to those who believed in and helped me write and revise this essay: Juan Guerra, Chrystos, Inés Hernández-Avila, and of course, Margo Solod.

1. Chrystos, *In Her I Am* (Vancouver, B.C.: Press Gang Publishers, 1993).

2. Alicia Ostriker, *Stealing the Language: The Emergence of Women's Poetry in America* (New York, N.Y.: Beacon Press, 1986).

3. For example, see *By Herself: Women Reclaim Poetry*, edited by Molly McQuade (Minneapolis, MN: Graywolf Press, 2000). McQuade, who writes that she 'attempts to redress that exclusion [of women] and uncover a novel and lasting body of knowledge while telling a story of women unheard until now' (xx) includes no articles by or about Native American women poets. *No More Masks! An anthology of twentieth-century American women poets*, ed. by Florence Howe (New York, N.Y.: HarperCollins Publishers, 1993), includes poems by three Native women poets out of 105 poets total; these are Paula Gunn Allen, Linda Hogan, and Joy Harjo (I discuss the dangers of repeatedly republishing the same poets and same poems later in this article). *Where we stand: women poets on literary tradition*, edited by Sharon Bryan (New York, N.Y.: W.W. Norton, 1993) has a short essay by Joy Harjo. Diane Middlebrook's *Coming to Light: American women poets in the twentieth century* (Ann Arbor, MI: University of Michigan Press, 1985), contains one article by, again, Paula Gunn Allen.

4. This era is generally agreed to have begun with the publication of Kiowa writer N. Scott Momaday's novel *House Made of Dawn*, which won the Pulitzer Prize for Literature in 1969. The word "renaissance" was first used in academic circles with the publication of Kenneth Lincoln's book, *Native American Renaissance* (Berkeley, CA: University of California Press, 1983).

5 Beth Brant, (Degonwadonti), *Mohawk Trail* (Ithaca, N.Y.: Firebrand Books, 1985); Anita Endrezze-Danielson, *Burning the Fields* (Lewiston, ID: Confluence Press, 1983); Rayna Green, ed., *That's What She Said: Contemporary Poetry and Fiction by Native American Women* (Bloomington, IN: Indiana University Press, 1984); Joy Harjo, *She Had Some Horses* (New York, N.Y.: Thunder's Mouth Press, 1983); Joy Harjo, *What Moon Drove Me to This* (Berkeley, CA: Reed and Cannon, 1979); Linda Hogan, *Seeing Through the Sun* (Amherst, MA: University of Massachusetts Press, 1985); Wendy Rose, *The Halfbreed Chronicles* (Los Angeles, CA: West End Press, 1985), *Hopi Roadrunner Dancing* (Greenfield Center, N.Y.: Greenfield Review Press, 1974), and *Lost Copper* (Banning, CA: Malki Museum Press, 1980); Leslie Marmon Silko, *Storyteller* (New York, N.Y.: Little, Brown & Co., 1981); and Roberta Hill Whiteman, *Star Quilt* (Minneapolis, MN: Holy Cow! Press, 1984).

6. Geary Hobson, ed., *The Remembered Earth: An Anthology of Contemporary Native American Literature* (Albuquerque, N.M.: Red Earth Press, 1979); Kenneth Rosen, ed., *Voices of the Rainbow: Contemporary Poetry by American Indians* (New York, N.Y.: Viking Press, 1975); Duane Niatum, ed., *Carriers of the Dream Wheel: Contemporary Native American Poetry* (New York, N.Y.: Harper & Row, 1975); Dick Lourie, ed., *Come to Power: Eleven Contemporary American Indian Poets* (New York, N.Y.: Crossing Press, 1974); James L. White, ed., *The First Skin Around Me: Contemporary American Tribal Poetry* (Moorhead, M.N.: Territorial Press, 1976); and Joseph Bruhac, ed., *Songs from This Earth on Turtle's Back: Contemporary American Indian Poetry* (Greenfield, N.Y.: Greenfield Review Press, 1983). Bear in mind that these works are only a list of publications I own or can find in library catalogues. There may be other similar collections of American Indian works of this period that are not listed here.

7. Marge Piercy, ed., *Early ripening: American women's poetry now* (New York, N.Y.: Pandora, 1987).

8. Marilyn Frye in *The Politics of Reality* (Trumansburg, N.Y.: The Crossing Press, 1983).

9. Joy Harjo and Gloria Bird in *Reinventing the Enemy's Language* (New York: W.W. Norton & Co, 1997), pp. 22–23. In light of Ostriker's large omission of Indian women in *Stealing the Language*, this title seems to count coup with some glee—and also subtly points out the differences between 'stealing' (and thus taking or appropriating) a language that has been withheld as opposed to the need to 'reinvent' a language that has been forcibly, violently imposed.

10. Conversation with Chrystos and the author (6/25/2000).

11. Conversation with Endrezze and the author (5/22/1999).

12. Eduardo Duran and Bonnie Duran, *Native American Post-colonial Psychology* (New York, N.Y.: SUNY Press, 1995).

13. For a well-documented and heartbreaking study of one point of encounter involving gendered violence, the California Missions, see Edward Castillo's text *Indians, Franciscans, and Spanish Colonization: The Impact of the Mission System on California Indians* (Los Angeles, CA: University of California Press, 1994), especially Chapter 4: "Resistance and Social Control in the Alta California Missions."

14. James W. Loewen, in his book *Lies My Teacher Told Me: Everything Your American History Textbook Got Wrong* (New York, N.Y.: Simon & Schuster, 1995) writes that, "As soon as the 1493 expedition got to the Caribbean, before it even reached Haiti, Columbus was rewarding his lieutenants with native women to rape" (65). Loewen quotes Columbus from a letter to a friend in 1500. ". . . there are plenty of dealers who go about looking for girls; those from [ages] nine to ten are now in demand." One woman was captured and given to colonist Michele de Cuneo as a gift slave from Columbus. Cuneo later recounted his experience in a now-infamous letter to a friend:

> Having taken her into my cabin, her being naked according to their custom, I developed a desire to take pleasure. I tried to put my desire into execution but she did not want it and treated me with her fingernails in such a manner that I wished that I had never begun. But (to tell you the end of it all), I took a rope and thrashed her well, for which she raised such unheard of screams that you would not have believed your ears. Finally we came to an agreement in such a manner that I can tell you that she seemed to have been brought up in a school of harlots. (qtd. in Paiewonsky, 50)

This same man was also witness to one of Columbus' huge round-ups of slaves. He notes that so many natives were taken captive that the Spaniards could not use them all, even after giving hundreds away as slaves. Cuneo writes, "For those who remained, we let it be known in the vicinity that anyone who wanted to take some of them could do so, to the amount desired; which was done." Finally, about four hundred natives still lived, and were told that they were free to go—for now. "Among them," Cuneo records,

> were many women with children still at suck. Since they were afraid that we might return to capture them once again, and in order to escape us the better, they left their children anywhere on the ground and began to flee like desperate creatures; and some fled so far that they found themselves at seven or eight days' distance from our community at Isabella, beyond the mountains and across enormous rivers . . .

Abandoning their infants and young children was, I believe, a form of infanticide for these Indian women, who were no doubt in shock from the capture and subsequent murdering and rape of many, and whose panic drove them to escape. Infanticide is a drastic step for any culture to take, and these scenes were only the beginning of a massive attack on Indian women's bodies and feminine powers. Besides the destruction of women's roles in the political and religious structures of traditional American societies, violence against women was a constant and brutal element of the *reconquista*, one that must be taken into account when examining the writing and publication of Native women's erotics.

15. See K. Tsianina Lomawaima, *They Called It Prairie Light: The Story of the Chilocco Indian School* (Lincoln: University of Nebraska Press, 1994); Devon Mihesuah, *Cultivating the Rosebuds: The Education of Women at the Cherokee Female Seminary, 1851–1909* (Urbana, IL: University of Illinois Press, 1993); and David Wallace Adams, *Education for Extinction: American Indians and the Boarding School Experience, 1875–1928* (Lawrence: University Press of Kansas, 1995).

16. I am not advocating that rawly sexual poems be included in anthologies for children. However, most high school and all college textbooks include a discussion of love poetry as the norm, yet typically exclude any American Indian literatures while frequently including other ethnic or sexual minority work.

17. Kateri Akiwenzie-Damm, "Publication News," private e-mail message to Deborah Miranda, 10 April 1999.

18. *Living the Spirit: A Gay American Indian Anthology*, edited by Will Roscoe (New York: St. Martin's Press, 1989) is sometimes mistaken for an anthology of erotica, but it is not; instead, it is a collection of very useful articles, essays and poetry about sociological aspects of gay Indian lives and histories.

19. Miriam Decosta-Willis, Reginald Martin and Roseanne P. Bell, *Erotique Noire/Black Erotica* (New York, N.Y.: Anchor Books, 1992), pp. xxxi–xxxii.

20. Ntozake Shange, ibid., p. xix.

21. Russell Leong, *On a Bed of Rice: An Asian American Erotic Feast* (New York, N.Y.: Anchor Books, 1995), p. xvi.

22. Ray Gonzalez, *Under the Pomegranate Tree: The Best New Latino Erotica* (New York, N.Y.: Simon & Schuster, 1996), p. xiv.

23. Ibid., p. xvi.

24. Russell Leong, *On a Bed of Rice*, p. xiv.

25. Audre Lorde, *Sister Outsider: Essays and Speeches* (Freedom, N.Y.: The Crossing Press, 1984), p. 39.

26. Chrystos, *In Her I Am* (Vancouver, B.C.: Press Gang Publishers, 1993), pp. 69–70.

27. Betty Louise Bell, *Faces in the Moon* (Norman, OK: University of Oklahoma Press, 1994), p. 192.

28. Audre Lorde, *Sister Outsider: Essays and Speeches*, pp. 53–59.

29. Chrystos, *In Her I Am*, p. 60. Permission to quote at length from the author.

30. Joy Harjo, *The Spiral of Memory: Interviews* (Ann Arbor, MI: University of Michigan Press, 1996), p. 108.

31. Chrystos, speaking at the University of Washington, Seattle, 5/10/1998.

32. Audre Lorde, *Sister Outsider: Essays and Speeches*, p. 56.

Seeing Red: American Indian Women Speaking About Their Religious and Political Perspectives

13

INÉS TALAMANTEZ

Deep within
I am wild in my sorrow
I am a woman
    a working woman
    a good Apache woman
    a gathering woman
    a Red World woman
    a brown Chicana woman
    a mother woman
    a loving woman
    a blue woman
    a eucalyptus woman
    a soft woman
    a loud woman
    a resisting woman
    a trouble making woman
    a hunting woman
    a moving woman
    a quiet woman
    a dancing woman
    a singing woman
    a pollen woman
    a spirit woman
    a mountain woman
    an ocean woman
    a White World woman

a trail making woman
a changing woman

Look around you
Look around you

What do you see
What do you see
What will you do
What will you do

When will we walk together
When will we walk together[1]

With the dawn breaking in the east over the Sacramento Mountains of New Mexico, the barrenness of the white gypsum sand dunes glimmers to the west. The early desert sun of the Tularosa Valley is already hot. I was born less than one hundred miles south from where I am now standing, and I am remembering what the women of this place have taught me. It is their stories that have helped me explore who I am today. They have given me the sense of self and place. Learning our stories as we move through our lives, collecting and gathering until we fill our baskets to the brim (or our files to overflowing, and we move on to entering our ideas on computer disks), we are reminded of the minds and imaginations of our ancestors and how they acquired the knowledge necessary to survive the struggle throughout the centuries.

Central to these teachings from Native American traditions are the elaborate explanations about the beginning of the cosmos and the role of female deities who were present at the time of creation. The role of many Native American women today is still influenced by the teachings passed on to us by those that went before us and their concern for the generations to follow. Acknowledging the perseverance of indigenous women for social justice and religious freedom is as necessary for Native American women as for American feminists. In a world where distorted images of native women's spirituality abound, spiritually impoverished American women often appropriate those aspects of our lives that fill their needs. Our struggle continues.

Those who write without knowing the truth provide glib, shallow accounts of what they consider to be "other," and the perspective they take places them beyond accountability to those on whose lives they draw for spiritual nourishment. Neither are they native women, nor do they want to be connected to their own female ancestors. They are detached from knowledge of their own past and seek meaning in the lives of others who are in no position to object. This is offensive and constitutes a form of intellectual imperialism. The belief that the traditions of others may be appropriated to serve the needs of self is a peculiarly Western notion that relies on a belief that knowledge is disembodied rather than embedded in relationships, intimately tied to place, and entails responsibilities to others and a commitment and discipline in learning.

Feminist explorations of the distinctive knowledge that women's distinctive experiences generate provide a helpful perspective on the struggle of native women to be heard and to see their traditions respected and their truths acknowledged. Diane Bell, Australian feminist, has argued that women's experience of subordination predisposes them to a reflexive stance on their lives and those of others.[2] Within this schema, Native American women may speak in a specially true and insightful voice. Of course, men as well may write of their experiences, which reflect their truths and their lives, but their narratives do not always represent the clearest expositions of what it means to be a gendered, colonized subject.

This work is not just a research project; it is part of my life. I am connected to these women and their truths. We are taught in our cultures that as young girls we are moving through the world with others, that we are moving in relationships with others, including the lives of the flora and the fauna. We are told to respect the lives and movements of others; the invisible forces at work in the natural world are revealed through the wondrous world created in the sacred narratives, the stories that provide the frame of reference through which we are instructed about our heritage as women of Native America. It is this aesthetic, created in the minds of our ancestors, that has given us a different way of looking at and thinking about time and place. The cycles of growth in the natural world or the movement of the sun, for example, explicate time as cyclical rather than linear, as represented on my digital wristwatch, on which of course I also depend.

The natural cycles of growth are closely watched, as is decay. Complex rituals embedded in our ceremonial structures provide a perspective into the world of the supernatural. The sacred is reflected in everyone and in everything, in our minds and worlds, in the moving bodies of dancers and in the voices of singers. However, we face profound political and sociocultural challenges in keeping our cultures alive through creative and religious introspection and work and not letting the devastating forces of change overwhelm us. Yet we know through understanding our ceremonies that transformation brings change. It is, however, the knowledge gained through ritual transformation that then gives us the responsibility to apply the lessons learned to our lives and the lives of those around us. It is here that we understand both the values and the social systems under which all individuals in diverse cultural locations must operate in order to maintain balance within their societies.

The indigenous framework within which many of us work reveals the systems of relatedness, obligation, and respect that govern the lives of many native women. There is a driving purpose behind our work; we know what we are expected to do. There are political commitments to social justice, concerns for what constitutes activism in our present day, complex issues of identity and naming ourselves. The political survival issues of the day—land claims, freedom of religion, environmental racism, lack of appropriate health care, education, and employment, for example—engage us as persons who labor under the twin oppressions of being woman and native. This narrative of inquiry requires deep reflection. It is an exploration in both humility and authority. Insight is gained through analysis, interpretation, and critique.

In practice today our lives are shaped by the complex intertwining of several controlling regimes that discriminate against us in a variety of ways. Native American women living on reservations are subject to the will of tribal governments, which are under the control of the Bureau of Indian Affairs, an arm of the Department of the Interior. The concerns of women are not a priority for the bureaucrats or the elected officials, any more than they are in the dominant society. For urban Indian women, who are not registered in federal government records—that is, have no number indicating that they are enrolled and are therefore "legitimate Indians" according to the government—social services and benefits are difficult or almost impossible to obtain. For example, those who do make it through the school system and plan to attend a junior college or university are denied access to scholarships unless they can prove that they are Indian. No one else in this country has to prove their ethnicity; why do we?

Health care issues are also viewed in this way. If you are enrolled, you qualify for federal Indian Health programs, but if you are not enrolled, you are just another minority woman seeking health care. In reforming the health care system, the particular needs of those of us who are women and native need to be addressed. We are American women. We are indigenous women. We share many of the health concerns of other American women, but we have been disproportionately exposed to some additional health risks. In seeking to heal our bodies, we look to religion, land, and medicine in ways that the present health care system finds difficult to accommodate. As Meredith Begay (document 1) tells us, medicine, health, ceremony are all intertwined, and her work as a cross-cultural communicator shows one path forward.

Churches are also guilty. Many Christian churches, especially in areas largely populated by Indians, still require that their parishioners give up participating in their own religious traditions if they wish to be Christians. This discrimination has been met in a variety of ways. Some native women continue to resist completely all forms of Christianity and practice their own native ways, which beautifully blend culture and spirituality in one complete worldview. Other women continue to follow their cultural ways and have found a method that allows them to be Indians from a specific culture but yet accept and embrace Christian dogma. And of course some Indian women have accepted Christianity completely and have opted for assimilation into the dominant American culture.

The struggle for religious freedom and a land-based pedagogy requires that we reconfigure the roles of native women and their distinctive features. We are looking at tangled historical processes and systems that integrate cultural, political, and ecological dimensions. We need a new schemata, one that frees us from the constraints of a Western patriarchal paradigm of control, one that takes us beyond victim status and blame. We need a framework that enables us to understand our own cultures as well as allows us to teach about them. We must not forget, however, that we are working within institutions that have continued to exert control over the very substance of our research, the publication of our work; institutions that have the power to determine what counts as scholarship. It will take reflection and a willingness to scrutinize the power of church and state before native and non-native, men and women can share in a meaningful way. It will be a long time before we can be equal partners in a dialogue. We women are at a historical juncture where as workers, mothers, scholars, healers, poets, we have the necessary tools to move forward. Our fight for religious freedom is a fight for life and for land. If you are fighting for social justice, you are fighting for our freedom. If you are raising children, you are fighting for our freedom. If you are writing as a woman, you are fighting for our freedom.

Voices of Wisdom

Having articulated the underlying philosophy, albeit in the abstract, and alluded to the complexity of the context within which we give expression to our beliefs, let me now ground this discussion in the specific writings of Native American scholars. Indian societies, long before the coming of Europeans to America, were in the process of significant and dynamic development in the areas of religious practice, economic production, and artistic and material achievements. These were hardly simple, savage, or "primitive" peoples. Alfonso Ortiz from San Juan Pueblo and professor of anthropology at the University of Albuquerque, remembers that in New Mexico,

> long ago, when first informing their worlds with meaning, the San Juan people took their three-tiered social order and projected it outwards and upwards to encompass the whole of their physical world as well by imbuing that world with a three-tiered spiritual meaning, one both reflecting and reinforcing their social order. The fit among their ideas of order in society, in the physical world, and in the

spiritual realm is ingenious, for these three orders interlock and render order into everything within the Tewa world.[3]

In Keres Pueblo, in New Mexico, Paula Gunn Allen (Laguna/Sioux, and professor of English at UCLA), tells us that Sun Woman, who was present at and participated in the creation of the universe, left to go to the east and it is said that she will return in times to come. At Laguna, Gunn tells us, people believe that she has already returned in the form of the atomic/hydrogen "suns," which were put together in her original lands. These are the lands that provided the uranium that was mined to create the atomic devastations.[4]

Vickie Downey, writing of her home pueblo, Tesuque, tells us about keeping alive the religious traditions of the Southwest Pueblos in spite of Spanish priests and soldiers:

> About our religion, yes, we've kept that alive even with exploitation that came in and tried to wipe out our religion. We've maintained that. Among the pueblos there's a church in each pueblo. With the Spanish they brought the priests along with the soldiers. Together they tried to exterminate our communities, our villages, our spirit. But we've maintained our way to this time. It's been a struggle, but we've maintained it. A lot of other Indian reservations, they've also maintained it.[5]

The settlers who came even later to this land felt the need to exploit it even further for its natural resources in the name of what they believed to be civilization. Their attitudes were very different from those of the diverse tribal societies they encountered. The sharp contrast in ideals and values that affected the way the newcomers viewed the religious practices of these societies is still felt today. The settlers feared nature and wilderness; they were, after all, from another land and ecosystem. Perhaps the settlers were haunted by memories of former times and the fear of going back to the earlier uncivilized states that had existed in Europe if they were not successful in mastering this new, strange land and its peoples.

The way these colonists acted toward this land had less to do with the natural world than with their ideals of individualism and independence and their desperate need for a new beginning in a new world. In shaping their own adjustment to this new environment, they inherited much from the Native American societies they encountered but were more concerned with conquering than understanding. Their belief that God had given them this natural world to exploit allowed them to rationalize their behaviors in the name of European manifest destiny, civilization, and Christianity. Everywhere, in every direction, the consequence was the laying waste of souls and natural resources.

Many Dene (Navajo) women today are dealing with these issues in an ongoing struggle for religious freedoms and social justice. To be a Dene woman requires living in and practicing the Dene way of life. The power manifested by Changing Woman, a female deity in the myth of the Blessingway ceremonial complex, is a power that Dene women call upon in their struggles today, especially their struggle for a land base, for they continue to be forced to relocate from what they consider to be their spiritual homeland. According to a Dene woman traditionalist and friend involved in this political, religious struggle, to be moved away from her place means to be living out of balance and harmony. The ideas set forth in the concepts of Blessingway provide the sanctions for Dene peoples' roles in human life and require participation in ceremonial life in a specific land base.[6]

In the *Kinááldá*, the girls' initiation ceremony, Dene girls are instructed to live their lives modeled after Changing Woman. Women's beliefs about the attributes of Changing Woman and the nature of her interconnectedness to all living entities is of great significance and clarifies for the initiates what their roles and responsibilities will be as Dene women. Female sponsors for the initiates derive their power from a codified body of ceremonial knowledge and personal experience. The ceremony itself requires of the women sponsors that they be responsible for ritually guiding the initiates from childhood through the doors of adolescence into womanhood. This is a tremendous task that requires rigorous, dedicated religious commitment if the ceremony is to be effective. Initiated women will sometimes gain prestige in the community by learning from their own sponsors how to carry on the *Kinááldá* ceremony. This, of course, takes years of apprenticeship if it is to be done correctly. The important fact here is that initiated women often become the carriers of the Dene female tradition. Dene woman, who are also known to perform the ceremonial roles of Hand Tremblers, praying over a patient's body with trembling hands as they search for answers, or of Diagnosticians, locating the source of an illness and then referring the patient to the appropriate ceremonies, are usually not free to pursue these demanding roles until after menopause.[7]

The struggle to pursue one's religion has many faces. For example, Flora Jones, a Wintu religious leader, like Pilulaw Khus, the Chumash elder (document 3), is concerned with desecration by the federal government and commercial interests of lands considered sacred and central to the continuity of their ceremonial life and practices. Flora has complained she has not been able to collect essential medicines in the forests of northern California.[8] Pilulaw has fought oil companies whose development would desecrate Chums ceremonial areas. When there are oil spills, she is the first out there to clean up the beaches and to assist the endangered animals. Knowledge of a sustainable environment, revealed in the languages in which the myths are told and in the concept of Mother Earth and the interconnectedness of all living things, is central to what it means to be indigenous to a place.

The tensions between the spiritual forces at work in Native America and the ideas of forced religious conversion, along with new introduced technologies, has had a tremendous impact on the lives of native women. In the sphere of religion, men were moved into positions of power over religious women leaders. Too often missionization meant the disempowerment of women. This is made explicit in *Jesuit Relations*, the journals of the Jesuit missionaries of the seventeenth century, which advocates placing men in religious leadership roles and counsels against dealing with women in positions of religious or political power.[9] Despite the pervasive power of these agents of change, the resistance of native women persists. Though often graciously stepping aside from former leadership roles, they continue in many places to be respected for their religious knowledge and women's wisdom.

The women of the Iroquois Longhouse, for example, have not permitted patriarchal distortion of the natural world or newly introduced technologies and commodities, such as fast food, disposable diapers, and television, to diffuse their powerful cultural positions as clan mothers and keepers of the Longhouse ceremonial complex. They are responsible for choosing the chiefs of the clan, who can govern only if they are in agreement with the rest of the clan members. The final decisions are made by the careful consideration of the clan mothers, who are concerned for the well-being of all the people, especially the young children.[10] This, of course, is a very different perspective on Indian women from one that blends many traditions into the stereotype of the Indian woman as subservient. It is important that we remember that women had many and varied tasks, ceremonies, and social roles, in different places, at different times, and in different nations. Yet, when we look to the historic record and ethnographic accounts, women are often invisible.

One notable exception is Ella Cara Deloria's (Yankton Sioux) novel *Waterlily*. Writing of the dramatic changes taking place in her society in the late nineteenth century, she paints a moving portrait of the elaborate rite *hunka, or* "child beloved," a ceremony for children who are selected for a place of honor in Teton society. Through this rite the girl, Waterlily, is taught the knowledge necessary for understanding the principles of daily life and why ritual practices are important for both men and women.[11]

In the American Southwest, inter-religious dialogue in churches and at conferences has ignored the religious life of Native American women and our relationships with other indigenous women of the borderlands. Historically, Chicana and Mexican women south of the border have been denied access to knowledge of their indigenous heritage in a manner similar to that of their sisters in the north. Church and state have combined in powerful ways to divide and conquer, yet the religious and medical practices of these women today demonstrate a rich, complex blend of ideas, commitments, and identities. Coatlicue (an Aztec female deity), Guadalupe (a melding of an Aztec deity and sixteenth-century Spanish

Catholicism), Curanderas (Mexican folk healers), Parteras (midwives), and more recently Mexican and Chicana Espiritualistas (document 5) stand as testimony to the strength and creativeness of women of the borderlands. Today, Chicana and indigenous women, in dialogue with our elders, are finding a place for ourselves as we redefine the history of our religious experience. *Mujeres Activas en Letras y Cambio Social* is an important forum for exploring these matters.[12] Rigoberta Menchu, Quiche woman of Guatemala, has so brilliantly named our struggle as the spirituality of the Western hemisphere.[13]

My own identity incorporates the richness of my Apache, Mexican Indian, and Chicana heritage. It was that background and my female kin that guided me along a path of even deeper reflection and understanding of the diverse roles of women. When I draw on the tradition of the Sun Clan at the Mescalero Apache Reservation in New Mexico, I make the linkages among myself, my research, and my political activism as a woman. In elaborate detail, the Sun Clan creation myth, when told in Apache, relates that from the very beginning of time, the earth existed and was in a process of continual change, which was seen and continues to be seen as the manifestation of the cyclical powers of nature.

In the ceremony, *'Isánáklésh Gotal,* which marks the transition from girlhood to womanhood, the symbols used to influence the young girls vary in their function, but their overall purpose is to convince the adolescent that she will undergo good and positive changes if she participates fully in the ceremony. However, it is up to the girl herself to decide if she wishes to undertake this responsibility. At this young age girls are thought of as soft and moldable, suggesting that they are still capable of being conditioned and influenced by female kin. It is easier to convince some girls to participate than others. Some need to be awakened to their female identity, while others need to be calmed down and taught to be more feminine. Within the ritual design of the ceremony, two concepts are at work: one is awakening the initiate to the world around her and to her abilities, and the other is to carefully calm down the unrestrained nature of adolescence. Both concepts are nurtured and encouraged in the young girl's everyday activities (document 4).

Preparation for the ceremony begins early in the life of a young girl. She is slowly and carefully made ready, then suddenly uprooted from her special privileged childhood in a family where female kin watch over her from the time of her birth. Menarche signals a physiological marker that the young girl immediately recognizes. Suddenly her life changes. Her first menstruation is usually celebrated by family and kin. At this time, she is sung over to emphasize the importance of this intimate celebration, the gift of *'Isánáklésh* to a young changing woman. Nearly all girls had this ritual in pre-reservation times. Today, a girl may look forward to a feast around the age of eleven or twelve years, at which time many members of her community will gather to honor her in the eight-day ceremony of *'Isánáklésh Gotal.*

The first time that I observed this ceremony was when, at the age of nine, I was taken by my mother and aunt to Mescalero to attend the feast of a relative. The image of the girl dancing in the tipi at night stayed with me and became the impetus for my present research.[14] Although I was born in Las Cruces in Doha Ana County, New Mexico, I grew up in Barrio Logan neighborhood in San Diego. My first paying job was at El Porvenir, a tortilla factory that is still there today. As I listened to the older women talk about the realities of their lives, they provided me with what I now know was an insightful critique of what they were experiencing. Our Lady of Guadalupe Catholic Church was the religious center for most of us. With both humility and religious authority, the women created beautiful personal home altars when they felt the need for a more intimate form of prayer and reverence. Many of these altars honored the Virgin de Guadalupe, the principal religious figure in all of her different manifestations.

It was in the Barrio Logan years later that I first heard about Sarita Macias. Her Templo Espiritualista was across the street from the Chicano Cultural Center. Mexican and Chicana/o espiritualismo, as practiced today, encompasses a complexity of religious and cultural elements. It uses pre-Columbian medicinal traditions, sixteenth-century Spanish Catholicism, and messianic and shamanistic ritual beliefs and practices. The practice of espiritualismo involves trance, soul voyaging, and visionary traits, such as *videncia* (spiritual sight). For believers, its teachings are legitimized by a divine charter that originates with an Ultimate Reality and other major Spirits who regularly speak through the spirit mediums (*guias*). The guias are, for the most part, women who act as spiritual guides, healers, and counselors. They have visionary experiences that become a source of power, according them respect and credibility in their congregations and the community at large.

Espiritualismo was first introduced into Mexico in the 1860s as a blend of native beliefs, Mexican folk Catholicism, and apocalyptic expectations that responded to the conflicts of church and state taking place in Mexico at that time. An ex-seminarian, Rogue Rojas, heralded the coming of the "Era de Elias," a messianic reign on earth that would bring salvation to the oppressed, called "espiritualistias Israelites." Rojas named his church "La Iglesia Mexicana Patriarcal Elias." Contemporary Mexican espiritualismo derives from this movement. My introduction to espiritualismo by Sarita in San Diego eventually led to my initiation by a guia in Mexico City. I did not myself seek to become a practitioner so much as to study the process of initiation, one that has deep ties to my Apache and Chicana heritages. Over time, Sarita became a source of strength, and it was her guidance that saw me through my doctoral examinations and dissertation (document 5).

I don't presume to speak for the women whose voices I document in this essay. Yet, I feel that their voices are also my voice, and I am in the process of understanding how to write the history that they speak about and how to describe their religious perspectives. I focus here on the voices of contemporary indigenous women. Too often we look to the old texts and feel comforted by the wisdom of those women who have now passed on. Yet there are indigenous women across this land whose religious and political perspectives can enrich us all today. The Chicano and American Indian Movement of the sixties produced writers who gave voice to our struggles and helped me to begin to find my own voice. Examining the warp and woof of a history whose tightly woven threads are not easily unraveled, I remember what a Dene weaver at the Hubbell Trading Post in Ganado, Arizona, once said to me as she sat before her loom. "Weaving," she said, "is about understanding power."

Documents

1. Meredith Begay: An Apache Medicine Woman
2. Inés Hernandez-Avila: Land Base and Native American Religious Traditions
3. Pilulaw Khus: Chumash Culture
4. The Presence of 'Isánáklésh and Apache Female Initiation
5. Espiritualista Initiation in Southern California and Mexico

Document 1. Meredith Begay: An Apache Medicine Woman

Meredith Begay is a contemporary medicine woman, spiritual adviser, and teacher of the traditions of the Mescalero Apache Reservation in New Mexico. The following is an interview on the role of medicine in Apache culture, recorded June 1994 on a trip to collect Indian Banana for an Apache female initiation ceremony.

Ines: Meredith, you're a Medicine Woman and very much respected by your people here at the Mescalero Reservation, and you're also trying to teach people beyond Mescalero. I am interested in talking with you to find out how you deal with it. A lot of people think of Medicine Women as something from the past, except for New Agers who keep inventing Medicine Women. So I would like to know what it is you do, why you do it and what your concerns are in terms of the present Apache Traditions and some of the political issues you face in being a Medicine Woman today.

Meredith: Medicine is Traditional Indian medicine. The focal point of it is healing. To be healed, the person has to live a healthy, good life. What I feel I am doing is just being an instrument to help heal. This is what I am doing for my people to help the young children. To help them understand that there is medicine and that there is Apache religion and that all of these cohese in order to be an Apache, a proud Indian. That's what it is. I don't profess to be the greatest medicine person. I don't profess to say that I know all medicines, no. I know my area; I know how far I can go with my medicines. And if somebody needs further medicine with a more stronger power, I refer that person. A lot of times I have helped other people heal. I have talked to them, or sometimes they ask for herbs, so I give them herbs, but I use them holistically. I don't just give it to them in a tea form and say here, drink this—no, I don't do that. I use it holistically. And I always stress that I am just a little person in this world trying to help my Indian people wherever they are, to help them understand that there is still good in traditional medicine and that medicine is all around us, the pharmacy is all around us, and it doesn't cost anything; it's free. It's for the people to get healed and live right. These are the things that I stress, and especially for the children I try to stress that they know their medicine, know that they have a heritage—something to be proud of and especially the Apache child. I always do this. I give them a lot of insight and teach them how to harvest medicine, when to get it, how to preserve it, and how to use it when they need it. This is what I do, but in order to become a medicine person you have to have lived the life on a reservation with Indian people. You have to know the intricacies of equalness between earth, plant, trees, rock, clouds. All of nature you have to know, have equalness with it and understand it, even the tiniest little insect. You have to understand that.

It is said that when a little black ant gets sacred pollen that has dropped to the ground, and the little ant is under you, and it gets pollen on it, it feels good. It's happy because it was blessed, and that's the way you have to be with Mother Nature. You don't over use it, and you don't under use. You equalize everything. That's the way you live. And a lot of these people that are now coming into medicine, it's not going to take one day or one night or one year to learn. It's going to take about 10, 15 years before they really understand and get to the focal point of what medicine is. You cannot practice Indian medicine at all in the United States unless you have been brought up into a particular life way. You have to have a background, people in your background, people that know how to heal, that tell you the story of the medicine, the way that it was applied, how it was used. You don't learn those things in just a matter of four days or five days. You learn it over a period of time, and then when you perform for other people, it will show.

A lot of it is fake today. You can tell the fake medicine from the real. A lot of people will copy you. Coyote copied a lot of people but he always came out at the short end of the stick. You have to do it with dignity, with faith, and if you don't have that, you are not performing right. Anybody can copy a sweat; anybody can copy a ceremony or dance; anybody can copy these things, but if they don't have the essence, it's no use; it's no good; it's a waste of time; it's a waste of money; it's just a lot of hogwash—because the end result is what you look at after you've performed something. The end results show the truth. If it was good, the person will feel good when they come out of it. If it was just an act, the person will still feel the same as when they went into the healing, dance or ceremony. That's how it is, and medicine is not to be played with because since you're an instrument or something to that effect—you're an instrument for the Supreme Being—you have to do within your own realm what you can do.

Like I said, if you can't do any more than what you've done, if you've helped the person as much as you can, you refer them to the next medicine person that has a little more power or maybe a different approach. Usually your true medicine people are poor—they don't have much. They don't have much in ways of physical things, maybe they don't have a big house and cars—things like that—they are poor people. Their spirit is very, very big. They are strong, they are giving, they are kind.

But a person that goes into medicine for money, then that person is in it for me, I and myself—nobody else matters. Their attitude is, I don't care. I'm just copying so I get the money. That's their whole idea. It's not like that. A true medicine person doesn't do that, doesn't put these things ahead. A true medicine person puts the sick person or whomever needs help ahead of me, I and myself. They put it ahead, they want to help. They give all that they can give, and the end result, like I said, is what comes out after the person is either healed or half healed or is on its way to healing. So this is why there could be a lot of people out there saying I'm a medicine person, but within their own life they are going to come to a crossroads.

Document 2. Inés Hernández-Avila: Land Base and Native American Religious Traditions

Inés Hernández-Avila is a Nez Perce/Tejana poet and scholar at the University of California at Davis. In the following document she presents a challenging understanding of the indigenous vision of the natural world. The excerpt is drawn from an address given at the 1993 annual meeting of the American Academy of Religion.[15]

Last June, I was present at a gathering, a "conversation," at Bucknell University that was called "Land and the Human Presence," which was attended by about forty people, seventeen of whom were Native Americans. One of the Native American elders present was Leon Shenandoah, Chief of Chiefs of the Six Nations people, the Iroquois Confederacy. One part of his message each time he spoke had to do with what happens when someone takes another person's life. The first time he spoke of this, I took his message very personally, because one of my relatives had just died violently (and possibly not accidentally), and I felt that his statements were helping me to make sense of the death. He and I spoke of these matters afterwards. The second time he repeated this portion of his message to us, I was struck by another level of its meaning.

What Chief Shenandoah said was this: When someone takes another person's life, that person cheats the Creator. He cheats the Creator because the Creator has his own plans for the person. If someone's life is taken, the one who dies has free passage to the beyond. All that the one who died left behind, all the errors, come on to the one who took the life.

As I emerged from my initial interpretation, I realized that there are many ways to take another person's life, aside from physically killing them. You take another person's life when you deny or distort their voice and appropriate their traditions for personal benefit without permission, or as a means to control them. You take another person's life when you use your institutional privilege to practice intellectual hegemony over them, or when you pretend that their discoveries and understandings are your own or valid only when you claim them.

In this regard, it strikes me as rather appropriate that the popular environmental movement as we know it has been carried out formally and initially by white people, given what we know of the historical trajectory of many of their ancestors with respect to degradation of the earth. It seems to me that the concepts of "landscape," "wilderness," "nature" all represent Western ideological perceptions, intellectualizations of the land, of the earth, and it occurs to me that when European Americans (in particular) intellectualize (and sometimes romanticize) in such a way, they are perhaps exhibiting a nostalgia for their own land bases, and for their severed relationship with these land bases. It is my understanding that native people in this hemisphere regard the earth not only as a mother, but also as a loving grandmother and strict teacher. As I have said in another essay,

> The distinct land base (in the sense of relationship, not ownership) of a people informs and nourishes their culture and in a precisely detailed manner directs the movement and meaning of their ceremonies. Through careful observation and the development of a respectful and intimate relationship with their land bases. . . . indigenous population[s] learn(ed) from their teachers how to live in harmony with their environment and how to sustain themselves through the changing seasons.[16]

This relationship, which was nurtured in a profoundly reverent and conscious manner, was/is founded on an understanding that the earth, indeed, the cosmos, was/is itself a complex, exact and intentional manifestation of the Creative Spirit. This understanding is one of the fundamental assumptions of indigenous belief systems. It is an assumption that speaks to the depth of the sacred relationships between indigenous peoples and their particular land bases, to their awareness of the interrelatedness of all life within the universe, and to their conceptual notions of identity, family, community, spirituality, and pedagogy.

. . . In other words, "God," or the Creative Spirit (called by many names) manifests a Sacred Science, due to the sacralized dynamics of inquiry, observation, and experiment upon which native "science" was/is based. These dynamics give shape to a cultural discipline that reflects the reciprocal relationship that exists between "we, the People, the Human Beings," and the entire cosmos. This discipline, which emanates from the Creative Spirit, is the creative pedagogy that informs native perceptions of the "natural world." In fact, the history (and even "prehistory" in Western terms) of mutual trust, intimacy of matter (or body) and spirit, constancy, loving attention, and respect between native peoples and their land bases here in this hemisphere, which are apparent in the understandings they came to have of their environment, speaks not only to their longevity on this land, but also perhaps represents the key to Native American conceptualizations of sovereignty.[17]

What are the implications of an appreciation that humans differ and that their experiences of the natural world also differ? I think of how an appreciation of the differences, in a sacralized and animated "natural world" might shape people's perceptions and experiences of the human world. I think also of how it is possible that it is humans who must be reinvented, especially humans who consider themselves to be civilized. "Civilized" to me means dominated, domesticated, tame, brought into order, brought into line, molded, indoctrinated in the art of appearance, the art of facade, trained to think in a "civilized" manner (read Western European). Perhaps it is a mark of "civility" that this dynamic is played out in the patriarchal manner in which the earth is treated. It has been my own observation that in this contemporary society the overall practice towards the earth has been to tame her, control her, manipulate her, degrade her, profane her, strip her, rape her, plunder her and deny her voice. There is, for me, a correspondence between the way the earth is perceived and treated and the way women, children, and any other "feminized" groups are perceived and treated, always by "civilizing forces."

Mexican feminist scholar, Maria Antonieta Rascon, reminds us that what Catholicism forced upon native people of Azteca descent was a male trinity in place of Ometeotl, in place of the Dual Duality that is the Supreme Being, MotherFather, FatherMother.[18] More pointedly, I would say that Christianity and Catholicism separated the mother (earth) from the deity and so separated the woman from the teacher. In separating the woman (as earth) from the teacher, we began to be separated from the Earth and from all of our animal, plant, water, and sky relations as well. The creative spirit has been perverted, commodified, and appropriated by those who can afford it or take it by entitlement. The logic of capitalist accumulation and consumption which antagonizes the earth contributes to the degradation of the creative spirit just as much as do institutionalized religions which abhor the flesh, perpetuate notions of sin, and dislocate humans from the earth. From many oral traditions I have heard elders say that the earth is a strict grandmother capable of love in abundance, and capable of discipline of the most rigorous kind. I have listened to them speak about human beings needing to know the humility that nurtures itself in respect. The earth purifies herself, either harmoniously or by blows; she does what she has to, as we saw with floods that recently hit the Midwest.

I would like to end by telling two stories. In 1987, I went to Cuba for two weeks as a participant in the 18th Contingent of the Venceremos Brigade. One of the days that we were given to visit different sites, I chose to go to the Santeria Museum. One part of the museum consisted of replicas of home altars as they had been cared for during the time when this religious expression was practiced more. On some of the altars I was surprised to see plaster of Paris statues of Plains-style Indians, which had been painted by hand. I was stunned to learn of the curator's response when people asked him why the statues were there. He said, "Oh, we always pay our respects to the original peoples of these lands and we always ask their permission to be here." Upon my return, I immediately rushed to tell a Paiute elder who is dear to me of the news; he simply nodded his head in affirmation. Last spring, at Easter time, my husband and I had the good fortune to be able to attend the Yaqui Easter *pahko* ceremonies in Arizona. On Easter Sunday, we were at Barrio Libre where we were privileged to see Luis Maso Cienfuegos as he was the Deer. As the procession began to get organized, we were invited to have responsibility; my husband was asked to carry one of the poles of the canopy that shaded the sacred image, and I was asked to carry one end of an arch of paper flowers under which the entire procession passed even as we walked. From my vantage point, I could see the Deer leading us; I could see his head clearly as he gestured to us and showed us the way, opening the paths for us. Even though I was raised Roman Catholic on my dad's side, my Nimipu mom has effectively (and effortlessly) subverted the rigidity of that training all my life, and I have certainly rejected the patriarchal foundations of Catholicism. I was still moved in a way I had not expected, however, when I saw the Deer lead us up to the altar and I understood what he had done, this emissary from seyewailo, this saila maso, little brother deer. He led his pueblo to pay respects to the imported religion, the Catholic religion; he led us respectfully to the altar; he took that responsibility on himself for the people.

In both of these stories there are lessons and examples. How many peoples, besides the santeros, have paid their respects to the spirits of this land and asked their permission to be here? How many religious traditions, which in many ways have been embraced by native peoples of this hemisphere, have in turn paid their respects to the traditions of indigenous peoples? Vine Deloria, Jr., says, in his "Afterword" to the volume *America in 1492*,

> From an Indian point of view, the general theme by which to understand the history of the hemisphere would be the degree to which the whites [I would add all immigrants] have responded to the rhythms of the land—the degree to which they have become indigenous.[19]

For me, this "becoming indigenous" does not have to do with the New Age movement, or with the appropriation, commodification, and consumption of native traditions. [20] It does have to do with the paying of respects (I am quite conscious of the English term "to pay" in this phrase), or the offering of respect in concrete gestures of solidarity with the contemporary struggles for sovereignty of indigenous peoples as well as in the validation of indigenous belief systems. These recognitions have been a long time coming.

Document 3. Pilulaw Khus: Chumash Culture

Pilulaw Khus is a highly respected Chumash elder who lives in Santa Barbara, California. In the following account she analyzes Chums culture from daily life in Chums villages before missionization until recent struggles for recovery of the sacred site of Point Conception. She also discusses her own role within that culture.[21]

Mother Earth, Hutash, is very important to us. It is hard to understand. I'm not saying that any other nation or area of the world is less. I just know that within our nation, there is an incredible amount of power. There are amazingly powerful sacred places within the Chums nation, and that is one of my primary jobs, that's the direction I've been given. The assignment I've been given is to protect the sacred places and to do the ceremonies. Point Conception, commonly known as Western Gate, is a very powerful place for our people, and not just our people; it also includes the stories of other native people.

When the Europeans came here, first there were the Spaniards, the military, and the priests. Secondly came the Mexican government and then the U.S. government. With each invasion our people suffered more. Within one generation, the population of our people was reduced by half: our systems were pretty much out the window. There was a well-thought-out and specific plan of genocide. Take a minute and think about it, that in one generation people were watching their world being destroyed. Their families were being pulled apart. If we went into a mission together there—because we were very spiritual people, of course we were interested in this new spirituality the people were bringing—we weren't allowed to leave. We became slave labor. And, later, when our people did leave, the military was sent out to bring us back. Frequently we were killed in those raids. Think about the holocaust coming down on us, in one generation. We'd been going along for thousands and thousands and thousands of years, doing things for the most part in the same way.

When a baby was conceived, that baby was beginning to be taught about people and about the baby's place within the group and the environment, and as soon as the baby was born, there would be ceremonies and there would be certain things to take care of that baby, to introduce that baby not just to the parents, but to all the people, to the environment and to the universe. And that baby would know its place, and it worked well.

The idea of changing by assimilating, by contact with others, it didn't work that much for us. We were a very integrated group. We were very satisfied with how it operated. We lived in a paradise, and so we had no real need to change a whole lot. We're still that way. We're what people might call clannish. We're not real interested in having people bringing their ways of doing things and doing it on our land. If you think about that consistency and that persistence coming through time, in that way, and that all of a sudden, something hits and everything is wiped out in one generation, that is devastation, that is holocaust. The death rate soared during that time and the birth rate dropped during that time, and that makes perfect sense to me. Who would want to bring a baby into the world when that world was no longer your own any more? Who would want to live in that kind of situation? When the U.S. government came in, they said okay, we want to make a treaty with you tribes, and they were really determined to take over all our land. In that treaty, the one thing we held onto (we said they could take everything if they would leave us one thing) and that was Point Conception, because it was so important. The Western Gate, that's where our spirits go through, pierce that veil and go into the next reality, and it's very important that it be left open so that we can go through.

In 1975/76, companies called Western Light and Natural Gas and Pacific Gas and Electric decided they were going to put a facility there, a big plant, and we didn't know anything about the treaties. The reason we didn't know anything was that when it got back to Washington, D.C., the politicians in California here prevailed on the officials back in D.C. to put our treaty under a seal of secrecy. This was done with about eighteen treaties here in California. So people treated in good faith with the representative of the government and believed that this was going to give some protection to the Western Gate, and the seal of secrecy allowed them to do what they want to and not live up to the conditions of the treaty. These treaties have only recently surfaced. Ours was found when we were on the occupation out there at Point Conception.

When these companies decided to put that facility out there, I had already been married, had children, divorced, and been in and out of the area. At about this time, I was pulled back to Santa Barbara and started to work on an educational project, and then this occupation came up, and that was pretty much when I began to work in a more public, open way. I went out in the occupation because we couldn't allow the plant to be put there. It would interfere with the spirits from this reality. We did everything the way you're supposed to do. We had lawyers, people from the Environmental Defense Center. We did everything, tried every legal way, but the court said this may be good for your spirituality but the greater good is for the natural gas plant to be put there. This was crazy, not just from a spiritual point-of-view, but from an environmental point-of-view, because a lot of earthquake faults are there and seas are very rough, and they were going to be loading and off-loading these volatile fuels out there, in what they called the graveyard of ships.

So, we were very innocent and naive. We said we'd go and occupy because we can't allow this to be put out there. So we were innocent, all of us, and we packed up our backpacks and sleeping bags and we went out there and we set up a sweat lodge and we sweated, and we prayed and we sat out there. We thought now they'll see we're really serious and they'll go away. But no, we ended up being out there for close to a year on that occupation, and that was an incredibly important period of time. There were people who came here to support us from all the different nations and from Alaska, Canada, Mexico, and over and over and over again, when I talked to people, they said we know of this place, that's why we've come to help you, because it's our story. We had a phenomenal amount of help out there. That was one the Native people won. They did not put their plant out there. We won that one, and it's still clean out there. Our spirits can still travel back and forth out there.

That's the way I got started on the protection of sites and battling in that way, for that particular place and that particular purpose. I feel very strongly about any place where our people were, whether it's just an ordinary village or a sacred site. Remember that at ordinary village sites people have been living there for thousands of years, and as people lived there, that place became more and more sacred. Why? Because they were birthing there, they were dying, they were doing ceremonies there, and they were going into spirits there. Their bodies were being returned to the embrace of our mother, and each time these kinds of things occur, a place becomes increasingly sacred . . . I tell my children, when I die I want to go like an Indian into the mother, because she gave me my life and sustained me all my life, and it is only right that I return to her and that the life cycles can continue. Somebody is returned to the earth in that way. They go into the earth. There is a change that begins to happen in that soil, and the longer the burial stays in the earth, the more that change occurs. That person's essence permeates throughout the soil, so even the grasses, trees, flowers are all that person, coming into all of that, and beyond, to even the birds and animals that are there and feed; all are being benefited by the essence of that person.

We can't stop the ceremonies. I've received my bundle in a ceremony. I was given the opportunity to walk away from it, because once accepted, I have responsibility that goes with that. I was told there would be times when no one would come, when I'd do it by myself, and that's the way it is. It doesn't matter if anyone else is there, I have a responsibility to earth, to ancestors, to spirits, the universe, the people, to earth, to myself.

The way I've been taught, if someone comes here, they need to be taught. I say to non-Native, you're welcome to come here and sit by the fire. All people are connected to the earth and recognize what people are doing, the destruction. Come and be part of this, but at some point you need to give up and leave my fire and find your own ancestors, become strong and knowledgeable in your own way.

Document 4. The Presence of 'Isánáklésh and Apache Female Initiation

The following account by Ines Talamantez examines the Apache belief in the female deity, 'Isánáklésh and the initiation ceremony for a young girl at puberty, 'Isánáklésh Gotal.[22] The songs and music of the ceremony are in collaboration with Ann Dhu McLucas.

THE PRESENCE OF 'ISÁNÁKLÉSH. In southern New Mexico, east of the great White Sands, stands Dzil gais'ani, or Sierra Blanca. This 12,000-foot sacred mountain is the home of 'Isánáklésh who has been revered as a powerful female deity since oldest Apache memory. At the time of creation, after the world was made safe for people, Apaches gathered together in small bands to receive knowledge and to learn the traditions. 'Isánáklésh then spoke and proclaimed her special ceremony:

> We will have a feast for the young girls when they have their first flow. Many songs will be sung for them, so that they will grow strong and live a long life.

This eight-day ceremony, called 'Isánáklésh Gotal, is celebrated in recognition of the significance of a young Apache girl's first menses. According to Apache myth, the ceremony was founded by 'Isánáklésh as a means through which the girl might temporarily experience herself as 'Isánáklésh and be honored as such by the people. The first four days of the ceremony are marked with elaborate ritual detail and festive social activities. The ceremony's songs, sacred narratives, and images combine to leave a powerful imprint of 'Isánáklésh, both on the girl herself and on attending relatives, friends, and family members. Throughout the final four days the girl secludes herself to reflect on her ritual experiences.

The name given to this ceremony, 'Isánáklésh Gotal, literally means "Ceremonial Sing for 'Isánáklésh. The Apache term *gotal*, "ceremonial sing," suggests not only a festive celebration, but also a raising of supernatural power to accomplish the many moments of transformation that the young girl experiences. Not only is the girl temporarily transformed during this rite of passage; she is also permanently transformed into a mature Apache woman by the end of the ritual.

This transformation into womanhood is accomplished by ceremonially awakening the initiate to the world around her. For some girls, the ceremony is said to calm their adolescent imbalances. The Mescalero conceive of "fixing" the young initiate, ridding her of her baby ways and helping her through the door of adolescence, for at this young age the girls are said to be soft and moldable, capable of being conditioned and influenced by their female kin and others around them.

Timid girls may need to be awakened to their female identities; others may need to be taught to settle down and be more sensible and feminine. Initiates are well aware that they have undergone special teachings during the ceremony. Analysis of the ceremonial procedures and their religious implications helps us to understand the transformative aspects of the ceremony. There is no single moment at which the transformation of the girl to 'Isánáklésh or to woman, occurs. It is the fusion of all the ceremony's elements, especially the songs sung over the eight-day period, that produces the desired goals. During the ceremony, great attention is paid to the ritual details, and the meanings of the symbols are carefully explained to the girls. As the Singer and sponsor explain these teachings to the initiate, the girl begins to understand important elements of Apache culture that from now on she will be charged to maintain. After her ceremony, she will be a keeper of Apache traditions and the pattern of everyday living in which they will continue to endure. Thus, she is not only taught and protected by this ceremony; like 'Isánáklésh who gave it, she will also ideally teach and work to protect her tribe.

Sometimes it is not easy to convince young girls to participate in 'Isánáklésh Gotal. Many are intimidated by the prospect of becoming such a center of attention. Thus, the mothers and grandmothers of the tribe's young girls try to prepare them psychologically and spiritually for the ceremony long before the girls reach their menarche. The women try to convince the girls that they will change in a positive way if they participate fully—and that the ceremony will bring them a good and healthy life. Older women will often encourage prepubescent girls to observe the ceremonies of other initiates closely so they will know what to expect. I have heard mothers or other female kin say to a girl, "Go up toward the front of the Big Tipi where you can see and hear everything better."

The family begins preparations for the ceremony several years in advance of their daughter's menarche. They begin collecting the necessary ritual objects, including sacred pollen, which can only be gathered during the season when cattails are ripe. It is no less important to gather relatives' support, because the ceremony will be a tremendous burden on family resources. When the proud day of the girl's first menstruation arrives, her family may celebrate with a small private dinner. In the ideal, a male Singer and a woman sponsor are secured in the proper ritual manner: four gifts must be given, and the proper words must be exchanged.

Throughout the year following menarche, the girl's women kin and female sponsor then teach her the proper Apache ways. These include the use of medicinal herbs and healing skills. The women also prepare her deerskin dress, like 'Isánáklésh dress, with elaborate symbolic beadwork; attached to the ends of the fringes are the tiny metal cones that now replace deer hoofs, which will gently jingle when she walks or dances. If the girl is to have a private ceremony or "feast," as it is called today, her family and kin will usually host it at a carefully selected site well away from congested areas. The girl also has the option to join the several girls honored at the annual public Feast; in this case, her ritual will occur on the ceremonial grounds of the Mescalero tribal headquarters on whatever weekend falls closest to the Fourth of July. In either case, friends and family gather, supplies are stored, temporary tipis and cooking arbors are assembled; and preparations are made to feed all who come to the first four days of the ceremony.

Prior to dawn on the first day of the ceremony, the girl is placed in her own private tipi and carefully attended by female kin and her sponsor. The sponsor blesses the initiate with pollen and ritually bathes and dresses her for the ceremony. She reminds the girl of how good it feels to be cared for, so that the girl will learn to care for others. The girl's hair is washed with *Ishee*, yucca suds; she is fitted with leggings and moccasins; she is ritually fed traditional Apache foods. She is given a special reed, or *uka*, through which she will sip water, since water is not allowed to touch her lips for fear that this will bring floods; she also receives a scratching stick, or *tsibeeichii*, for she is not to scratch with her fingernails.

Meanwhile, outside on the ceremonial grounds, the Singers and the girl's male kin begin to construct the sacred tipi. This will be the central structure where most of the rites take place. It is called the ceremonial home of 'Isánáklésh or the Big Tipi. According to Apache sacred songs, only when this tipi's four main poles are properly erected can 'Isánáklésh reside there. Then the power of the songs will go out from the tipi to carry the ceremony's benefit out to all of the people on earth. To raise these poles, first four rocks are used to mark the sacred place that was touched by the first rays of the sun. Then the four poles are sung into place. A song is sung for each pole as it is placed into the earth and tied to the others at the top of the structure. Thus, the Apache sacred number four is established musically as well as visually. Ideally, the first songs should be sung approximately at dawn, as the sun rises to the east, where the opening of the tipi must face. This way both song and sunrise mark the beginning of sacred time. Since the voice of the Singer can only carry so far in an outdoor setting, the songs also serve to mark off a sacred space for the circle of participants, who must move close enough to hear as well as to see.

The sacred tipi is now completed and readied for 'Isánáklésh who has been symbolically approaching from the east with the early dawn light. The tipi's upper portion is wrapped with a clean white canvas cloth, and its lower portion is filled in with oak branches. The eastward opening is built out to the sides, as wings, in order to let the sun's light inside. After the tipi is in place, the initiate in her ritual garment appears with her sponsor and family. She is freshly bathed and dressed and carries a blanket and white deerskin to be unfolded and placed in front of the tipi. The initiate, now taking on the role of 'Isánáklésh, then blesses everyone who wants to be blessed with yellow cattail pollen, and the people in turn bless her. An essential component of this rite is the *tadadine*, the cattail pollen, which is the pollen that 'Isánáklésh used in the creation story. The girl motions in the Apache way to the four directions and then applies the yellow life-giving substance over the bridge of the person's nose, moving from the right to the left side; she may also apply it to other parts of the person's body. This blessing assures the people of a good long life. Hence, to remind the girl of her role as healer, the sponsor, Meredith Begay, now tells her:

> When you become 'Isánáklésh in the ceremony, you will have her power to heal because it is 'Isánáklésh who handed this knowledge to us. There is a sacred story about this. Since you will be 'Isánáklésh you will be asked to heal and bless people who come to see you. You must always remember how you felt during your ceremony, when you were the living 'Isánáklésh; then, later in life, you can call on her for help whenever you face problems; you will remember how you felt when you were her, when you became her.

The initiate's young, soft body is next "molded," that is, massaged and aligned by her sponsor to insure the transformation of the girl to 'Isánáklésh as well as for continuing health and strength and a long, productive life. The Singer then draws four naturally paced footprints on the deerskin with pollen. While a sacred basket is put in place to the east of the tipi, the initiate steps on the pollen prints and is then gently "pushed off" to run around the basket and return to the tipi. This sequence symbolizes walking on the pollen path, again to bring the initiate a long, healthy life. The initiate runs around the basket four times, as four verses of the ritual song are sung. Before each run, the ceremonial basket is moved a little closer to the tipi. Meanwhile, the girl's female sponsor makes the "ritual marker" during the song, a long high-pitched sound, to draw the attention of the supernatural. For, as she runs, the initiate meets the approaching 'Isánáklésh and escorts her back to the Apache people.

After the first morning's rituals, the initiate ideally appears in public only during the next four nights. During the day, she may not have any ordinary social contact; only relatives, close friends, and those who wish to be blessed or healed may visit her in her private tipi.

When dusk arrives on the first night of the ceremony, male dancers appear to bless the young initiate, the tipi, and the central ceremonial fire. These dancers have been ritually transformed into *hastchin*, supernaturals, who live inside the mountains near Mescalero.

At about 10 P.M., the initiate, her sponsor, and the Singer appear at the sacred Tipi. The Singer leads the girl into the home of 'Isánáklésh by extending an eagle feather, which he holds in his right hand. The girl takes hold of the other end of the feather and follows as he takes four steps into the tipi; each step is accompanied by the verse of a song that refers to the tipi as the home of 'Isánáklésh. Inside, facing the fire at the center of the tipi, the initiate and her sponsor sit on deerhides and blankets. The Singer prays and then kneels in front of the girl with his back to the fire and prays as he blesses the initiate.

As other songs are sung in groups of four, the initiate dances back and forth across a deerhide, looking always just above the fire or at the Singer's rattle, as the ritual rules prescribe. Accompanied by the light, the regular pulse of the Singer's deerhoof rattles, each song and dance lasts for about four to six minutes. Between songs, the girl rests for three to four minutes; sometimes the Singer and sponsor will talk, but usually they are silent. As each group of four songs ends, a short formula is sung to mark its conclusion. Then the Singer lights hand-rolled cigarettes of ritual tobacco, and a longer break is taken, during which the initiate is sometimes offered water through her drinking tube. During nights two and three, the same pattern occurs, with no morning or daytime activity. Only the content of the songs varies with each nightly performance as the initiate moves through the ceremony.

A closer look shows that this seemingly endless repetition is a tightly structured and deliberate ritual form. The repetition establishes a stable place, quite literally when combined with the dancing, which is restricted to the area of a small deerhide. In the matrix of this stability, thoughts are free to wander. The young 'Isánáklésh appears to be in a trancelike state as she dances more vigorously each night. The Singer tells her to think in images about the tribe—to visualize troubles and illness and to send them over the mountain and away from the tribe. She is to set her mind and spirit in motion, even as her physical space is confined.

Similarly, the repetition also alters the sense of time. All necessary elements for a good life are said to be present in the ceremony; all the important symbols of Apache culture and of the world of women are contained in the songs that are sung each night. By calling on these symbols with the songs' powerful words, participants evoke images that are sometimes literally seen in the sacred space. The mind can travel between these two images. When similar tunes are used, it is as if no time has elapsed between one set of songs and the next—or between the present ceremony and the first ceremony ever sung. 'Isánáklésh is there; and her healing power is present, as it was during the first moments of the world's creation.

The ceremony lasts almost until dawn on the fourth day. Songs are counted by wooden markers that are driven into the ground around the fire. Many of these songs, both words and tunes, are repeated from the previous evenings. Then, on the fifth and final morning of the ceremony's public segment, the ceremonial circle is completed by actions that reverse the pattern of the first morning. The initiate, the sponsor, and the Singer assemble in the tipi just as dawn is about to break. 'Isánáklésh has again been freshly bathed. The sacred basket is beside them, holding pollen, the girl's eagle feather, tobacco, a gramma grass brush, several kinds of clay, and galena, a shiny black lead ore found in the mountains of Mescalero. Using the clays, pollen, and galena, the Singer paints an image of the sun on the palm of his hand. As he sings, he holds his hand up to the sun, so that the galena glitters as the early sun's rays hit it. When the song is finished, the Singer turns and touches his sun-painted hand to her shoulders and chest. Then he touches each side of her head and rubs the sun-image into her head.

Singing another song, the Singer paints her with white earth clay, covering all the exposed skin on her arms and legs, as well as the lower half of her face. As this is happening, other participants remove the cloth and branches covering the sacred tipi, so that only the four main poles remain. Within this skeleton structure, the ritual blessing and healing of the tribe again take place. Taking red clay from a basket beside him, the Singer blesses members of the community (and anyone else seeking blessing) by marking them with the clay, taking special care for young children, the elderly, and the sick.

The next and final ritual sequence occurs very quickly. 'Isánáklésh is led out of the tipi to the same tune and eagle feather that led her in; she walks on pollen footsteps, which are again painted on the deerskin. The sacred basket is once again placed to the east of the tipi, at the same distance from the tipi as it had been during the final run of the ceremony's first morning. Once again 'Isánáklésh takes the four ceremonial pollen footsteps and runs off, accompanied by the four verses of her running song. This time, after each run, the basket is moved further to the east. On the last run, she runs to the basket—now far to the east. She picks up her eagle feather from the basket and runs to the east as far as she can, then turns around and begins to rub the white clay from her face while returning to her private tipi, where she will stay during the next four days. During the past four days she has symbolically left behind her childlike youth and has been ritually transformed into 'Isánáklésh. Now, 'Isánáklésh has herself departed into the east. After the next four days of quiet reflection, the initiate will emerge from her tipi as an adult Apache woman.

As the girl performs her last run, the Singer chants as the rope that tied together the tipi poles is loosened and undone. Now the tipi's last four poles fall to the ground with a great crash. During all of this excitement, the Singer has continued to sing, accompanied by his rattle. However, the crowd, which knows the traditions of this ceremony, has by now moved toward the cooking arbor. Here, pickup trucks have driven in, loaded with candy, fruit, and household goods. These are thrown to the crowd as gifts from the family sponsoring the feast. The effect of the final run, the dismantling of the sacred tipi, and the giveaway with all of its accompanying excitement are meant to decisively break the sense of sacred space and time.

Document 5. Espiritualista Initiation in Southern California and Mexico

In the following account Inés Talamantez recounts her introduction to espiritualismo in Barrio Logan in San Diego, California, which led to her eventual initiation by a guia in Mexico City. The
two guias who provided information for this analysis are Sarita Macias from El Templo Amor Poder
y Sabiduria in San Diego and Manuela Cegudo "la Guia de Guias" at El Templo del Mediodia in
Mexico City. Both were interviewed in their respective templos, offices, and homes, where they talked
of their training, professional methods as healers, and attitudes toward their calling. These guias belong to the movement of Mexican Espiritualismo that emerged from the teachings of Rogue Rojas,
founder of La Iglesia Patriarcal Elias.[23]

The approach for recruiting initiates to espiritualismo and the steps taken in
the process of shaping and performing the initiatory ritual known as La Marca
tells us how the female practitioners, or guias, manipulate provocative symbolic
images to transform and move the initiates from one religious and social status to
another.

The initiation follows a three-part pattern common to rites of passage: (1) the
preliminal phase of separation from the initiate's community and everyday activities; (2) the liminal phase of transition, in which the initiate is ritually marked
with consecrated oils and holy water; and (3) the postliminal phase or incorpora-
tion back into society with a new social and religious status.[24]

According to Guia Macias, the following teachings are still practiced today at
all the templos:

Desarrollo, or the practice of spiritual development that leads to "La Marca,"
defines the nature of the initiate's task in life. It is a gift of spiritual inheritance
that is validated at the time of the ritual initiation. It focuses on the development
of the initiate's powers in what are called the *siete virtudes y etapas graduadas* (seven
virtues and graduated stages):

1. *Recibir el ser espiritual:* to take a name provided by her protector
2. *Ungeamiento:* anointing by the help of the Holy Spirit
3. *Dar consejo curacion:* modes of spiritual and psychological counseling
4. *Curar con medicina:* healing with herbs and homeopathic techniques
5. *Tomar el Rayo:* receive the sacred touch *(toque espiritual)* in preparation for
   trance—women receive this from Mary and men from *el Padre Elias*
6. *Radicion del maestro:* ecstasy or trance
7. *Alta luz:* pure spiritual *communication* with the Ultimate Reality, the Eternal
   Father, Jehovah; this refers to enlightenment and communication between
   spirits

According to Guia Cegudo in Mexico City, only those who attain the highest
spiritual development of *alta luz* become guias, and they are sanctioned by the ma-

jor *templo* of espiritualismo, Templo del Mediodia in Mexico City, to open and operate templos or *recintos.* At their templos, these authorized guias implement the teachings and initiate others through the process of "La Marca."

"La Marca" is an invisible sign that "marks" or bestows upon initiates their task in life; it serves as a *confirmation* that the initiate has completed the necessary stages of spiritual development. La Marca opens the initiate's understanding of the "third eye," which *contains* the knowledge and teachings of God. The guia knows through her *videncia (vision)* if the initiate is ready to be marked. La Marca thus becomes a public *recognition* of one's spiritual ability, which is further recognized by a special certificate. A practicing guia usually displays in her templo the certificate verifying she has received La Marca.

In La Marca, the initiate receives the Holy Spirit (recibir el ser espiritual) and is given a spirit guide by the guia in trance. It introduces the initiate into the world of mediumship through trance, *curaciones unidas* (healing with the help of other guias), and *ungeamiento espiritual y físico* (spiritual and physical cleansing with holy water only). The process occurs as follows. *Guias* who operate on a highly developed spiritual plane go into trance and lend their consciousness so that the spirit may work through them. This *toque espiritual,* or sacred touch, is known as the word or breath of God, which represents all truth. While in trance, the *guia,* with the help of her own spirit guide, speaks and counsels the initiate, answering whatever questions she may have. The *guia* gives advice and sometimes provides a spiritual guide if the person is considered to be appropriately prepared.

During the ritual, a person appointed as *la pluma de oro* (golden pen) records the message coming through the medium. Later the transcription is used to decode the *carga* (task in life). This *carga* ritually marks the person who must then seek to analyze and understand the message. Sometimes no message comes through. In this situation, the person is rejected and informed that no spirit has come forth. This is interpreted as meaning that something in that person's life is out of harmony or that she may lack spiritual preparation.

Guia Sarita in San Diego explained to me that the spiritual "calling" may come to the *guia* through personal crisis at a young and impressionable age. Sarita, for example, was ill as a child and was cured by a curandera (Mexican folk healer). At the time, she did not believe in the healer's powers and rejected *curanderismo* as nonsense. Later, as an adult, she became ill with chest pains and a heart murmur. Rejecting the idea that she needed an operation, she instead went to a *templo espiritualista* and through a psychic operation was healed. Informed that the procedure was entirely spiritual, she was eventually transformed into a believer of *espiritualismo.*

Sarita apprenticed herself to the healer Petra Castro in Tijuana, Baja California, for three years and then moved to Mexico City, where she studied for the next eight years with Guia Cegudo at Templo del Mediodia. At the end of this time, she was instructed by the directors of the Templo to go to San Diego to set up the first *templo* in California in Barrio Logan to provide for Mexicans and Chicana/os a place of refuge.

As a guia *espiritualista*, Sarita serves two sets of clients: those who need to have health or spiritual problems met, and those members of the community at large who are in need of a communication network and support system. Her clients are usually, but not exclusively, Mexicans or Chicana/os. Sarita performs *limpias* (cleansings) using the burning of incense over a charcoal fire and various plants such as sage, pepper tree branches, and geraniums in an effort to remove malevolent spirits. Her clients are mostly women, including white women who sometimes are believers in holistic healing or other alternative healing systems.

For physical ailments, Sarita uses *curaciones* (healings), healing with massage, manipulation, kneading, rubbing, rotating and aligning the body, and spiritual operations and injections. The latter are healing maneuvers in which she uses her thumb and forefinger to function as a syringe and needle. She also employs *balsamo de curacion* (holy water), oil, garlic, chile, lemon or eggs, as well as a variety of herbs in her healing. In addition, she prays while in trance to her spirit guide and other divinities to work through her for the healing of her clients.

On Sundays, she holds *catedras* (doctrinal teachings) from ten in the morning until noon in her *templo* in San Diego. Usually, twenty to thirty people are present. When they enter, they take the *balsamo de curacion* (holy water) and rub it between their hands, wiping the water over their heads and down the sides of their bodies, after making the sign of the cross. At the front of the *templo*, a tiny altar symbolically represents the major canons of *espiritualismo*: seven steps (which correspond to the above-mentioned *siete virtudes y etapas graduadas*) leading to a triangle above the altar with an *ojo de dios* (God's eye) in the center and rays of divinity shining down. The altar is covered with burning candles, ritual objects, and freshly cut flowers, the aroma of which permeates the air.

The "Pedro," or pillar of the church, and the "Guardian" assist Sarita by leading the congregation in several songs or hymns. After the singing, Sarita, who is now in trance, delivers the *catedra* or *mensaje de Cristo* (the word of Christ). Then the chosen *vidente* (visionary), who is selected by Sarita for the day, stands with eyes closed, lifts her palms, and begins to channel the message of the spirit. When she finishes telling what she envisioned, five or six participants from the congregation, including Sarita, describe the spiritual visions that they received with their eyes closed during the channeling. These revelations often use the iconography of the *templo*: the altar, the *ojo de dios* (the God's eye) over the seven steps, and the symbols of the *templo* banner. Then, more hymns are sung and everyone gathers for social interaction before leaving the *templo*.

In her *templo*, Amor Poder Sabiduria (love, power, knowledge) in the Barrio Logan in San Diego, at Sarita's invitation, I participated in a *catedra*. Listening to her words while she was in trance possession, words of charismatic force yet tender kindness, I was fascinated by the metaphorical aspects of her speech and beautiful incantations. For Sarita, spirits are essential; she works very hard to contact her spirit guide through powerful language. In her role of medium, under the possession of her spirit guide, *patas de aguila gris* (Gray Eagle Foot), she has attained status in her community as well as in other cities where she heals and advises.

A woman of keen awareness and personal warmth, Sarita always welcomed me to her *templo* with an *abrazo* (warm hug) and told me initially that she knew I would be coming to see her. She claimed to know what my role in life was, and she, of course, knew exactly how far I had come in my spiritual development simply by laying her hands on my head. This information she acquired by seeing and interpreting my aura, gently pulling down my lower eyelids, and gazing intently into my eyes. She was already in the process of pulling me into her flock.

Sarita claimed that I was in a bad way and that I seemed to be undergoing stress. I was in the last days of completing work on my dissertation. Indeed, I had very red eyes. After a sage smoke, cleansing *(limpia)* and prayer sessions using candles and holy water, she invited me to come to the next *catedra* on the following Sunday so I could witness her at work.

I returned many times to Sarita's *templo*. She soon sensed my interest in her work and often enlisted me to help her. I frequently interviewed patients about their primary reasons for coming to a *templo*; sometimes I served as translator for non-Spanish speaking patients, escorted them into Sarita's presence, and prepared the articles she used in her healing. An incident related to translating was especially memorable. One day an African American man arrived at the *templo*, seeking a cure for his terminal illness. Since he did not speak Spanish and Sarita does not speak English, she turned to me and said, *"Hermana, ayudame con el hermano"* (Sister, help me with our brother). I agreed, and she then went into trance for the healing and I was confronted with the task of translating the message from the spirit world. Such participation increased my interest in *espiritualismo*. It was Sarita who initially insisted that in order for me to understand, I should prepare myself for initiation into *espiritualismo*. As I resisted, she reminded me, "If you want to truly understand, the best way is to experience it." I was reminded of African American sociologist Bennetta Jules Rosetta's initiation into the African Apostolic Church under similar circumstances. The next thing I knew, she was insisting that I go to the Templo del Mediodia in Mexico City to meet the *guia* there to determine if I was eligible for La Marca. Since this experience with Sarita, I have often observed how *guias* actively recruit and give special consideration to those in teaching, medical, or counseling professions in order to further legitimize their positions in the community.

In my case, La Marca required two months of preparation and daily concentration on meditation and body purification to try to raise my spiritual awareness. I was told to fast one or two days a week, to take sweat baths, and to put a glass of water covered with a white cloth at the head of my bed every night. This water would draw away any negative force around me and help me spiritually. In the morning, I was instructed to pour the water down the drain.

Finally, after two months of *consejo* (spiritual counseling) and meditative training, I was ready, according to the *guia* Manuela, to leave this state of preparation and enter the state of transition as described by Van Gennep. Dressed in a white dress with the emblem of Templo del Mediodia in red letters enclosed by a triangle, I was escorted up to the altar to undergo La Marca.

After a warm welcome before the congregation of about 1,200 people, I was introduced as *"la Hermanita Piel Roja* (Red-Skin Sister) from California." They sang hymns as Manuela went into possession trance. I was instructed by a *materia* to come forward and kneel before the *guia*, who was by now in trance. The *materias* are those women from the congregation who are carefully selected by the *guia* because of their higher state of spiritual development. They are groomed through a special training process to become *guias*. As part of their special training, they assist the *guia*. The material being of the guia serves as the instrument of the spirit.

Kneeling before Manuela, I was given the name of the tribe of Abraham as the tribe to which I would belong from then on. Then she delivered the message from the spirit world to me. The message contained what I was given as a *herencia espiritual* (spiritual heritage); that is *videncia* (vision), *ensenanza* (teaching), and *curacion* (healing). To not develop these gifts, I was told, would produce dire consequences.

Manuela then laid her hands on my head, shoulders, and chest; she wiped my hands with holy water and touched my body with a flower, all in an act of purification. I was then prayed over and advised to incorporate my *carga* into my everyday life. I was asked to return to my seat walking backwards. As I did so, I noticed that the *materias* occupied the first ten pews, acting as a protective barrier for the *guia* who was in trance.

After this, other *videntes* (visionaries) in the congregation revealed what they had experienced while the *guia* was in possession trance seeking my message from the spirit world. Five people related their experiences. All of them claimed to see me in the role of teacher or healer. A final hymn was sung and the ceremony was over. The congregation moved to the back of the *templo*. I was soon surrounded by people who wanted to meet me and welcome me for coming such a long distance to be with them. Many asked questions about Apache culture and language because they had Apache spirit guides.

The entire possession trance and ceremony was taped, and I was told to return in two weeks for a transcription of the text and an interpretation of its content.

The person who has this task at Templo del Mediodia is the participant, usually a male, who takes the role of Pedro (Peter), the foundation of the templo. Several weeks later, after the reading and analysis of the text, I received a personal copy of La Marca with the seal of the *templo* as well as a new status—that of *marcada* (spiritually marked). I now had a new responsibility: to carry out the message of my *marca* and my *carga* as uncovered by the ritual of La Marca.

Notes

1. Inés Talamantez, "The Longest Walk," *Shantik: Journal of International Writing and Art* 4, no. 2 (Summer–Fall 1979).

2. Diane Bell, *Daughters of the Dreaming* (Minneapolis: Univ. of Minnesota Press, 1993).

3. "San Juan Pueblo," *Handbook of North American Indians, Vol. 9* (Washington, DC: Smithsonian Institution, 1979).

4. Paula Gunn Allen, *Grandmothers of the Light: A Medicine Woman's Sourcebook* (Boston: Beacon Press, 1991).

5. Vickie Downey, "Tewa-Tesuque Pueblo," in *Wisdom's Daughters: Conversations with Women Elders of Native America*, ed. Steven Wall (New York: HarperCollins, 1993), pp. 2–21.

6. Personal communication with Shirley Montoya.

7. Personal communication with Shirley Montoya.

8. Flora Jones is a Wintu religious leader and healer in northern California.

9. *Jesuit Relations and Allied Documents: Travels and Explorations of the Jesuit Missionaries in New France, 1610–1791* (Cleveland: Burrows Brothers, 1896–1901).

10. See Beatrice Medicine and Patricia Albers, eds., *The Hidden Half: Studies of Plains Indian Women* (New York: Univ. Press, 1983).

11. Ella Cara Deloria, *Waterlily* (Omaha: Univ. of Nebraska Press, 1988).

12. MALCS, *Mujeres Activas en Letras y Cambio Social* (Women Active in Letters and Social Change), is the major network for Latina women academics, writers, and social activists.

13. Rigoberta Menchu, *I, Rigoberta Menchu: An Indian Woman in Guatemala*, ed. by Elisabeth Burgos-Debray, trans. Ann Wright (London: Verso Press, 1984).

14. See forthcoming book by Ines Talamantez, *'Isánáklésh Gotal: Introducing Apache Girls to the World of Spiritual and Cultural Values*.

15. Ines Hernandez-Avila, address given at the 1993 Annual Meeting of the American Academy of Religion, Washington, DC.

16. Original note to the document: Ines Hernandez-Avila, "Tejana Intonations/Nez Perce Heartbeat: Notes on Identity and Culture," *A/B Autobiographical Studies* 7, no. 2 (Fall 1993): 298.

17. Steven Crum writes: "Because of their hunting and gathering way of life, the extended families moved about inside their larger tribal territory." Also, Crum states, "Although the Newe moved about throughout the year, they still had a strong sense of place. In fact, they were deeply attached to particular valley areas and the nearby mountain ranges. They did not wander aimlessly but remained within niches inside the larger tribal

territory." *Po'i Pen-Tammen Kimmappeh/The Road on Which We Came: A History of the Western Shoshone* (Salt Lake City: University of Utah Press, 1994), p. 8.

18. Original note to the document: Maria Antonieta Rascon, "La Mujer en la Lucha Social," *Imagen y Realidad de la Mujer* ed. by Elena Urrutia (Mexico City: SeptDiana, 1977), p. 150.

19. Original note to the document: Vine Deloria, Jr., "Afterword," in Alvin M. Josephy, *America in 1492: The World of the Indian People before the Arrival of Columbus* (New York: Alfred Knopf, 1992), pp. 429–30.

20. Original note to the document: Simon Brascoupe says, in "Indigenous Perspectives on International Development," *Indigenous Economics: Toward a Natural Order, Akwekon Journal* 9, no. 2 (Summer 1992): 429–30, "For the West to adopt Indigenous knowledge, they do not have to become 'indigenized,' but they do need to reflect on their own culture and benefit from lessons learned. The field of Indigenous knowledge extends to ecology, hunting and gathering, medicine and fishing."

21. This document is taken from Pilulaw Khus's lecture to a religious studies class on myth and symbols at the University of California at Santa Barbara, April 7, 1994. The lecture was transcribed by D. Bell.

22. See forthcoming study in Inés Talamantez, *'Isánáklésh Gotal.*

23. For the beginnings of Mexican spiritualism, see Isabel Lagarriga Attias, *Magia y Religion entre los Espiritualistas Trinitarios Marianos* (Mexico City: Departamento de Etnologia y Antropologia Social, Instituto Nacional de Antropologia e Historia, 1974).

24. These stages are described in Arnold van Gennep, *Rites of Passage* (1909; reprint, Chicago: Univ. of Chicago Press, 1960), pp. 3–4.

Out of Bounds: Indigenous Knowing and the Study of Religion

14

MARY C. CHURCHILL

No longer relegated to the margins of academic importance, the study of American Indian women has finally found a home in the newly emerging area of Native American women's studies. Historically,[1] it has been anthropology, more than any other field, that has staked its claim as the turf of Indian America. Hopi-Miwok writer Wendy Rose, for instance, points out that when she wanted to study American Indian literature she was forced to do so in anthropology, not in English or comparative literature.[2] Despite anthropology's predominance, however, its treatment of Native women has not paralleled the intensity of its study of American Indians overall. The fact that male anthropologists have had limited opportunity to observe and speak with American Indian women has no doubt contributed to this situation, but the field's failure to recognize the importance of indigenous women, especially beyond the confines of home, may speak more clearly to the underlying epistemological reasons for the rather limited information.

While the emergence of American Indian studies and women's studies has remedied this situation to a noticeable degree, each has its own limitations as well. Analysis of gender issues has not necessarily been a central aspect of American Indian studies, although individuals have made it a point to specialize in the study of American Indian women or to employ a gender analysis in their work. Women's studies has also failed to prioritize the study of Native American women. The history of women's studies demonstrates its interest in the concerns and experiences of white middle-class and elite women over those of women of color and working-class and poor women. When feminist academics turn their attention toward Native American women, these researchers generally do not write out of indigenous frameworks. Even as the scholarship on women of color develops within women's studies, the voices of American Indian women remain few and far between. Therefore, Native American women's studies has the potential to best address the unique intersection of race, gender, and class as well as sexuality and religion that characterizes the life experience of American Indian women.

Central to the foundation and development of this area are the perspectives of indigenous people, especially women. As a mixed-blood Cherokee scholar trained in religious studies, I find this assumption of vital importance, for the primacy of Native perspectives cannot be assumed in my own field. One would think that with the dedicated efforts of Native scholars before us we could move beyond the narrow limits of the "white path" of academia, but such is apparently not the case. One recent example is an article by religious studies scholar Sam Gill, who argues that prioritizing the perspectives of believers and practitioners, including those of American Indians, African Americans, and women, for instance, is detrimental to the development of the academic study of religion. He offers several "bounding criteria" for religious studies that disparage the scholarship of Native scholars and others as "the religious study of religion" and hence not significant for the future of the field. In this chapter, I examine and respond to Gill's claims, arguing that the academic study of religion cannot develop adequately without the study of American Indian religious traditions, among other forms of scholarship, as studied by "insiders" themselves. As an example of the potential for such scholarship, I offer an analysis of the poem "Prayer of the Poet-Hunter" by Cherokee writer Marilou Awiakta. It is my hope that both this response to academic claims that are oppressive to Native American people and my emphasis on the work of an American Indian woman will serve as an example of the necessity of Native American women's studies and of the kind of scholarship that might fall within the scope of this valuable emergent field.

Disappointed by the direction the academic study of religion has taken, Sam Gill offers a vision for the development of religious studies. He argues that what has flourished in the field is the "religious study of religion"—scholars studying religious traditions for the same reasons that religious practitioners practice religious traditions—while the *academic* study of religion has not developed adequately.[3] While this assessment of what kinds of studies have thrived is debatable, Gill does delineate several "bounding criteria" for the study of religion that appear on first reading to be very reasonable: the academic study of religion should not depend on the identity of the researcher, but it must be sensitive to multicultural issues; religion must be understood as an "academically constructed rubric," not synonymous with any religious tradition or with the sacred; the study of religion is a comparative endeavor; and the motivations for the study of religion are dual— the wish to understand specific religions as well as the desire to use the comparative category of religion to comprehend ourselves as human beings.[4] Christopher

Jocks, a Mohawk scholar of religious studies, has written an excellent critical response to Gill's schema, and to Jocks's voice, I would like to add my own, which both complements and supports his assessment.[5]

It seems plausible that any scholar of religion could find a way to work inside the boundaries Gill circumscribes, whether or not particular works are especially comparative or devoted to religion as a subject of universal human concern. Yet, behind these seemingly neutral prescriptions is a religious studies that reinscribes problematic aspects of Western thought and generally dismisses emic, or "insider," approaches in the study of American Indian religious traditions, women and religion, African American religions, Asian religions, and so forth as important but secondary in value in the academic study of religion.[6] Gill's central argument, articulated in the premier American journal of religious studies, is that the academic study of religion is a Western endeavor.[7] As he puts it, "The academic study of religion has often failed to acknowledge what it is. It is academic; it is Western; it is intellectual."[8] Many of us who study religion in the academy are well aware of religious studies' emergence out of Western Enlightenment thought, and we regularly employ—although critically—academic methods and intellectual ways of knowing that are infused with Western thought. The academic study is indeed Western, as Gill argues—but only historically and, to a certain extent, methodologically. Yet, Gill suggests that it should be Western *necessarily* (i.e., based on "rational discourse, hypothetic inference, and the application of scientific method").[9] As a result of the academy's failure to study religion within the boundaries he creates and the Western frame he privileges, the academic study of religion has fallen short of its potential, according to Gill; it is "less inspired," "not . . . a mature academic field," and its development is "repressed and retarded."[10]

This emphasis on Gill's part on Western ways of knowing is somewhat surprising, considering some of his previous work. In "The Trees Stood Deep Rooted," for instance, Gill implicitly argues for the importance of indigenous thought in understanding indigenous traditions. He asserts that in American Indian religious traditions "the events of creation are somehow paradigmatic, and the knowledge given in the creation stories permeates the life of the people."[11] He demonstrates this contention by discussing how the Diné (Navajo) conceive of creation. "To the Navajo," Gill writes, "the world was not created by some powerful earth-making god, but through the creative powers of thought and the ritual language of song and prayer."[12] He goes on to show quite effectively that how the Diné thought about creation is central to understanding their religious traditions, such as the Blessingway ceremony and the practice of drypainting. In another article, "'It's Where You Put Your Eyes,'" Gill also emphasizes the "insider" perspective. In regard to viewing a drypainting, Gill states that "the most important point of view is that of the person being cured, and this person sees the painting from the inside out because he or she sits in the middle of it."[13] And for a masked dancer, Gill explains that "the full meaning [of the mask] is gained by looking through the eyeholes of the mask and seeing the effect it has on the world."[14] These two articles, I believe, illustrate the power of taking seriously indigenous ways of knowing and perceiving in the academic study of religion. Incidentally, they also demonstrate that a non-Indian, in this case a Euro-American, can contribute effectively to the emic study of American Indian religious traditions.

These articles suggest, therefore, that Gill and scholars who stress the importance of indigenous perspectives share a common ground. Even in "The Academic Study of Religion" and the rejoinder, Gill makes assertions these scholars could agree with. His contention that religion should not be considered synonymous with Christianity is one such example.[15] Those stressing an indigenous emic approach could also support Gill's point that studies that utilize "indigenous categories, indigenous rationality and so on . . . . are not only important but essential *to* the academic study of religion."[16] Where Gill draws the line, however, is that such studies do not constitute "mature academic studies *of* religion."[17]

Mature academic studies of religion, Gill would have us believe, are governed by the scientific method. This way of knowing includes, for example, such notions as objectivity, subject-object separation, empiricism, cause and effect, and rationality.[18] Ironically, however, by promoting this epistemology, Gill endorses what feminist philosopher Donna Haraway refers to as the "god trick"—of "seeing everything from nowhere," of supposing there is a perspective from above, a view independent of the observer and his or her location.[19] Haraway argues instead for the concept of "situated knowledges," knowledges that are partial, locatable, accountable, and capable of joining other partial views.[20] Situated knowledges make the observer and his or her visual apparatus or frame apparent. "Only those occupying the positions of the dominators," observes Haraway, "are self-identical, unmarked, disembodied, unmediated, transcendent."[21] In other words, the privilege of domination, be it male, Euro-American, Western, or elite, is that those in power consciously or unconsciously consider their vision to be neutral and their visual apparatus or frame transparent, enabling them to see what really is. They fail to acknowledge the ways in which their perceiving or knowing is incomplete, reflective of their location, and influenced by their commitments, whether they be ideological, philosophical, or otherwise. For Haraway, true objectivity is "critical positioning" (i.e., perception that is "least likely to allow denial of the critical and interpretive core of all knowledge").[22] She is in effect arguing for the importance of ways of knowing other than the scientific method. These forms of knowing include critical and interpretive epistemologies, the first of which stresses the roles that social, economic, and political forces play in the construction of knowledge and the second of which emphasizes the role of interpretation in knowing. It is often the subjugated or marginalized who have such "critical positioning" because their locations have the promise of demystifying the "god trick" and generating models that question or undermine structures of power.[23] Haraway, however, admits that such positioning is not unproblematic:

> There is a premium on establishing the capacity to see from the peripheries and the depths. But here there also lies a serious danger of romanticizing and/or appropriating the vision of the less powerful while claiming to see from their positions. To see from below is neither easily learned nor unproblematic, even if "we" [feminists] "naturally" inhabit the great underground terrain of subjugated knowledges. The positionings of the subjugated are not exempt from critical reexamination, decoding, deconstruction, and interpretation; that is, from both semiological and hermeneutic modes of critical inquiry.[24]

The idea of situated knowledges therefore entails that scholars engage in critical inquiry while being a part of the field of inquiry itself. Feminist philosopher Sandra Harding has come to this same conclusion, arguing for the stance of "strong objectivity," which "requires that the subject of knowledge be placed on the same critical, causal plane as the objects of knowledge."[25] These ways of knowing in effect undermine the scientific method and its traditional assumptions of objectivity and subject-object separation. The scientific method advocated by Gill is therefore at best only one perspective among many. It has something to contribute to the academic study of religion just as critical and hermeneutical perspectives do. At worst, however, its roots in structures of domination make it a less useful perspective. That it is more mature than critical or interpretive frames—on which emic approaches often rely—is therefore doubtful.

With these understandings in mind, let us return to Gill's five bounding criteria for the academic study of religion and examine them more closely. On the face of it, Gill's first contention that "the academic study of religion must not depend upon or require of its researchers, teachers, or students any specific religious belief or affiliation, race, culture, or gender" is indisputable.[26] Surely anyone admitted to an academic institution who wants to study a particular religious tradition can indeed do so, regardless of his or her identity. When Gill's first criterion is read in light of the Western frame he privileges, however, it becomes clear that Gill implies that one's identity *should be* divorced from the academic study of religion. To believe that one's religious, racial, cultural, or gender identity or location even *could* be divorced from one's study is to remove the observer from the field of study and subscribe to the "god trick." Rather, it is the relationship of this identity to one's scholarship that is important. Gill's argument, therefore, is an appealingly disguised way to discredit the scholarship of American Indians and other "insiders" as suspect because it fails to live up to the Western standard he privileges. Unfortunately, Gill's position as an outsider does not

offer him a better perspective—only a different one. He cannot escape the particu-
larities of his location any more than American Indian scholars can.

The second of Gill's criteria is that the academic study of religion "must be
sensitive to multi-culturalism: the awareness that there are many peoples, cultures,
and religions, none of which has any exclusive claims to be made with regard to religion as an academic subject."[27] Certainly it would seem that sensitivity to multiculturalism should be a part of the academic study of religion, concerned as it is
with a variety of cultures and practices. However, frameworks of multiculturalism,
diversity, and ethnic pluralism are highly problematic because they fail to take into
account how power and privilege structure race, gender, and class relations. Margaret L. Andersen and Patricia Hill Collins argue that analyzing race, class, and gender in relation to structures of power and privilege moves beyond such frameworks:

> Analyzing race, class, and gender is more than "appreciating cultural diversity." It
> requires analysis and criticism of existing systems of power and privilege; other-
> wise, understanding diversity becomes just one more privilege of those with the
> most access to education—something that has always been a mark of the elite class.
> . . . It means recognizing and analyzing the hierarchies and systems of domination
> that permeate society and that systematically exploit and control people.[28]

The academic study of religion, like most fields, is structured by such systems of
power and privilege. Sensitivity to multiculturalism or awareness of diversity without analyses of, and challenges to, these systems simply perpetuates inequity because it locates the problem in the realm of individual psychology—whether one
is well-meaning or sympathetic, for example—rather than in hierarchal systems
that advantage some (the Euro-American, male, and elite) over others. Even the
most sensitive of people could not negate his or her unearned privilege. The kind
of analysis proposed by Andersen and Collins reveals that such structures of domination are in part responsible for Christianity's "exclusive claims" to the nature of
religion and the divine. American Indian religious traditions, feminist forms of religious practice, and the like simply have not had the power or status to make "exclusive claims" about the nature of religion. It should also be noted that mere
sensitivity to multiculturalism fails to adequately address the roles that religious
belief, action, and institutions play in structuring, perpetuating, and undermining
inequality and domination. Analyses that fail to take these interrelationships into
account will unfortunately not lead to the development of the field as a whole.

The other aspect of Gill's second criterion, the notion of religion as an academic
subject, is more extensively discussed in Gill's third criterion. According to Gill,

> The term "religion" must be understood as designating an academically con-
> structed rubric that identifies the arena for common discourse, inclusive of all re-
> ligions, as historically and culturally manifest. "Religion" cannot be considered

synonymous with Christianity or with the teaching of religion to members of specific traditions. "Religion" must not be thought of as the essence of the subject studied. "Religion" is not "the sacred," "ultimate concern," or belief in god (or some disguising euphemism). There is nothing religious about "religion." Religion is not *sui generis*. There are no uniquely religious data.[29]

Here Gill argues that religion is in a sense a function of academic discourse, a term constructed by scholars to organize data. That it should not be the same as any specific religious tradition makes sense; after all, the components of Christianity may not be the same as those of other religions. For instance, doctrine may play an important role in some forms of Christianity and little or no role at all in forms of American Indian religious traditions. By limiting religion to an academic construct and discourse, however, he denies the inductive processes that have gone on in shaping our understanding of the term to date. In other words, Gill's approach fails to acknowledge the dialogical relationship between religion as invented by scholars and religion as engaged in by practitioners and believers. It seems that at this seemingly arbitrary point in time, Gill intends to supplant this inductive process with a deductive one. This intervention conveniently preserves a sense of religion infused with Western values, gained through inductive processes that have excluded the contributions of American Indians, African Americans, women, and others to discourse development. Obviously, both induction and deduction play important roles in the process of definition. But it is those voices that have been denied in the past that must be sought out for the academic study of religion to mature in a balanced way.

Gill's fourth criterion is that "the methods of the academic study of religion are necessarily comparative. Religion is a category whose subdivisions are categories that demand comparison. Comparison must be understood as the play of fit and non-fit, of congruity and incongruity, rather than conformity with a pre-existing pattern."[30] That the academic study of religion is a comparative endeavor is generally accepted in the academy; a problem arises, however, when other forms of the study of religion are considered secondary to this comparative enterprise. Unfortunately, Gill seems to hold precisely this view:

> I am operating on the assumption that religion is a modern distinctively Western academic category born of the imagination that aspires to embrace the whole of human history and geography to ask the demanding and ultimately unanswerable question: "What does it mean to be human?" It is my view that until we address the academic study of religion at this level, in these terms, it cannot be considered a mature academic field and that the work on specific traditions, however academically credible or valuable, simply cannot benefit by or contribute to the broader study of religion.[31]

Under this model, studies of particular religious traditions are beneficial to the extent that they advance this comparative project. Ideally, all research projects to some degree should attempt to contribute to both the comparative and particular dimensions of the study of religion. To do that, however, scholars who study religious traditions of subjugated groups, such as American Indians and women, must first have a thorough understanding of how the Western biases that permeate much of the data affect the data. Unfortunately, studies with this emphasis have only begun to emerge and receive critical acclaim. More than compensatory studies, however, this work has the potential to undermine accepted structures of academic knowledge, providing new ways of understanding. The study of women and religion, for instance, has already proven this to be true. It is these studies that are in the process of maturation, in large part due to the gradual decentering and discrediting of the hegemonic Western model by the subjugated and marginalized and their allies. It is these studies that are in need of encouragement. Only with the loosening of religious studies from the binding aspects of Western epistemology can indigenous, or emic, models fully develop. Without this development, etic, or outsider, approaches will fail to mature.

The final element of Gill's vision for the academic study of religion concerns the scholar's motivations for the study of religion. Gill argues,

> Once it is comprehended that religion designates a significant aspect of a major portion of the human population throughout its history, dual motivations arise for the study of religion. On the one hand is the desire to appreciate, understand, and comprehend specific religions in their historical and cultural particularity. On the other hand is the opportunity afforded by the broadly comparative category, religion, to learn more about ourselves as human beings.[32]

While I agree that these are valid motivations for the academic study of religion, Gill's position is nevertheless contradictory. The problem here is that only certain motivations are permissible and not others. In particular, Gill rules religious factors as unacceptable motivations. In actuality, many motivating factors have the potential to influence our research—from promotion and tenure to recognition to a desire for mastery.[33] To suggest that only some motivations are acceptable denies the reality that many motivations do in fact influence our work, whether we intend them to or not, and that some of these motivations may indeed fall outside of the scientist's penumbra. Gill fails to explain, however, why religious motivations are more perilous than say, economic, psychological, or hegemonic motivations. Even Gill's permissible motivations could be construed as religious. The appreciation or understanding of religious traditions is part and parcel of American civil religion, which appears to permit "appreciation" of other cultural traditions as long as the dominance of Christian monotheism remains strong. The desire "to learn more about ourselves as human beings" is also part of many spiritual philosophies. Instead, to the extent possible, the variety of factors that motivate one's study of religion, religious or otherwise, should enter into our field of view and should be available for interrogation.

Gill's bounding criteria for the study of religion, therefore, fail to advance the field of religious studies in any significant way. While it could be argued that they merely maintain the status quo, I believe they are a reflection of, and contribute to, the current backlash against emic approaches, whether these ways of knowing are utilized in religious studies, American Indian studies, or women's studies.

In light of this response to Gill's argument, I would like to offer an example that suggests the possibilities of emic work. My own research focuses on Cherokee religious traditions and the development of emic theories, approaches, and models for the study of Cherokee religious expression, especially in literature. As a person of both Euro-American and Cherokee backgrounds educated in Western institutions, I naturally find indigenous and Western perspectives valuable in my work. However, I believe it is possible to develop academic tools that privilege Cherokee values, conceptions, and orientations yet draw on and make parallels to Western scholarship as well. The scholarship of feminists and people of color has already laid the groundwork for the development of theories, approaches, and models based on a particular group's experiences, locations, perspectives, or worldviews. For instance, the idea of a "feminist standpoint," as developed by Dorothy E. Smith, Nancy Hartsock, Patricia Hill Collins, Donna Haraway, Sandra Harding, and many others, provides the basis for creating these types of academic tools.[34] And Collins's articulation of a Black feminist standpoint and an Afrocentric feminist epistemology offers insight into how to develop such models.[35] Henry Louis Gates Jr.'s theory of African American literary criticism has also been helpful.[36]

In the study of religion, American Indian scholar Inés Talamantez stresses the importance of generating "from the culture itself the theory for studying it."[37] In regard to studying religious expression in American Indian literature, the generation of such theories may have been inhibited by the lack of a critical mass of writing by the members of one Native nation. However, in a growing number of indigenous nations, including the Cherokee, this critical mass now exists, enabling the works of writers from one nation, as a group, to be discussed in relation to indigenous traditions. My current project, "In the Spirit of Corn: Indigenous Theory and Cherokee Women's Literature," focuses on religious expression in the writing of Cherokee women.[38] In it I employ what American Indian critic Kimberly M. Blaeser calls "a tribal-centered criticism."[39] Specifically, I draw from Cherokee religious traditions to generate a model for interpreting the literature of contemporary Cherokee women. A brief summary gives a sense of the process. I begin by demonstrating that experts on Cherokee culture have incorrectly interpreted

Cherokee religious traditions as focusing on achieving purity and overcoming pollution. I argue, on the contrary, that Cherokee traditions are based on concepts of opposition, unity, and boundary-crossing found in Cherokee myth, ritual, and social organization. In developing this model, I draw on the work of Cherokee scholars Jack and Anna Kilpatrick, particularly Jack Kilpatrick's statement that "balance and synthesis, and the acceptance of the non-material nature of existence lie at the foundation of the Cherokee thought-world."[40] I also look to one of the most important bodies of stories in Cherokee religious traditions, the myths of the origin of corn, *Selu*. From these stories and other Cherokee understandings of the cosmos, I have realized that a dialogical process is at the heart of Cherokee religious traditions. In the ritual cycle, for instance, there are moments in which opposition or separation (balance) is stressed and other times when unity (synthesis) is important. These two processes are related to each other in a complementary, dialogical way, meaning that neither exists separate from the other; both are needed for the full ceremonial cycle. Opposition and synthesis are dialogically related in many Cherokee sacred stories as well. From the dialogical model generated from Cherokee mythic, ritual, and cosmological conceptions, I then suggest a template to apply to interpreting Cherokee women's literature.[41]

The potential for this Cherokee-centric approach is apparent in the interpretation that this model enables. An analysis of Marilou Awiakta's "Prayer of the Poet-Hunter" serves as a useful example. Eastern Cherokee writer Marilou Awiakta is probably best known for *Selu: Seeking the Corn-Mother's Wisdom*, published in 1993.[42] However, she has been writing on Cherokee themes for many years, her works appearing not only in a variety of anthologies and periodicals but also in her collection of poems and prose, *Abiding Appalachia: Where Mountain and Atom Meet*.[43] While *Selu* is full of evidence attesting to the importance of opposition, unity, and boundary-crossing in Awiakta's thought, *Abiding Appalachia* provides an interesting yoking of traditional Cherokee ideas with a postmodern sense of humans as potential victims, at a moment's notice, of nuclear disaster or attack. Awiakta's "Prayer of the Poet-Hunter" suggests how opposition, unity, and boundary-crossing are part of her response as a Cherokee to the nuclear age.

> "Prayer of the Poet-Hunter"
>
> O Ancient White, Spirit of Light, come and lay down my path.
> Awi Usdi, small chief of the Deer, ancestor of the unicorn,
> sacred spirit of the Cherokee, draw near and hearken.
>
> For you have said, "When I shall hear my grandchildren I shall
> hold up their heads." Because you have said it, draw near   [5]
> and listen. . . .

I seek the White Path where trees bend their branches in the
wind and the heart lifts up its voice. I seek light in the
mountain, in the star that shines above and deep within.
I do not know the way. I cannot direct my steps.   [10]

O Ancient White, come forth from the heart of the mountain.
Hold up my head. Give me the wind. Give me the light.
Lay down my path.[44]

"Poet-Hunter" takes the form of a Cherokee ritual incantation, an i:gawé:sdi
("to say, one"). In it Awiakta calls upon two Cherokee beings, "Ancient White,"
the Cherokee sacred fire, and "Awi Usdi," Little Deer. James Mooney notes that
Ancient White refers to the fire's "antiquity and light-giving properties and perhaps also to the fact that when dead it is covered with a coat of white ashes."[45]
That Awiakta calls it to "come forth from the heart of the mountain" (11) can
be understood as an allusion to the sacred fire as it lies smoldering within the temple mound. Historically, firekeepers could cause the fire to rise up from the depths
of the mound with the use of the stalks of the ihyâ'ga weed.[46] This process was
accompanied by prayers.[47] The light "in the star that shines above and deep
within" (9) is also a reference to the sacred fire, which exists both within the
mound and in the form of the sun, the fire above.

Awi Usdi, literally "Deer, Little," is the immortal chief of the deer people.
White and about the size of a small dog, Awi Usdi travels with ordinary deer and
can only be seen or wounded by those who have sacrificed of themselves and have
great spiritual knowledge.[48] It seems that the main purpose of this spirit animal is
to ensure that the deer are treated with respect. As Mooney describes it,

> The Little Deer keeps constant protecting watch over his subjects, and sees well to
> it that not one is ever killed in wantonness. When a deer is shot by the hunter the
> Little Deer knows it at once and is instantly at the spot. Bending low his head he
> asks of the blood stains upon the ground if they have been heard—i.e., if the
> hunter has asked pardon for the life that he has taken. If the formulistic prayer has
> been made, all is well, because the necessary sacrifice has been atoned for; but if
> otherwise, the Little Deer tracks the hunter to his house by the blood drops along
> the trail, and, unseen and unsuspected, puts into his body the spirit of rheumatism
> that shall rack him with aches and pains from that time henceforth.[49]

The origin of Awi Usdi's concern about the treatment of the deer is found in the
story that explains the origin of sickness and medicine. According to this myth, the
animal people met in councils to discuss how to protect themselves from humans
who were overpopulating the earth and preying on and trampling them. The result

was to inflict sickness on humans who mistreated the animals. The plants, however, hearing the animals' plans, offered themselves as remedies to the illnesses.[50]

In light of the appearance of Ancient White and Awi Usdi in "Poet-Hunter," it is possible to interpret Awiakta's role in relation to the poem as three-faceted: she is firekeeper, hunter, and poet. But the fire she tends, the deer she calls, and the consciousness she evokes are not Cherokee only, for Awiakta was raised on the atomic frontier. In 1945, at the age of nine, her family moved to Oak Ridge, Tennessee, the site of a then secret nuclear reactor in which the atom was split for purposes of war and peace.[51] With this upbringing and the role of nuclear themes in her work, it is not surprising why she is regarded as "mother of atomic folklore."[52] And as the subtitle of her work *Abiding Appalachia* indicates, she regards her homelands as "the place where mountain and atom meet."

Awiakta recalls when she began to make a connection between mountain and atom. She explains her experience at the Museum of Science and Energy at Oak Ridge in 1977:

> For a long time I stood in front of a giant model of an atom—an enormous, translucent blue ball with tiny lights whirling inside, representing the cloud of electrons. Stars whirling . . . whirling . . . whirling . . . drew me into an altered state of consciousness.
> Suddenly, I saw Little Deer leaping in the heart of the atom.[53]

She translated this vision into an image, a deer jumping in the center of the atom, surrounded by whirling electron orbits. As an emblem, this image graces the cover of *Abiding Appalachia*, which appeared in 1978, the year following her experience at the museum.

In a sense, "Poet-Hunter," appearing as it does near the beginning of *Abiding Appalachia*, suggests the beginning of Awiakta's journey to what she calls "the mystery's heart."[54] While the fruit of this journey has matured by the time both she and her reader arrive at the work's last poem, "Where Mountain and Atom Meet," the seeds of the understanding she gained are nonetheless planted below the surface of "Poet-Hunter."

Seeking to understand the mystery, Awiakta calls upon Ancient White and Awi Usdi in "Poet-Hunter." She asks the sacred fire to "lay down [her] path" (1) and Little Deer to "draw near and hearken" (3). Part of Awiakta's insight stems from the parallels she draws between Cherokee beings and concepts and the atom and ideas related to it. The images in "Poet-Hunter" of the "Spirit of Light" (1) and the "star that shines above and deep within" (9), for instance, refer both to Ancient White and atomic energy. The fire, like the atom, emits light. The trace of the atom, writes Awiakta, is "a fine blue glow."[55] She also refers to the reactor as a temple.[56] The townhouse in which the sacred fire was kept burning was, similarly, a spiritual site.

Awiakta also makes a comparison between Awi Usdi and the atom. In reference to Little Deer, she writes, "From the heart of the mountain he comes."[57] Like the hunter, Kana´t, Awiakta knows where the deer live, deep in the heart of the mountain. Other Cherokee stories tell of how humans are taken inside mountains by deer, particularly deer women. And it is deep within the mountain that the atom abides. The reactor at Oak Ridge, explains Awiakta, is a mountain, a full three stories high, "an altar, majestic, immense—with seven feet of concrete shield to guard the black body deep within. And across the front a thousand eyes that once were channels to her heart now stare stark and cold and dead."[58] These tunnels, where particles once bombarded atoms, are the pathways of the white deer. It is through the beings of Ancient White and Little Deer, therefore, that Awiakta gains an understanding of the atom and its power.

In uniting the Cherokee with the atomic, Awiakta also begins to articulate what she feels a proper relationship with the atom should be. She is deeply aware of the destructive potential of splitting the atom. Of Hiroshima, for instance, Awiakta writes: "Destruction. Death. Power beyond belief, released from something invisible."[59] She also recalls the disaster drills and test cows, "radioactive now and locked / behind a fence."[60] The potential for nuclear attack and disaster is imprinted on her mind like the flash of a radioactive mushroom cloud. However, she recognizes the atom's creative power, too. Awiakta writes that her mother told her as a child that the atom is in everything.[61] The atom is a central part of creation. Awiakta also refers to an even smaller particle within the atom, the quark, as "the atom's mother heart."[62] This heart, like a grain of corn, "bears new life."[63] As she explains,

> Nuclear energy is the nurturing energy of the universe. Except for stellar explosions, this energy works not by fission (splitting) but by fusion—attraction and melding. With the relational process, the atom creates and transforms life.[64]

She also points to the medical benefits of the atom, writing, "It could . . . heal ten thousands at a time."[65]

So how does Awiakta resolve the binary opposition presented by nuclear technology: its potential for both destruction and creation? She treats it as a traditional Cherokee treats something powerful: she learns to live in balance with it. So *Abiding Appalachia* concerns Awiakta's ability to live with the atom and, by implication, humanity's ability likewise to exist harmoniously with it. As she puts it, "*Abiding* raised the question: Do humans have enough reverence for life to cope with the atom?"[66] As firekeeper, hunter, and poet, Awiakta seeks to show the way to this reverence.

Reverence is an important aspect of firekeeping. The fire must be constantly tended, kept smoldering or allowed to burn, but simultaneously respected for the potential conflagration it could become. Such attention is accompanied by prayers. In Cherokee ceremonies, the sacred fire was rekindled every year and a place made for it in each household. The fire was also ritually fed, not only in communal ceremonies but also by hunters after a kill. But the treatment that hunters were to give the deer makes the idea of reverence even clearer. If a hunter failed to offer the proper prayers when a deer was killed, imbalance occurred. If he acted with reverence, Little Deer would not harm him, but if not, his retaliation was crippling. In the poem "Disaster Drill," for instance, Awiakta asks, "Have you heard, Little Deer . . . / the words of pardon . . . have you heard?"[67] If he has, no danger will occur—the alarm is indeed a drill, not impending destruction. Awi Usdi, therefore, is a symbol of reverence for Awiakta.[68] "I understood that he embodied the sacred law of taking and giving back with respect, the Sacred Circle of Life," she writes. "I was certain that Little Deer and his story would reveal ways to make harmony in my own life and in the world around me."[69]

As a poet, Awiakta tries to foster a new kind of consciousness in her readers. She aims to see with the eye of Little Deer and to promote reverence in humanity's treatment of the atom. The consciousness enacted and evoked in *Abiding Appalachia* is one of nonbinary thought. The potential to construct binaries in regard to nuclear energy is evident in such examples as war/peace, death/life, and technology/nature. Awiakta crosses the boundaries that separate technology from nature, for instance. The reactor and the mountain are one for her. More important, however, she is not willing to divorce science from religion. She recognizes that "to split the atom from the sacred is a deadly fission that will ultimately destroy nature and humanity."[70] This is the heart of Awiakta's reverential consciousness.

So, Awiakta brings together seemingly opposing ways of understanding the world. Just as science has embraced the theory of the wave/particle duality of the electron—that is, that an electron sometimes acts as a wave and other times as a particle—Awiakta inhabits a reality that is not unidimensional. She abides by what would have been called, prior to quantum physics, a "magical" way of knowing. For her, the atom is Ancient White and Little Deer. And the power at its core is the "I Am."[71] Awiakta, therefore, has little concern for boundaries that separate Cherokee tradition from Western science and from Christianity. She manages to make a home where they converge—in power. What does matter is that the atom, the spirits, and God, along with Awiakta, all inhabit Cherokee country/Appalachia, and she feels she must coexist peacefully with them. So, Awiakta asks Ancient White and Little Deer for guidance to the "White Path." She quotes Albert Einstein as saying, "The unleashed power of the atom has changed everything save our modes of thought, and thus we drift toward unparalleled catastrophe." Through her poetry, she asks us to take up the White Path with her and to walk away from the darkening land of catastrophe.[72] As she has written, stories create a "path in the human mind and heart."[73] The powerful tale of Little Deer is one such story.

This analysis of Awiakta's "Poet-Hunter" is helpful as we return to the question of disciplinary futures. The future of religious studies envisioned by Sam Gill effectively excludes the contributions of believers and practitioners to the development of the academic study of religion, especially if those believers and practitioners are scholars themselves. Employing a Western frame of reference, he imposes a binary opposition that separates scholars from adherents when in reality such a separation cannot be made. As feminist scholarship has shown, all of us exist as both "insiders" and "outsiders" of a variety of contexts that influence our perception, and both locations have the potential to be valuable. The example of "Poet-Hunter" reveals similarly that in Cherokee tradition, opposition is a momentary state within a dynamic that cycles between separation (balance) and unity (synthesis). Both locations and the process that connects them are absolutely necessary to the whole.

It is this "both/and" philosophy that signals a promising future for Native American women's studies. It has the potential to respond not only to indigenous traditions but also to Western thought. And it can draw from the best that both ethnic studies and women's studies have to offer. But, as with any other field, it must begin to develop its own foundation. In light of the misinformation about and misunderstanding of American Indians in general and Native women in particular, this foundation must consist of indigenous traditions and philosophies and indigenous women's experiences and perspectives. Or, to use Awiakta's language, we must follow the "White Path" at the heart of our Native traditions while we negotiate and redirect the white path of academia.

Notes

1. I would like to thank Marcia Westkott and Michelene Pesantubbee for their insightful feedback on drafts of this chapter and the University of Colorado at Boulder for financial support of my research on Cherokee religious traditions and literature.

2. Wendy Rose, interview by Laura Coltelli, in *Winged Words: American Indian Writers Speak*, American Indian Lives (Lincoln: University of Nebraska Press, 1990), p. 124.

3. Sam Gill, "The Academic Study of Religion," *Journal of the American Academy of Religion* 62, no. 4 (1994): 966.

4. Gill, "Academic Study of Religion," pp. 965–66.

5. Christopher Jocks, "American Indian Religious Traditions and the Academic Study of Religion: A Response to Sam Gill," *Journal of the American Academy of Religion* 65, no. 1 (1997): 169–76. For Gill's rejoinder, see Sam Gill, "Rejoinder to Christopher Jocks," *Journal of the American Academy of Religion* 65, no. 1 (1997): 177–81.

6. For a discussion of emic and etic approaches, see Kenneth L. Pike, "Etic and Emic Standpoints for the Description of Behavior," in *Language in Relation to a Unified Theory of the Structure of Human Behavior*, 2nd ed. (The Hague: Mouton, 1967), pp. 37–72.

7. "The Academic Study of Religion" appeared in a special issue of the *Journal of the American Academy of Religion* on "Settled Issues and Neglected Questions in the Study of Religion."

8. Gill, "Academic Study of Religion," p. 967.

9. Gill, "Academic Study of Religion," p. 968.

10. Gill, "Academic Study of Religion," pp. 966–67; "Rejoinder to Christopher Jocks," p. 177.

11. Sam Gill, "The Trees Stood Deep Rooted," in *I Become Part of It: Sacred Dimensions in Native American Life*, ed. D. M. Dooling and Paul Jordan-Smith (New York: Parabola Books, 1989), p. 23.

12. Gill, "Trees Stood Deep Rooted," p. 23.

13. Sam Gill, "'It's Where You Put Your Eyes,'" in *I Become Part of It: Sacred Dimensions in Native American Life*, ed. D. M. Dooling and Paul Jordan-Smith (New York: Parabola Books, 1989), p. 79.

14. Gill, "Where You Put Your Eyes," p. 82.

15. Gill, "Academic Study of Religion," p. 965.

16. Gill, "Rejoinder to Christopher Jocks," p. 178 (Gill's emphasis).

17. Gill, "Rejoinder to Christopher Jocks," p. 178 (Gill's emphasis).

18. Joyce McCarl Nielsen, introduction to *Feminist Research Methods: Exemplary Readings in the Social Sciences*, ed. Joyce McCarl Nielsen (Boulder: Westview Press, 1990), pp. 1–37.

19. Donna Haraway, "Situated Knowledges: The Science Question in Feminism and the Privilege of Partial Perspective," *Feminist Studies* 14, no. 3 (1988): 581.

20. Haraway, "Situated Knowledges," pp. 584, 590.

21. Haraway, "Situated Knowledges," p. 586.

22. Haraway, "Situated Knowledges," pp. 584, 586.

23. Haraway, "Situated Knowledges," pp. 584–85.

24. Haraway, "Situated Knowledges," pp. 583–84.

25. Sandra Harding, "Rethinking Standpoint Epistemology: 'What Is Strong Objectivity'?" in *Feminist Epistemologies*, ed. Linda Alcoff and Elizabeth Potter (New York: Routledge, 1993), p. 69.

26. Gill, "Academic Study of Religion," p. 965.

27. Gill, "Academic Study of Religion," p. 965.

28. Margaret L. Andersen and Patricia Hill Collins, preface to *Race, Class and Gender: An Anthology*, 2nd ed. (Belmont, CA: Wadsworth, 1995), p. xiii.

29. Gill, "Academic Study of Religion," p. 965 (Gill's emphasis).

30. Gill, "Academic Study of Religion," p. 965.

31. Gill, "Rejoinder to Christopher Jocks," p. 177.

32. Gill, "Academic Study of Religion," pp. 965–66.

33. Linda Martín Alcoff argues that the impetus to speak for others in academic or other contexts can stem from a desire for mastery or domination. See her article "The Problem of Speaking for Others," in *Who Can Speak? Authority and Critical Identity*, ed. Judith Roof and Robyn Wiegman (Urbana: University of Illinois Press, 1995), p. 111.

34. Dorothy E. Smith, "Women's Perspective as a Radical Critique of Sociology," in *Feminism and Methodology: Social Science Issues*, ed. Sandra Harding (Bloomington: Indiana University Press; Milton Keynes: Open University Press, 1987), pp. 84–96; Nancy C. M. Hartsock, "The Feminist Standpoint: Developing the Ground for a Specifically Feminist

Historical Materialism," in *Feminism and Methodology: Social Science Issues*, ed. Sandra Harding (Bloomington: Indiana University Press; Milton Keynes: Open University Press, 1987), pp. 157–80; Patricia Hill Collins, *Black Feminist Thought: Knowledge, Consciousness and the Politics of Empowerment* (London: Unwin Hyman, 1990; reprint, New York: Routledge, 1991); Donna Haraway, "Situated Knowledges"; and Sandra Harding, "Rethinking Standpoint Epistemology."

35. Collins, *Black Feminist Thought.*

36. Henry Louis Gates Jr., *The Signifying Monkey: A Theory of African-American Literary Criticism* (New York: Oxford University Press, 1988).

37. Inés Talamantez, "An Insider's Point of View," in *Center for the Study of Women in Society Review: Annual Magazine for the Study of Women in Society* (Eugene, OR: Center for the Study of Women in Society, University of Oregon, 1990), p. 20.

38. This project stems out of my dissertation, "Walking the 'White Path': Toward a Cherokee-Centric Hermeneutic for Interpreting Cherokee Literature" (PhD diss., University of California, Santa Barbara, 1997).

39. Kimberly M. Blaeser, "Native Literature: Seeking a Critical Center," in *Looking at the Words of Our People: First Nations Analysis of Literature*, ed. Jeannette Armstrong (Penticton, BC: Theytus Books, 1993), p. 53.

40. Jack Frederick Kilpatrick, *Sequoyah of Earth and Intellect* (Austin: Encino Press, 1965), p. 3.

41. On the subject of a template, see Paula Gunn Allen, "'Border' Studies: The Intersection of Gender and Color," in *Introduction to Scholarship in Modern Languages and Literatures*, ed. Joseph Gibaldi, 2nd ed. (New York: Modern Language Association of America, 1992), pp. 303–19.

42. Marilou Awiakta, *Selu: Seeking the Corn-Mother's Wisdom* (Golden, CO: Fulcrum Publishing, 1993).

43. Marilou Awiakta, *Abiding Appalachia: Where Mountain and Atom Meet* (Memphis: St. Luke's Press, 1978; reprint, Bell Buckle, TN: Iris Press, 1995).

44. Marilou Awiakta, "Prayer of the Poet-Hunter," in *Abiding Appalachia: Where Mountain and Atom Meet* (Memphis: St. Luke's Press, 1978), p. 17. Reprinted by permission of the author.

45. James Mooney, "Sacred Formulas of the Cherokees," in *Myths of the Cherokee and Sacred Formulas of the Cherokees* (Nashville: Charles and Randy Elder, 1982), p. 359.

46. James Mooney, "Myths of the Cherokee," in *Myths of the Cherokee and Sacred Formulas of the Cherokees* (Nashville: Charles and Randy Elder, 1982), p. 396.

47. Mooney, "Myths of the Cherokee," p. 396.

48. Mooney, "Myths of the Cherokee," pp. 263–64.

49. Mooney, "Myths of the Cherokee," pp. 263–64.

50. Mooney, "Myths of the Cherokee," pp. 250–52.

51. Awiakta, *Abiding Appalachia*, p. 95.

52. Awiakta, *Abiding Appalachia*, p. 95.

53. Awiakta, *Selu*, p. 32.

54. Awiakta, *Abiding Appalachia*, p. 84.

55. Awiakta, *Abiding Appalachia*, p. 89.

56. Awiakta, *Abiding Appalachia*, p. 84.

57. Awiakta, *Abiding Appalachia*, p. 18.

58. Awiakta, *Abiding Appalachia*, p. 84.

59. Awiakta, *Selu*, p. 66. The nuclear accidents at Three Mile Island and Chernobyl occurred after publication of *Abiding Appalachia* (*Selu*, p. 33).

60. Awiakta, *Abiding Appalachia*, pp. 65, 57; Awiakta, *Selu*, p. 68.

61. Awiakta, *Selu*, p. 66.

62. Awiakta, *Selu*, p. 69.

63. Awiakta, *Selu*, p. 71.

64. Awiakta, *Selu*, p. 69.

65. Awiakta, *Abiding Appalachia*, p. 84.

66. Awiakta, *Selu*, p. 33.

67. Awiakta, "Disaster Drill," in *Abiding Appalachia* (Memphis: St. Luke's Press, 1978), p. 65.

68. Awiakta, *Selu*, p. 71.

69. Awiakta, *Selu*, p. 32.

70. Awiakta, *Selu*, p. 71.

71. Awiakta, *Abiding Appalachia*, p. 89. God appears to Moses, revealing himself as "I Am Who I Am" (Ex. 3:14).

72. Awiakta, *Selu*, p. 70.

73. Awiakta, *Selu*, pp. 21–22.

Credits

Joy Harjo's poem "Remember" first appeared in *She Had Some Horses*, by Joy Harjo. Copyright © 1983, 1987 by Thunder's Mouth Press. Appears by permission of the publisher, Thunder's Mouth Press.

Elizabeth Cook-Lynn's essay "The Big Pipe Case" appeared first in Elizabeth Cook-Lynn, *Why I Can't Read Wallace Stegner and Other Essays: A Tribal Voice*. © 1996. Reprinted by permission of the University of Wisconsin Press (pp. 110–25).

Gloria Bird's essay "Toward a Decolonization of the Mind and Text: Leslie Marmon Silko's *Ceremony*" first appeared in *Wicazo Sa Review*, Vol. IX, No. 2 (Fall 1993): 1–8.

Joanne Barker and Teresia Teaiwa's essay "Native InFormation" first appeared in *Inscriptions* 7 (Fall 1994): 16–41.

Inés Hernández-Avila's essay "Relocations Upon Relocations: Home, Language, and Native American Women's Writings" first appeared in *American Indian Quarterly*, Vol. 19, No. 4 (Fall 1995): 491–507. Copyright Inés Hernández-Avila.

Deborah Miranda's essay "Dildos, Hummingbirds and Driving Her Crazy: Searching for American Indian Women's Love Poetry and Erotics" first appeared in *Frontiers: A Journal of Women's Studies*, volume 23, no. 2 (2002) (University of Nebraska Press), in a special issue on indigenous women co-edited by Gail Tremblay and Inés Hernández-Avila.

Inés Talamantez's essay "Seeing Red: American Indian Women Speaking about Their Religious and Political Perspectives" first appeared in *In Our Own Voices: Four*

About the Authors

Joanne Barker (Lenape) completed her PhD in the history of consciousness department at the University of California, Santa Cruz, in 2000 where she specialized in indigenous jurisprudence, Women's/Gender Studies, and Cultural Studies. She has published articles in *Wicazo Sa Review: A Native American Studies Journal*, *Cultural Studies*, *Inscriptions*, and *this bridge we call home: radical visions for transformation*. She has edited a collection of essays titled *Sovereignty Matters* that is being published in the fall of 2005. Joanne is working on energy policies and conservation issues in relation to California Indian tribes with the California Energy Commission and California Indian Legal Services. She is an assistant professor in American Indian Studies at San Francisco State University.

Gloria Bird (Spokane) is a poet, essayist, and editor. She co-edited, with Joy Harjo, the anthology of Native women's writing *Reinventing the Enemy's Language*. Her books include *Full Moon on the Reservation* (1993) and *The River of History* (1997). She is an associate editor for *Wicazo Sa Review* in which her critical work has appeared. She resides on the Spokane Indian Reservation in eastern Washington state.

Victoria Bomberry (Muscogee/Lenape) received her PhD in modern thought and literature from Stanford University, June 2001. She is on the faculty of Ethnic Studies at the University of California, Riverside. She is a past recipient of the University of California President's Postdoctoral Fellowship (2001–2003) with the Native American Studies department at the University of California, Davis. Victoria is an advisor and coordinator of Neshkinukat (California Native Artists Network), a statewide group.

Mary C. Churchill (mixed-blood Cherokee) is a visiting assistant professor in American Indian and Native Studies at the University of Iowa. She is also an assistant professor of Women's Studies and Religious Studies at the University of Colorado at Boulder. Mary received her PhD in Religious Studies at the University of California, Santa Barbara, specializing in the area of Native American religious traditions. Her work has appeared in *American Indian Quarterly* and the *Journal of the American Academy of Religion*, among other publications. She was a Bunting Fellow at the Radcliffe Institute for Advanced Study, Harvard University.

Elizabeth Cook-Lynn (Crow Creek Sioux-Dakota), professor emerita, is a major voice in Native American Studies. She is an essayist, novelist, poet, and founding editor of *Wicazo Sa Review: A Journal of Native American Studies* (since 1984). She is one of the writers of the Twentieth-Century Native Literary Renaissance and is the author of three novellas: *From the River's Edge*, *Circle of Dancers*, and *In the Presence of River Gods*, published as *AURELIA* in 1999. Her collection of essays, *Why I Can't Read Wallace Stegner and Other Essays: A Tribal Voice* (1996), was awarded the Myers Center Award for the Study of Human Rights in North America. Elizabeth is a recipient of an Oyate Igluwitaya award given by native university students in South Dakota, an award that refers to those who "aid in the ability of the people to see clearly in the company of each other." Since her retirement from Eastern Washington University in 1990, she has been a visiting professor and consultant in Native Studies at University of California, Davis, and Arizona State University in Tempe and a writer-in-residence at several universities. Her latest book is *Anti-Indianism in Modern America: A Voice from Tatekeya's Earth* (2001). She lives in the Black Hills of South Dakota.

Carolyn Dunn (Cherokee/Muskogee/Seminole) is the co-editor (with Carol Comfort) of *Through the Eye of the Deer: An Anthology of Native Women Writers* (1999) and *Hozho: Walking in Beauty* (2001) with Paula Gunn Allen. Her first poetry volume, *Outfoxing Coyote* (2002), was named Book of the Year for poetry by the Wordcraft Circle of Native Writers and Storytellers. A wife and mother of three small children, Carolyn is pursuing a PhD in American Studies and Ethnicity at the University of Southern California, where she is an Irvine Fellow. She is a founding member of the all-woman Northern-style drum group, the Mankillers.

Reid Gómez (Navajo), creative writer and scholar, received her PhD in Ethnic Studies from the University of California, Berkeley. Her dissertation was titled "Rewor(l)ding Indian Survival: Language and Sovereignty in Native American Literature." She is currently completing her novel *Cebolla*. Her first novel, *A Woman's Body Was Found There*, is forthcoming.

Janice Gould (Konkow) earned degrees in linguistics (BA) and English (MA) at the University of California, Berkeley, and her PhD in English from the University of New Mexico. She is the recipient of grants for poetry from the National Endowment for the Arts and from the Astraea Foundation; her scholarly work has been recognized with awards from the Roothbert Fund and the Ford Foundation. Janice's poetry has been widely anthologized, and she has written three books of verse: *Beneath My Heart* (1990), *Earthquake Weather* (1996), and *Alphabet*, an artbook/chapbook. A book of essays on American Indian poetry, *Speak to Me Words*, which she co-edited with Dean Rader, is forthcoming this fall. Janice is an assistant professor and the Hallie Ford Chair in Creative Writing at Willamette University. She lives in Portland, Oregon.

Joy Harjo (Muscogee), distinguished award-winning poet and musician, is the author of several collections of poetry, including the most recent, *How We Became Human: New and Selected Poems* (2002). She has a new CD of music, *Native Joy for Real*, and performs nationally and internationally solo and with her new band. Joy is the recipient of the Lifetime Achievement Award from Native Writers Circle of the Americas among many other awards. She is on the faculty of English at UCLA and lives in Honolulu, Hawaii.

Inés Hernández-Avila (Nez Perce/Tejana) is a poet, cultural worker, professor of Native American Studies, and director of the Chicana/Latina Research Center at the University of California, Davis. She is an elected member of the National Caucus of the Wordcraft Circle of Native Writers and Storytellers, and she was a consultant for the National Museum of the American Indian, which opened in the National Mall in Washington, DC, on September 21, 2004. Inés is a member of the Latina Feminist Group who produced *Telling to Live: Latina Feminist Testimonios*, which won an award from the Gustav Meyer Center for the Study of Human Rights and Bigotry as one of the ten outstanding books of 2002. She and Gail Tremblay co-edited a special issue on *Indigenous Women for Frontiers: A Journal of Women's Studies* (2002), and she and Domino Renee Perez co-edited a special issue for *SAIL: Studies in American Indian Literature* titled *Indigenous Intersections: American Indians and Chicanas/os in Literature* (2003). She has several works in progress, and she thoroughly enjoys working with her graduate students.

Jean LaMarr (Paiute and Ilmawi band of the Pitt River Nation) lives and works on the Susanville Indian Rancheria. She is a respected print-maker and installation artist.

Deborah A. Miranda is a mother, poet, scholar, and mixed-blood woman of Esselen, Chumash, and European ancestry. Her collection of poetry *Indian*

Cartography won the First Book Award from the Native Writer's Circle of the Americas. Her new collection of poetry, *The Zen of La Llorona*, is forthcoming. Deborah was named Poet of the Year by the NWCA for 2000. She has been published as a scholar and poet in several journals, including *Calyx, Weber Studies, Frontiers, Through the Eye of the Deer*, and the new anthology *This Bridge We Call Home: Radical Visions for Transformation*, edited by AnaLouise Keating and Gloria Anzaldua. Deborah received her PhD in English at the University of Washington and is an assistant professor of English at Washington and Lee University in Lexington, Virginia. Projects in progress include a critical study of the indigenous erotic found in Native women's poetry and fiction.

Luana Ross (Salish) was raised on the Flathead Indian Reservation in Montana and is an enrolled member of the Confederated Salish and Kootenai Tribes. She has a PhD in sociology and is associate professor of Women's Studies and American Indian Studies at the University of Washington. Luana was the first scholar in the nation to conduct a study on imprisoned Native American women and the first to research the Women's Correctional Center in Montana. She has several publications from this research including a book, *Inventing the Savage: The Social Construction of Native American Criminality* (1998), which won the Best Book of 1998 award from the American Political Science Association. She is co-director of Native Voices, a graduate program for Native students studying film, and is also involved in producing films and has assisted on several projects, including the documentary *White Shamans, Plastic Medicine Men*.

Andrea Smith (Cherokee) was the co-founder of the Chicago chapter of Women of All Red Nations (WARN). She is formerly the Women of Color Caucus Chair for the National Coalition Against Sexual Assault and is a founding member of Incite! Women of Color Against Violence. She is an assistant professor of American Culture and Women's Studies at the University of Michigan.

Inés Talamantez (Mescalero Apache, Sun Clan) is a professor of Religious Studies at the University of California, Santa Barbara, and a Senior Fellow at the Center for the Study of World Religions at Harvard University. She specializes in Native American Religious Studies and philosophies, Chicana/o Studies, women and religion, and religion and healing. Her publications include "The Presence of Isanaklesh: The Apache Female Deity and the Path of Pollen," in *Unspoken Worlds: Women's Religious Lives*, and "Transforming American Conceptions about Native America: Vine Deloria, Jr., Critic and Coyote," in *Native Voices: American Indian Identity and Resistance*. Recently she co-edited *Hypatia: A Journal of Feminist Philosophy* (Volume 18, Number 2, Spring 2003) with M. A. Jaimes Guerrero and Anne Waters.

She has also just completed the manuscript *Becoming: Initiating Apache Girls to the World of Spiritual and Cultural Values.*

Teresia Teaiwa is senior lecturer and program director, Pacific Studies, in the School of Maori, Pacific and Samoan Studies/Te Kawa a Maui, at Victoria University of Wellington/Te Whare Wananga O Te Upoko O Te Ika a Maui. Teresia is of Banaban, I-Kiribati, and African American descent, born in Hawaii and raised in the Fiji Islands. She earned her PhD in history of consciousness from the University of California, Santa Cruz. Teresia co-edited the volume of *Inscriptions* with María Ochoa on women of color's collaborations and conflicts, in which her co-authored work with Joanne Barker in this volume first appeared. Teresia has published widely on contemporary Pacific politics and culture.

Hulleah J. Tsinhnahjinnie (Seminole/Muscogee/Diné) is an established artist known for her vanguard work and for her sharp critique of PL 101-644, the Indian Arts and Crafts Act. She has exhibited nationally and internationally and was a Rockefeller Fellow in the Humanities with the Department of Native American Studies at the University of California, Davis.

Date Due